An Economic History of the American Steel Industry

The American steel industry was a prototype for many economic sectors that have risen from the economic growth of the nineteenth and twentieth centuries, and its product, steel, has become the lowest cost and most used metal in the world. The industry became a major supplier to such leading sectors as railroads, automobiles, and military equipment. Later, the demand composition of the economy moved to less steel-intensive goods and services, attenuating the importance of the industry. Additionally, other countries such as Japan and Korea became the major steel innovators, and the American industry was forced to make drastic adjustments in order to compete. Consequently, an industry that had once been a source of economic growth and high-paying jobs became a problem sector leading to a long series of government policy actions and debates.

This book covers the 160-year history of the steel industry in America. It starts with the 1830s when the American iron and steel industry resembled the traditional iron-producing sector that had existed in the old world for centuries. It then examines the development of the industry and its influence on the Industrial Revolution, through the First and Second World Wars and the post-war period, up to 2001. The book describes how the industry changed from a cornerstone of the economy into a problem sector, and how it responded to new conditions.

Rogers' new monograph will be of particular interest to undergraduate and postgraduate students of business, economics, and history, as well as steel and metal producers, researchers and policy makers.

Robert P. Rogers is associate professor of Economics at Ashland University, Ohio, USA.

Routledge explorations in economic history
Edited by Lars Magnusson
Uppsala University, Sweden

An Economic History of the American Steel Industry

Robert P. Rogers

Routledge
Taylor & Francis Group

LONDON AND NEW YORK

First published 2009
by Routledge
2 Park Square, Milton Park, Abingdon, Oxon, OX14 4RN

Simultaneously published in the USA and Canada
by Routledge
711 Madison Avenue, New York, NY 10017

Routledge is an imprint of the Taylor & Francis Group, an informa business

© 2009 Robert P. Rogers

Typeset in Times New Roman by Swales & Willis Ltd, Exeter, Devon
First issued in paperback in 2013

British Library Cataloguing in Publication Data
A catalogue record for this book is available from the British Library

Library of Congress Cataloging in Publication Data
A catalogue record for this book has been requested

ISBN 13: 978–0–415–74352–5 (pbk)
ISBN 13: 978–0–415–77760–5 (hbk)
ISBN 13: 978–0–203–88103–3 (ebk)

Contents

Tables

Figures

Preface

The purpose of this book is to give a concise account of the American steel industry between 1860 and 2001. In this period, modern science led to the low-cost production of steel, making it the most used metal in the world. While many very good books and articles have been written about shorter periods in the history of this industry, no work tries to cover the whole period except for William T. Hogan's five-volume *Economic History of the Iron and Steel Industry in the United States* written in 1971. My book gives the reader a description of events in the industry in a much shorter and more accessible format, and it covers events until 2001.

The steel industry especially in the United States has been identified with the industrial revolution. It was a prototype for many economic sectors that arose out of the economic growth of the nineteenth and twentieth centuries. While not necessarily the inventors, Americans were the major developers of the nineteenth- and early twentieth-century steel technology. Subsequently, steel became one of the largest industries in the country, and a pivot point for the economy. It was a major supplier to such leading sectors as railroads, automobiles, and armaments. At the same time as the industry was seen as a paragon of the modern economy, fears arose of its power and dominance. These fears led to the development of a series of policies limiting its influence, the main one being antitrust.

Subsequently the American steel industry followed a pattern typical of many markets, going from being a leading innovative sector to a group of firms faced with new foreign competitors and domestic substitutes. Thus, insights on other markets can be gleaned from our narrative.

The demands of the economy moved to less steel-intensive goods and services attenuating the importance of the industry. Furthermore, other countries, mainly Japan and Korea, became the major steel innovators, and the American industry was forced to make drastic adjustments in order to compete with the new competition. Thus, an industry that had once been a source of economic growth and high-paying jobs became a problem sector leading to a long series of government policy actions and debates.

Thus, this book describes how the industry went from being a cornerstone of the economy to a problem sector and how it responded to new conditions. The book gives a concise outline of the actions and events that affected it in the 160 years between 1860 and 2001. It will help scholars and policymakers understand the industry.

Acknowledgements

This project has been a goal of mine for almost two decades. Many people have helped and encouraged me in my study of the steel industry: colleagues at the Federal Trade Commission, fellow professors and students at the University of the South, Monmouth College, and Ashland University and others.

I wrote my dissertation on the steel industry at George Washington University where I was very much helped by Professors Robert Goldfarb and John Kwoka. At the Federal Trade Commission, my place of employment in the 1970s and 80s, many people taught me much about the steel industry and the methods to analyze it. Notable among them were Richard Johnson, Hans Mueller, and David Tarr.

When I took at a job at Monmouth College, my colleagues and I developed a series of industry history courses, among which was steel. The basic outline of this book came from that course. Instrumental in developing these courses were Rodney Lemon and Andrew Weiss.

At Ashland University, many people helped me with ideas on this project; among them were Robert Stimpert, Richard Symons, Mark Nadler and Jeff Pinkham. Erin Bistline and Thomas Hunter provided invaluable editorial assistance. Lastly, three students were especially helpful, Jennifer Hoekstra from Monmouth College and Kevin Quinn and Tim Wolford from Ashland University.

I must acknowledge a scholar who, while I never met him, did much to make this book possible, and that is William T. Hogan of Fordham University. His thorough studies of the steel industry written in the 1970s, 1980s, and 1990s provided much valuable information for this book.

Last, I would like to recognize the many people with whom I have talked who worked in the industry, both at the management and plant level. I have met them not only in Ohio, Pennsylvania and Illinois, where one would expect to find them, but also in Washington, D.C. and other places. Their insight and opinions did much to increase my feel for and knowledge of the steel industry, but in some ways I will never have the innate understanding that most of them have.

Acknowledgement

1   Introduction

Plan for chapter

This book outlines the history of the American steel industry. The narrative starts with the 1830s, when the American iron and steel industry resembled the traditional Old World iron sectors, and it ends with 2001. In this period, steel, an alloy of iron and carbon, became the most commonly used metal in the world. Its very size and position give the steel industry an unusual relevance to modern society.

After explaining why the industry is important, this chapter describes its basic technology and presents the taxonomy used in subsequent chapters to describe the history of steel in America.

The importance of steel

The size and position of the steel industry give it an unusual economic, historical, and political importance. Thus, one can examine the reasons for studying steel under these three categories.

Economic

Steel is important in the economy. In 2000, the value added in the steel industry constituted over one percent of GDP originating in manufacturing. In 1970, the steel industry employed 531,196 people and even after its decline in 2000, it still had 225,000 on its payroll. Steel also influences other parts of the economy. As shown in Table 1.1, it is an important input into large industries such as automobiles, construction, oil, and machinery. Thus, what happens in steel affects the whole economy.

Another reason for the importance of steel is that its market structure is typical of modern industrial markets. Historically, the steel industry has been so concentrated among a few firms that one could readily accept the hypothesis of noncompetitive pricing. Table 1.2, showing the market shares of some of the large firms in 2000, gives one an idea of the present concentration of the American steel industry. Much of this concentration can be accounted for by the large plant size needed for low-cost operation, but more of it results from mergers. Some of these mergers were

Table 1.1 The major buyers of steel product, 2000

Year	2000
Total shipments	109,051,000 tons
Steel service centers & distributors	27.6
Construction, including maintenance	18.6
Automotive	14.7
Oil & gas	2.7
Agricultural	0.8
Machinery, industrial and electrical	3.5
Household and communications equipment	2.8
Containers, packaging and shipping material	3.4
Other	23.3
Exports	2.6

Source: American Iron and Steel Institute, *Annual Statistical Report*, 2001.

likely undertaken with the objective of concentrating the market in order to control output and raise prices.

Nevertheless, no one firm or group of firms has ever totally controlled the industry. When growth occurred in the industry and new technologies were developed, new firms often entered. For instance, Steel Dynamics listed in Table 1.2 was only founded in 1996. Table 1.2 also shows the prominence of the minimill firms which arose from a new technology. Furthermore, the presence of imports often did much to decrease the ability of domestic firms to raise prices. Thus, steel is typical of many parts of the economy in that prices are neither perfectly competitive nor totally monopolistic.

Table 1.2 The production and market shares of selected large American steel firms, 2000

Company	Total and company production	Market share
Total U.S. production (in tons)	112,242,000	
USX/US Steel	11,791,000	10.5
Nucor*	11,020,000	9.8
Bethlehem (now part of Mittal Steel)	8,900,000	7.9
LTV (now part of Mittal Steel)	8,155,000	7.3
National Steel (now part of USX/US Steel)	6,171,000	5.5
AK Steel	6,392,000	5.7
Birmingham* (now part of Nucor)	3,100,000	2.7
North Star* (now part of Gerdau Ameristeel)	2,900,000	2.6
Steel Dynamics*	2,000,000	1.8

Source: Cooney, 2003, p.10.

* The primary plants of these firms were minimills, while the other firm listed here were mainly integrated producers.

Some of these companies have been merged into other firms; the parenthetical expressions tell which firms now own them.

Historical

The historical importance of the steel industry can be illustrated by many examples. The growth of the industry did much to change the United States. By providing the steel for factories, office buildings, and other major construction projects, such as subways, highways, and large bridges, the industry facilitated the growth of the industrial and urban economy. Many of the leading growth sectors such as railroads in the late nineteenth century, automobiles in the 1920s, and armaments in the 1940s were heavily dependent upon steel.

New industries developed that used steel as a major input; examples include canning, steel drums, bicycles, and machinery. The increasing availability of steel led to great changes in construction, agriculture, and ocean shipping. While the introduction of the auto industry increased the demand for steel, innovations in the steel industry did much to foment the development of the automobile.

The demand for steel inputs led to great changes. The labor requirements of the steel industry provided impetus for the migration into Pennsylvania and the Midwest from Eastern and Southern Europe and the Southern states. The sheer size of the labor force led to conflicts over governance between the companies and the unions. The development of the Michigan and Minnesota iron ore deposits facilitated the growth of navigation on the Great Lakes. The demand for coal from the steel industry led to great increases in that industry.

There were also many examples of technological spillovers from the steel industry to other industries resulting from its emphasis on teamwork and exact chemistry and technologies. For instance, the first large aluminum company, Alcoa, was located in Pittsburgh, a major steel center.

Political

The geographic concentration of steel firm employment makes politicians highly sensitive to the fortunes of the particular companies and unions. There is also a perception that a modern nation needs a large steel industry. The uses of steel in warships and later armored land vehicles and airplanes have lent a national defense implication to the industry's situation. Furthermore, many policymakers believe that a modern manufacturing sector requires a domestic source of steel.

These things have led to government measures to protect steel firms from foreign competition. Almost from the founding of the United States, there has been pressure to put tariffs on iron and steel products. Furthermore, the government used other trade barriers such as quotas, trigger price regulations, and locality preference in government procurement.

The technology of the industry

Two sectors exist in the modern steel industry: the integrated sector which transforms iron ore into steel products, and the minimill sector which uses iron or scrap steel to make the final product. The former accounts for about half of the steel production, but the latter is growing.

The integrated steel mill is a combination of four components: the smelting furnace which changes the iron ore into raw or "pig iron," the steel furnace which refines the iron into steel, the continuous casters, and rolling mills; the latter two form the steel into the shapes useful to mill customers. The minimill sector, which mainly uses scrap steel as an input, has three components: the steel furnace, the caster, and the rolling mills. A few minimill firms, however, have integrated backwards by building the direct reduction steel smelters described below.

Here, the parts of the steel production process are described. In the last 170 years, there were three ways of smelting iron ore: the Catalan furnace, the blast furnace, and the direct reduction furnace. The Catalan furnace used a combination of air blast and hammering to purify iron ore to get a product that can be shaped into a useful iron implement. This furnace was used in isolated areas by firms called bloomaries until the mid twentieth century. Even in the nineteenth century, however, this process was obsolete, accounting for only a small portion of the total production.

The most common type of iron smelter was (and is) the blast furnace, in which a mixture of iron ore, limestone, and coke (purified coal made by cooking the coal without burning it) is oxidized by a blast of air. As a result of this reaction, a mixture of molten iron and carbon collects at the bottom of the furnace, and it is periodically tapped and drained out of the furnace. Historically the resulting iron was cast into shapes called "pigs" before being moved to the steel furnace – hence the term "pig iron." In recent times, however, the iron has been moved to the steel furnace in a molten form.

The third method of smelting iron is the direct reduction process. In this process, hydrogen and carbon monoxide are passed over iron ore, and the oxygen is taken out of the ore. A mixture of iron and carbon is then left in the form of briquettes or pellets. This process requires a source of cheap natural gas; thus, it is used in Venezuela and Saudi Arabia. It is not all that common in other areas, but it does have a presence in the United States.

The steel furnace, the next step in the production process, exposes molten pig iron to oxygen or air and carbon. This gets the excess carbon and other impurities out of the metal and, then, it raises the level of carbon to that needed to form a specified grade of steel. Historically, six types of steel furnaces have been used in the United States, the blister furnace, the crucible furnace, the Bessemer converter, the open hearth process, the basic oxygen furnace, and the electric arc furnace.

The first two were used in the period before steel became a basic industrial product. Blister steel was made by heating bars of iron covered with charcoal in a furnace for several days (Ashton 1968, p. 54). Crucible steel was made from blister steel by melting it in clay pots or crucibles. When it was cooled, it was a much harder and more useful product. Both these products were very expensive, resulting in a very limited use.

In the period of mass steel use, the other four furnaces dominated the industry: the Bessemer, open hearth (OH), basic oxygen (BOF), and electric furnace (EF).

The latter two account for all present-day American production, but the other two have great historical importance. In the Bessemer process, molten iron, scrap, and some other trace ingredients are put into a vessel; air is then blown through the bottom of the vessel, and the impurities are oxidized. The process takes about 50 minutes. The Bessemer process was important historically because it was the first process by which steel could be produced at a cost low enough for wide use.

The open hearth furnace still accounted for about 19 percent of American production in 1975, but the last American OH shut down in 1992. In the OH, scrap, pig iron, and other ingredients are put in a vessel, and air and other gases are blown and burned over the top of the pool of molten metal to eliminate the impurities and leave steel. It takes from five to eight hours to get these impurities out.

For two reasons, OH accounted for the largest amount of steel in the early twentieth century. First, with this process, the charge of scrap steel was variable, and thus mills could take advantage of variations in the price and availability of scrap. Second, the OH process could be altered to take into account the exact nature of the steel output demanded by the customer. In contrast, the Bessemer process worked within very restricted parameters.

The basic oxygen process accounted for the largest amount of steel produced in 2000: 53 percent of U.S. production. This process puts molten iron, scrap steel, and other ingredients into a vessel. Oxygen is then blown into the mix from the top of the vessel, and the impurities are oxidized out of the mixture, creating steel. The process takes about 50 minutes. In some ways, it is a modern version of the Bessemer process. Nevertheless, due to the modern ability to engineer metal, it can produce the wide variety of steel desired by the customers.

The last type of furnace, the electric furnace, transforms iron into steel by exposing the input, usually scrap, to an electric charge. With this process, a charge of iron and/or scrap is put into furnaces, and an electric arc heats the mix. Oxygen then is fed into the furnace to combine with carbon and other non-iron elements in order to leave the combination of carbon and iron that constitutes steel. The process usually takes from one to two hours depending on the amount of electricity used.

In 2000, the EF accounted for 47 percent of the total steel production. As stated above, the steel industry is divided into two sectors: the integrated mill sector and the EF sector. At present, the first sector mainly uses BOF furnaces, but integrated mills often use electric furnaces to produce specialty items and to absorb scrap created within the mill. Thus, the different types of furnaces are often combined into one conventional integrated mill.

In contrast, companies in the EF sector use only the electric furnaces. These firms usually start with recycled or scrap steel rather than newly smelted iron. This sector accounted for about 19 percent of the total steel consumption in 1976, but its share had risen to 47 percent by 2000 and 52 percent by 2004. The plants in this sector are usually smaller than other steel mills: hence the term, minimill.

In the late 1960s and 1970s, the production of stainless steel led to a variant on the EF, called the AOD (argon-oxygen decarburization) vessel. The process allows the refining of stainless steels with very low carbon levels (0.01 percent).

For both the integrated plant sector and the EF sector, the next step has been the continuous caster. This large complex machine, through a combination of cooling and rolling, shapes molten steel into the hard pieces that can be readily changed into the eventual products.

The casters produce three intermediate shapes: billets, blooms, and slabs. Billets are steel pieces about 6 feet long with dimensions of less than 6 by 6 inches, and blooms are steel pieces about 6 feet long with dimensions varying from 6 by 6 inches to 12 by 12 inches. Both shapes are used to make wire, rods, rails, and structural shapes. Historically, slabs are pieces of steel, 2 to 6 inches thick, 2 to 6 feet across and 10 to 30 feet long, though these sizes could vary. In recent years, new technology is casting thin slabs as little as a $\frac{1}{2}$ inch thick. Slabs are used to make sheet steel products, plates, and welded pipe and tubes.

Continuous casters are a relatively recent development (in the last forty years). In the past, the mills used a less direct process to shape molten steel. First the steel from the furnace was cast into molds called "ingots." Then, a separate set of rolling mills, called the primary rolling mills, rolled the ingots into billets, blooms, and/or slabs.

At present, what were once called secondary rolling mills roll these intermediate shapes into final pieces used by the customers. Examples of these shapes include wire rods, bars, rebar, small structural shapes, large structural shapes, rails, tubes, axles, and wheels. There are several types of rolling mills. The sheet mills make sheet, and the other mills make bars, rods, plates, and tubes.

A taxonomy for examining the steel industry

This book divides the history of the industry into reasonably appropriate chronological periods and then applies Michael Porter's taxonomy to each period. (See Porter 1980 and 1998.) Porter suggests that an efficient way to analyze an industry is to divide the subject up into the areas with which firms must deal to operate effectively.

Thus, a chapter is devoted to each period, and in each chapter a section covers each of the following aspects of the steel industry: the product and its production process, the product demand, the industry firms, substitutes for steel, the input suppliers, and the industry's relationship with the government. To operate successfully, firms in a given industry must concern themselves with each of these areas. A conclusion on overall issues ends the chapter.

The section on product examines changes in the production process. Then, a second section considers the demand for the product. In effect, this section examines developments among the particular steel customer sectors.

A third section analyzes the industry competitors and market structure. The section also describes developments with given firms that had industry-wide implications.

The next section examines developments among the substitute products such as aluminum. Under the heading of suppliers, the situations in industries supplying major input to the steel industry are discussed. Among these industries are iron ore, coal, electricity, and scrap steel. In addition to what are normally called suppliers, this section examines the market for steel labor, perhaps the most important input.

Then, the relationship of the industry to government is discussed. The government deals with many other issues impacting steel firms such as trade restrictions like tariffs, antitrust, the environment, safety, and taxes. Finally, in each chapter, a concluding section reviews the major issues facing the industry at that time.

Each chapter applies the Porter taxonomy by describing each of the above components of the market for its period. It is difficult to divide the history of the steel industry into concise periods. Nonetheless, the following chronological divisions are defensible: the early history (from about 1830 to 1860), the take-off (1860–1900), The time of consolidation (1900–1920), the 1920s (1920–1930), the Depression (1930–1940), the war years (1940–1945), post-war prosperity (1945–1970), troubled times (1970–1988), and uneasy stability (1989–2001).

During the first period, the early history (1830–1860), iron was used for many of the functions for which steel is now used, and steel itself was an almost semi-precious metal used in very expensive special products. In the second, or take-off, period (1860–1900), the steel and iron sector became a large industry with raw iron production growing by almost seventeen fold. The great growth was due to increases in both demand and supply.

In the time of consolidation (1900–1920), the industry became consolidated with the formation of U.S. Steel and other companies. In the next period, the 1920s, some smaller steel firms such as Bethlehem and Armco came into their own. The 1930s were the years of depression and the rise of the labor movement. The next stage in the history of the industry was the war years, 1940–1945, when World War II drove events in the steel industry.

Next came post-war prosperity, 1945–1970, when the major issue confronting the industry and the government was the impact on the economy of steel pricing. Then, came the years of decline, 1970–1988, when stagnant demand and imports caused a loss in production and profitability. Last came a time of uneasy stability when there were some signs of recovery but also ongoing problems. In the last chapter, events in the last seven years are reviewed, and conclusions drawn.

The application of the Porter taxonomy to the chronological periods allows for a concise and comprehensive narrative of the last 170 years of the American steel industry.

2 The early history
1830 to 1860

Introduction: technology, growth, and imports

To put the later history of the steel industry in context, we examine the period between 1830 and 1860 just before the introduction of mass steel production. During this period, the American iron sector transformed itself from a group of traditional iron producing firms into a sector capable of innovation in an industrialized economy.

At this time, the iron and steel industry faced issues that would remain into the future. (It is termed, below, the iron sector because most production went to iron use; at that time, steel was only a minor product.) First, the industry experienced great growth. Second, important technological changes took place. A third issue was the foreign competition from mainly British mills which led to a campaign for protective tariffs.

In this period, iron was used for many things for which steel is used today. The increase in iron use can be seen in production totals for the United States which increased from 30,000 tons in 1776 to 200,000 tons in 1830 and 821,000 tons in 1860, an increase of 2,600 percent over 1776. (This contrasts with a U.S. total steel production of 112,242,000 tons in 2000.) Two interacting phenomena explain this growth. First, technological progress in the iron industry itself led to lower prices increasing the use of iron. Second, the demand for iron increased due to growth and technological progress in the customer industries. Thus, both the supply and demand increased in this period.

To understand these developments, we divide the chapter into the following sections: product and production process, demand and users, the firms, substitutes, suppliers – iron ore and labor, government relations, and the conclusion.

Product and production process

This section examines the product, iron, and its manufacturing process. In this chapter, the usual sequence is changed in that the fuel used for smelting and refining is examined here rather than in the suppliers section because the choice of fuel was intimately connected with changes in the production process. First, however, this chapter examines the types of iron or ferrous metals produced in this period.

Other than steel, two types of iron were used in this period: cast iron and wrought iron. Essentially, cast iron was pig iron cast into the shape of the desired product. After being taken from the furnace or shipped to the processor, the pig iron was cast into the shape of the final or intermediate product. An example of a cast iron product was the old-fashioned cook stove.

Wrought iron was pig iron further processed to lower the carbon content. Until the nineteenth century, most wrought iron was made by a sequence of heating, hammering and reheating, and further hammering. The establishments in which this took place were called forges. The blacksmith shop was essentially a small forge, its primary product usually being the horseshoe. The other types of forges made more complex products.

The great bulk of the ferrous products in weight and value came from the above two iron types, but there were uses for steel. It was a semiprecious metal used for specialty items requiring especially hard metal. Of the two types of steel, blister steel was used to make cutlery, files, saws, and scissors, and crucible steel was used for sharp hard items like swords, razors, and pen knives.

In this period, the following major changes took place in the production process: coal replaced charcoal as the major fuel; hot air blasts were adopted for blast furnaces, and the puddling process replaced the forges for many types of wrought iron. At the time, the iron process was divided into two parts: the furnace where iron ore was smelted into pig iron and the refining process where the iron changed into the shape and consistency needed by buyers. The refining stage consisted of three types of processes differentiated by the area in which they take place: the foundry where cast iron products were made, the forge where wrought iron was created by heating and hammering, and the puddling mills where wrought iron was refined by stirring.

Two types of smelting furnaces, the blast furnace (BF) and the Catalan furnace, accounted for all the production. The latter was used in bloomaries which were usually located in isolated areas. The BF produced most of the pig iron. In the middle of the nineteenth century, it was a 30-foot high hollow tower into which large bellows blew an air blast from its bottom. In the 1800s, the bellows were at first powered by water wheels and later by steam engines. The burden or feedstock, consisting of iron ore, limestone, and fuel, was fed into the BF from the top. The air blast resulted in the oxygen being taken out of the ore, leaving a mixture of iron and carbon at the bottom of the furnace.

Two major innovations occurred with the BF in this period. The first was heating the air blast before blowing it into the furnace, and the second was using coal or coke rather than charcoal. Heating the air for the blast lessened the amount of fuel needed to smelt the iron. The blast air was heated by piping it around a flame or heated area. The hot air blast was adopted usually by companies with furnaces using coal. The eastern parts of the country adopted heated air more quickly than the western part of the country. (For our purposes here, the West is defined as the district west of the Appalachian mountains, and the East is defined as the district east of the Appalachian mountains.)

In the 1840s, the United States iron industry began to switch its smelter fuel from charcoal to coal. The British had made this transition in the late 1700s. The United

States had two types of coal. The first, anthracite, required no coking, and initially it produced a better quality of iron than bituminous coal. Anthracite deposits are concentrated in eastern Pennsylvania, where much of the industry was located near customers and iron ore. In contrast, bituminous coal which had to be made into coke, was mainly adopted in the West.

By the late 1850s, most BFs in the East used coal, while most in the West still used charcoal. In the East, the furnace firms using anthracite coal made iron comparable in quality to charcoal iron and imports. In the West, however, the firms using coke from bituminous coal were not able to produce as high a quality iron as the charcoal firms. Consequently, the price of coke-based iron was lower than that of either charcoal or anthracite iron.

In the late 1850s, the West started to adopt coke as a fuel. With improved transportation, iron from the East and Britain penetrated the West. To compete, the western mills had to lower costs. Thus, some firms adopted bituminous coal in order to survive. This led to the development of ways to use coke to make high-quality iron and to explorations for bituminous coal suitable for high-quality iron. Such coal was found in the Connellsville area southeast of Pittsburgh.

The refining part of the iron-making process is divided into two sectors: one producing cast iron products and one producing wrought iron. The cast iron sector consisted of foundries which essentially remelted the pig iron from the BFs and poured it into casts of its products.

In the nineteenth century, the American wrought iron sector had three types of firms: bloomaries, independent forges, and puddling furnaces (puddlers). A bloomary was an integrated company with a Catalan smelting furnace and a forge; it started with iron ore and ended with saleable wrought iron (Ashton, 1968, p. 2 and Smith, 1922, pp. 17–21). These operations were usually located in areas isolated from larger more sophisticated iron firms. In these areas, the usual demand was from simple agricultural items like horseshoes and plowshares. This demand did not justify a BF, but it could justify the smaller Catalan smelter.

The second source of wrought iron was unintegrated forges. Here, the metal purchased from BFs or puddlers was alternatively heated and hammered until it had the right consistency. Then, it was shaped into the pieces demanded by the customers.

The third method of refining pig iron into wrought iron was the puddling process. In puddling furnaces, iron from the BF was remelted and stirred by men standing outside the furnace until the right consistency was reached. An important feature of this process was that the flame from which the heat came was separated from the iron itself. This lowered the possibility of contamination. Then, the iron was hammered in a forge into the shapes wanted by the customers. The puddling was usually at a separate location from the BF. Often, it was at the same location as the shop making the final product.

The major change in the refining during this period was that puddling replaced forges for many uses. By 1856, 85 percent of the wrought iron was produced by the puddling technique. Additionally, over this period, a larger portion of the wrought iron was shaped in the rolling mills instead of forges. Part of this change came about from the increase in the production of railroad rails.

Uses and users

The demand for iron originated in five sectors: (1) household goods, (2) agricultural implements, (3) non-agricultural machinery, (4) construction, and (5) transportation. In the household sector, stoves, pots, and pans were made of cast iron. Other items were made of wrought iron and steel. In the agricultural sectors, ploughs and other implements were made of cast iron. Thus, early on, the demand from agriculture was for cast iron, but there were still some items made of wrought iron, including horseshoes and hoes. With the development of the reaper and the iron plow, the agricultural demand for wrought iron increased.

The use of iron in non-agricultural machinery consisted of many items, the primary one being the steam engine. Table 2.1 shows the uses for the steam engine in 1838. The use of steam in industrial plants, especially textile mills, increased the other uses of iron. More iron was needed to allow for the greater speed resulting from the use of the steam.

In construction, nails were the most important iron items. Nails in the middle 1800s were proportionately more important than today. Other uses for the metal, however, were increasing. Beams and posts made of wrought and cast iron were beginning to be used on bridges and buildings instead of wood. Even on the wood structures, bolts were used. Among the builders of iron bridges and large buildings, there was a movement from cast iron to wrought iron.

In the transportation sector, iron had four uses: the fittings for horse wagons, boats, steam engines, and railroad rails. The first rails were wood, and then a combination of wood and iron, and finally they were made totally of iron. There were two elements of the demand for rails: the original rails when the railroads were first built and the replacement demand when the old rails were worn out. In the 1850s, iron rails had to be replaced every two years. By 1856, rails accounted for 27 percent of U.S. production and, due to imports, 38 percent of wrought iron consumption.

The firms

Between 1830 and 1860, several types of firms operated in the iron and steel industry. Most of them were unintegrated. One type of firm was based on the BF. The other types were organized around the next step in the iron process. For cast iron, foundry firms cast the iron product. For wrought iron, there were four firm types, bloomaries, independent forges, puddlers, and rolling mills.

Table 2.1 Distribution of steam engines by use, 1838

Use	Number
Stationary	1860
Steamboats	800
Locomotives	300
Total	3010

Source: Temin, 1964, pp. 40–1.

Two types of BFs existed during this period. The first that burned charcoal were often called iron plantations. The average charcoal BF produced about 1,000 tons a year. The demand for iron in the United States allowed for about 200 firms in 1830, when total production was about 200,000 tons a year.

Charcoal BFs were located in wooded areas near iron ore deposits. The demand for wood was determined by the charcoal requirements of the furnace. The average BF required 3,500 acres of forest land to sustain a supply of charcoal and other inputs, hence the name, iron plantation. (See Temin, 1964, pp. 83–86). The BF was usually near a stream or river. The air blast engines ran on either water power or steam, both of which required a good source of water. Such a BF had about 54 workers – almost always men. The capital for these furnaces ran between $5,000 and $100,000 depending on the size of the furnace. (In 2007 dollars, that would be between $143,000 and $2,900,000.)

When coal BFs first came into production, coal firms had their own iron ore and coal mines. Using anthracite coal, the earliest of these firms were located in eastern Pennsylvania where both iron ore and coals were available. In the 1850s, two changes led to the ownership separations of the furnaces and mines. First, the development of railroads and canals made it much easier to transport coal and iron ore. Second, larger coal mines had lower costs, and the separate BF could obtain low-cost coal on the market. These improvements also led to the development of iron ore markets.

In the refining part of the iron sector, the foundries which made cast iron products bought pig iron from BFs and sold their cast products to the final users. Bloomaries and independent forges made wrought iron that was sold to the next manufacturer or to the final user. The bloomary smelt iron with a Catalan furnace and then forged it into the desired type of wrought iron. The independent forges worked at two points in the process. Some forge firms took pig iron from the furnaces and transformed it into the wrought iron desired by the customers. Others bought wrought iron from the puddlers and shaped it. These firms stayed about the same size and continued to use the traditional technology, but they garnered a much smaller share of the market. In 1856, bloomaries and independent forges respectively accounted for 29,000 and 53,000 out of the 520,000 tons of wrought iron produced. In Pennsylvania, a typical bloomary produced 91 tons of wrought iron a year and employed 16 employees, and the typical independent forges produced 360 tons a year with 26 employees. For details, see Table 2.2.

Table 2.2 The geographic distribution of bloomaries, independent forges, and rolling mills in Pennsylvania as of 1849

Type of firm	East Number	Average employment	Capacity	West Number	Average employment	Capacity
Bloomaries	6	16	91	0	0	0
Forges	118	26	360	3	14	127
Rolling Mills	56	65	1640	23	131	3130

Source: Temin, 1964, p. 107–108.

The puddlers essentially reheated pig iron and stirred it until it reached the carbon consistency of the desired wrought iron. Then, they sold or moved their product to forges and rolling mills. Many puddlers owned their own rolling mill or vice versa. The puddlers accounted for the bulk of the wrought iron produced in the United States (438,000 tons out of 520,000 tons in 1856).

The rolling mills formed the shapes desired by customers by rolling. At that time, their main product was railroad rails, but they sold other things. Often rolling mills used all of the production of a puddler, and mills rolling rails usually used the total production of a BF. Therefore, rolling mills began to buy up puddlers and BFs.

The geographic distribution of the firms in the refining sector sheds much light on the industry. Table 2.2 shows the distribution of various types of refining firms in Pennsylvania. In contrast to the BF use of coal, the West readily adopted the rolling mills. In doing this, it also adopted the use of coal in the puddling processes. Given the technology of the times, coal in the West could be more readily adopted for puddling and rolling than for the BF. In these two processes, the combustion of the coal took place in a container separate from the melting of the metal.

The degree of vertical integration in the industry depended on the particular fits and resources of the firms in the markets. At first, the BF firms integrated backwards in order to secure a steady supply of iron ore and fuel. When markets developed in coal and iron ore, the BF firms separated from the coal and iron ore mines. The BF firms, however, did not integrate forward because independent forges and puddlers could market final products more efficiently than did BF firms. The independent forges were not integrated backwards because the firms were generally too small to have their own BF. The average size BF (about 1,000 tons a year) could supply three average-size forges (about 300 tons a year). Not needing so much wood or proximity to the iron ore, they could be located near the customers.

When charcoal was the major fuel, puddlers were not integrated with blast furnaces, because the combination of the two used too much land. This pulled them away from woodlands and mines toward the markets for iron products.

In contrast to their relationships with the BF firms, the puddlers and the rolling mills seemed to fit together as integrated organizations. A rolling mill could usually use all the production of a puddling furnace. The larger rolling mills also were starting to buy or build their own BFs. Apparently, one and one-half BFs could supply a typical rolling mills-puddler combination. Nonetheless, as long as there was a wide market for pig iron, meaning a large number of independent BFs and puddlers, no great incentive existed for rolling mills to totally integrate into BFs.

Table 2.3 summarizes the situation in the iron sector in 1860. In Pennsylvania, there were 206 establishments, most of which were independent forge firms. Even in Pennsylvania, where the iron industry was very well developed, there still were some bloomaries with Catalan furnaces. The puddler-rolling mill sector, however, was becoming the dominant part of the industry.

Table 2.3 The adoption of coal as a fuel for blast furnaces: national ratios

	Percentage 1854	*Percentage 1860*
Anthracite & charcoal	46	57
Bituminous coal & charcoal	7	13
Charcoal only	47	30

Source: Temin, 1964, Table C3, p. 268.

Substitutes

Wood was probably the major substitute during this period. Wooden pegs were often used instead of nails. Often machine cogs could be either wood or iron. In buildings, wooden beams, studs, and other pieces were often substitutes for wrought and cast iron. In other cases, wood was used in conjunction with iron; some beams were combinations of wood and iron. Thus, wood was a complement for iron in many other uses. In this period, there were few developments in the wood industry that particularly affected iron use.

Steel and iron had not yet gotten into many uses such as canning. Aluminum, the major substitute for steel at present, was still a rare semiprecious metal used for little other than jewelry and decoration. So, while many of the present uses of iron and steel were not yet on the scene, neither were many of the substitutes.

Suppliers: Iron ore and labor

This section focuses the iron ore and labor markets. The fuel and coal markets were discussed above. During the period (1830 to 1860), iron ore deposits large enough for use by the current technology were found in many areas of the country. Among them were both eastern and western Pennsylvania, New Jersey, New York, the South, Michigan, and Missouri. In many locations, bloomaries and BFs were organized to take advantage of the local sources. The Missouri iron ore, however, was moved to BFs in western Pennsylvania by steamboat. Michigan ores were also starting to be moved by Great Lakes boats. Thus, while most iron ore was owned by BF firms, regional and even national iron ore markets were developed.

There were three labor markets in the iron sector: unskilled labor, skilled labor, and management. Unskilled labor was drawn from a very large pool consisting of rural people and immigrants to the United States. As with the labor for other types of industries, people found jobs in the iron sector through a grapevine consisting of their family and neighbors.

Labor skilled in particular iron and steel making jobs were drawn from a more narrow set of areas. Other than parts of the United States where iron was made, these people tended to come from Wales, Sweden, and Germany.

In the iron and steel sector, management came from a small community of people and families known throughout the nation and sometimes the Western world. Managers tended to move great distances to get the best jobs. For instance, the leading pioneer of the anthracite BF, David Thomas, moved to Pennsylvania from Wales in 1838.

Government relations

With the government, the major issue concerning iron and steel was the tariff. Invariably, iron sellers wanted it raised, while iron buyers wanted it lowered or abolished. The political interplay between these groups made it appear that variations in the tariff led to ups and downs in the industry. When tariffs were raised, the industry boomed. When tariffs were lowered, the industry faltered, and bad times ensued.

Essentially, when the iron market was down, the sellers pressured the government to raise tariffs. This would be done through lobbying and expert advice. Often conventions of iron manufacturers would be organized to pressure the government. Also experts were used to show how the tariffs helped the industry. Henry Carey, the first noted American economist, an owner of an iron furnace himself, often worked with the iron industry on this issue.

When the iron market boomed, prices would go up and buyers would find themselves squeezed. They then would put pressure on the government to lower tariffs. When the cycle repeated itself and the market went back down, the political pressure to raise tariffs would repeat itself. The coincidence of high and low tariffs with rising and falling iron markets led contemporaries to believe that high tariffs helped the industry. Some studies (see Temin, 1964, pp. 23–24) posited that the state of the market may have affected the height of the tariffs and not vice versa, but other studies supported the contemporary assessment (Fogel and Engerman, 1969).

Summary and conclusion

This chapter has shown the state of the iron industry in the thirty years prior to the emergence of the modern steel industry in the 1860s and 1870s. While the industry was small and primitive compared to what came later, it was dynamic as demonstrated by innovations such as puddling and coal fuel.

These changes plus the increase in demand made for an ever-changing environment in that most firms had to be prepared for shocks. At the same time, other firms could succeed by continuing on with their traditional methods. This was similar to the situation faced by the steel and iron industries in the later parts of the nineteenth century.

3   The great take-off

1860 to 1900

Growth and low-cost steel

The period (1860–1900) covered by this chapter can be termed as the take-off because of the great growth in the iron and steel industry. This growth was due to increases in demand and the development of two low-cost methods of making steel, the Bessemer and open hearth (OH) processes. These processes led to the replacement of wrought and cast iron by steel in most uses.

The great increase in the use of iron and steel products came from growth in all parts of the economy. Some historians have termed this period, "the Great Transformation" and the "Take-Off" (See Polanyi, 1957 and Rostow, 1971). In this period, the United States became the world's leading industrial nation.

A look at the actual numbers on iron and steel production conveys an idea of the magnitude of these changes. As shown in Table 3.1, iron production industry grew by 1,580 percent, and steel production increased by 88,000 percent. Steel was transformed from a small sideline of the iron sector into its major product. In 1860, steel production was 13,000 tons, 1.41 percent of the American iron production, and by 1900, it was 11,412,000 tons, 73.9 percent of the iron production.

The development of the Bessemer and open hearth led to changes in the other parts of the iron-making process. The operations of the Bessemer converter required a precise sense of timing and knowledge of chemistry. These attributes were used in many other parts of the production process, especially the blast furnaces and the rolling mills. Even the older crucible steel process increased its

Table 3.1 Production of iron and steel, 1860–1900

Year	Iron	Steel	Process used to make steel
1860	919,770	13,000	Blister and crucible steel
1870	1,865,000	69,000	Mostly Bessemer
1880	4,295,414	1,497,000	Mostly Bessemer
1890	10,307,027	4,790,800	Mostly Bessemer and open hearth
1900	15,443,951	11,412,000	Mostly Bessemer and open hearth

Source: Hogan, 1971, pp. 14, 184, and 185, and Temin, 1964, p. 207, and U.S. Bureau of the Census (1975), p. 694.

production. To see the impacts of these changes, this chapter goes through the six elements of the Porter taxonomy.

Changes in the product and the process

This section looks at the technology of making iron and steel between 1860 and 1900. One major change in this process was the introduction of the Bessemer converter. After describing the development of this process, this section analyzes how its introduction led to changes in the other parts of the steel plant. Then, it goes on to the OH process.

In the 1850s, Henry Bessemer, an Englishman, came up with the idea of making steel by blowing air into the cauldron filled with molten iron. Then, he developed the machinery needed to use this process, including the blower for getting the air into the cauldron. For the Bessemer process to work, however, a dose of pure carbon had to be introduced, and certain chemical reactions were needed for the carbon to mix properly with iron. Bessemer never did find the right mix, and, thus, his original process could not reliably make steel. Nevertheless, in England and some other European countries, he obtained the patents for both the process and machinery.

Robert Mushet, a British metallurgist, discovered and patented the proper chemical mix of iron, carbon, and other ingredients to make steel in the Bessemer vessel. In the meantime, an American, William Kelly, independently discovered the Bessemer process and obtained the U.S. patent on the process ahead of Bessemer, even though he used it to make only wrought iron.

Neither the Kelly nor the Bessemer patents were effective at consistently making steel without the Mushet patent. In England, one firm held both the two Bessemer patents and the Mushet patent. In the United States, however, two groups held the relevant patents. One, including William Kelly, owned the Kelly and Mushet patents. This group has been called the Wyandotte group because their original Bessemer steel plant was built at Wyandotte, Michigan.

A second group obtained the U.S. rights to the machinery patent of Henry Bessemer. Because their plant was originally located in Troy, New York, this group was called the Troy Group. To make steel, the Troy Group needed the Mushet Patent, and the Wyandotte group needed the Bessemer machinery patents. The two groups, then, merged into the Pneumatic Steel Association which held all three patents: the Kelly, the Bessemer machinery, and the Mushet. With these patents, the association licensed other firms, and the diffusion of the invention began.

By 1873, ten Bessemer converter plants were operating in the United States under license from the Pneumatic Steel Association (see Table 3.2). Six-ton Bessemer converters such as the ones placed in the Johnstown, Pennsylvania plant would produce about 30,000 tons of steel a year. With two converters, a plant could produce about 60,000 tons a year. In comparison, an average blast furnace BF at that time produced 1,000 tons a year. Thus, the Bessemer converter processed a lot more material than any other part of the steel and iron process.

The Pneumatic Steel Association became a remarkable mechanism for the diffusion of technology. When the association granted a firm the right to operate a

Table 3.2 The first eleven Bessemer steel plants in the United States

Company	Location	Number of converters	Size of vessel	Date plant opened
Kelly Pneumatic Process Company	Wyandotte, MI	1	$2\frac{1}{2}$ tons	1864
Albany and Rensselaer Iron and Steel Company	Troy, NY	1	$2\frac{1}{2}$ tons	1865
Pennsylvania Steel Company	Steelton, PA	2	$6\frac{1}{2}$ tons	1867
Freedom Iron and Steel Works	Lewiston, PA	2	5 tons	1868
Cleveland Rolling Mill Company	Cleveland, OH	2	$6\frac{1}{4}$ tons	1868
Cambria Iron Company	Johnstown, PA	2	6 tons	1871
Union Iron and Steel Company	Chicago, IL	2	$5\frac{1}{3}$ tons	1871
North Chicago Rolling Mill Company	North Chicago, Il	2	$6\frac{3}{4}$ tons	1872
Joliet Steel Works	Joliet, IL	2	$5\frac{1}{3}$ tons	1873
Bethlehem Iron Company	Bethlehem, PA	2	7 tons	1873

Source: Hogan, 1971, p. 35.

Bessemer converter, it sent a group of experts to build the converter and, then, get it running. In setting up these plants, the Pneumatic Steel Association men not only taught others to operate the plants but also increased their own knowledge of the processes. All this activity led to improvements in the process.

Many of these men became outstanding contributors to the development of the iron and steel industry. Examples of these people were Alexander Holley, Captain William Jones, and John Fritz. Holley worked for several years for the Pneumatic Steel Association and developed a number of innovations that improved the Bessemer process. The major one was the patented removable bottom to the converter.

Often, these men took jobs at the new steel companies. Captain Jones became the manager of the Edgar Thomson Works, the main mill of Carnegie Steel, and John Fritz became the chief executive of the Bethlehem Iron Company.

The Bessemer process required three things not needed by the older iron processes: a higher degree of precision and coordination in the operation of the plant, a knowledge of engineering, and a thorough knowledge of metallurgy. The

Table 3.3. Production of steel by type, 1865–1900

Year	Type of process Bessemer steel	Open hearth	Crucible and blister
1860	0	0	13,000
1880	1,203,000	113,000	81,000
1885	1,702,000	149,000	66,000
1890	4,132,000	575,000	84,000
1895	5,498,000	1,274,000	77,000
1900	7,487,000	3,806,000	118,000

Source: Hogan, 1971, p. 185.

upshot was the great increase in steel production shown in Table 3.3. As of 1880, 22 converters made 1,203,000 tons, and as of 1892, 110 converters produced 4,700,000 tons.

The procedures and ideas needed for the Bessemer process were applied to other areas (See Temin, 1964, Chapter 7). The very large amount of material handled by the Bessemer process created a demand for more production from the other parts of the iron and steel system. The higher heat used in the Bessemer converter led engineers to apply these temperatures to other processes. The mastery of chemistry necessary for the Bessemer process was then applied to processes such as the BF and the rolling mills. This led to a great increase in productivity.

The large throughputs required by the Bessemer process led to increases in the sizes of the BFs. It demanded controlled combustion, changing the character of the BFs. They became larger – reaching a height of 70 feet and a width of 20 feet. Additionally, the blast engines were now powered almost everywhere by steam instead of water wheels.

The need for hotter blast led to the introduction of the Cowper stove. It was a brick structure through which the air is blown both when it is going into the furnace and when it is leaving it. The stove was set up so that the air leaving the BF further heated the air entering it.

The Bessemer incentive to raise the BF production led to a practice called "Hard Driving." In the 1870s, the plant managers began pushing the production beyond the rated furnace capacity. The capacity was set by the construction engineer, when the plant was built, and before 1860, the plant managers rarely pushed their production beyond the rated capacity.

"Hard Driving" was achieved by three methods. First, the managers just pushed more material through the furnace. Second, they employed chemists to study the BF process and find ways to increase the furnace output. Third, over time, as repairs occurred, they modified the furnace in ways that they thought would increase the effective output. This was an experimental process where sometimes the changes increased output and sometimes they did not. The managers also fed information to the engineers and firms building new furnaces.

The long-term results were impressive. By 1880, the pioneer Isabella and Lucy Furnaces of the Carnegie Steel Company were producing about 37,000 tons a year. Later, the Duquesne furnace of the same company reached a production of 100,000 tons a year. By 1890, the average production of the BFs in the United States was a little bit less than 25,000 tons a year. This compares to the 1850 average of 1,000 tons. (Today, the largest furnace produces about 3,000,000 tons a year.)

Supplementing the greater throughput of the furnace itself were improvements in material-handling equipment. The BF firms started to use hoists to get the material to the top of the furnaces. Conveyors, trains, and hand cars were also moved about the furnace or mill yard. Furthermore, often the product, the pig iron itself, was altered to help increase the total furnace output.

The rolling mills also were changed greatly during this period. The metallurgy developed for the Bessemer converters was often applied to the rolling mills. One of the people that did much to improve the rolling mills was John Fritz who in the

1850s invented the three-high rolling mill machine to make rails. In this period, the rolling mill part of the iron or steel plant became divided into the two divisions, the primary rolling mills which produced the intermediate pieces, slabs, blooms, and billets and the secondary mills which produced the pieces used by the customers. Among them were the rails, plates, and sheets. The latter were produced by a slow process with the metal being rolled and re-rolled many times. Furthermore, when necessary, the rolling mills were used to put coatings on the sheets.

The last major change in technology was the introduction of the second major steel-producing technique, the open hearth. It developed somewhat later than the Bessemer process. In some ways, it was an outgrowth of the puddling process.

Emile and Pierre Martin of France and William Siemens of England developed the OH process. In 1868, Abraham Hewitt introduced the process to the United States, and in 1875, the Otis Steel Company of Cleveland, Ohio started the first successful American OH plant. From zero in 1865, the amount of steel produced by the OH process grew to 113,000 tons in 1880, to 574,000 tons in 1890 and to 3,086,000 tons in 1900.

There were two reasons for this increase: the first being the availability of iron ore with a high phosphorous content in Minnesota. With the OH furnace with basic lining, it was possible to use this ore. The second reason was the perceived superior quality of OH steel. While some contemporaries and later historians claimed that this was an erroneous folk tale, metallurgical research has confirmed the scepticism about Bessemer steel. This research found that the major problem with Bessemer steel was its high nitrogen content. It was the result of the air blown into the material by the converter. Some customers, however, continued to use Bessemer steel.

Changes in the uses of iron and steel

The uses for iron and steel changed greatly in this period, 1860 to 1900. The following sectors became important: transportation, agriculture, machinery, construction, and two new sectors, oil and containers.

There were two major components of transportation sector demand for steel, railroads and ships. The railroad demand for steel and iron can be divided into that for rails and that for locomotives and train cars. Rails accounted for most of the Bessemer steel until 1880. Table 3.4 indicates the extent of the growth of rail use. It also shows the levels of railroad mileage, a rough indicator of demand.

From the time they became fairly cheap, steel rails had a great advantage. While iron rails lasted from two to four years, steel ones lasted from twenty to forty years. Rails were a very large part of steel demand in this period. In 1880, almost all steel except the crucible type went to rails, but less than 50 percent of the steel went to rails by 1900.

There are two parts to the demand for rails, new railroad construction and replacement demand. The change in mileage is a good indication of the new construction demand for rail. It varied a great deal averaging about 8,000 miles a year but rising in some years to as much as 15,000 miles. The demand for rails played a very important role in the development of the modern steel industry. Being the

Table 3.4 Production of rails and mileage changes in railroad, 1860–1900

1. Production of rails

Year	Rails	Steel rails
1860	205,000	0
1870	620,000	34,000
1880	1,462,000	968,000
1900	2,386,000	2,385,000

2. Railroad mileage

Year	Mileage
1860	30,626
1880	93,267
1900	258,784

Source: Hogan, 1971, pp. 112, 114, 305, and Temin 1964, p. 275.

chief product of Bessemer steel, rails led to the early and fairly rapid adoption of the Bessemer process.

The other parts of the railroad system using steel were the locomotives and cars. The production of locomotives rose from 300 in 1838 to 1,962 in 1880, and to 3,153 in 1900. At first, these machines were made mainly of iron but later mainly of steel.

The amount of steel used in freight cars increased; it was not as much steel replacing iron as steel replacing wood. Early on, a railroad car could be described as a wooden house on iron or steel wheels. Helping the growth of steel in railroad cars was the development of the hard OH steel items like plates. Over time, also larger and larger proportions of each car were made of steel. By 1900, the bulk of the 113,000 cars produced were mostly composed of steel.

The development of the steel car illustrates the feedback effects of iron and steel industry growth. The first steel railroad cars were gondolas used mainly for coal and iron ore. Much of the coal went into the steel industry, and therefore, the growth of the steel industry fed on the increase in railroad cars.

The second transportation sector that used steel and iron was ocean and Great Lakes shipping. The number of iron and steel ships built in a year increased from one in 1867 to 31 in 1880, and to 90 in 1900. The United States, however, lost its edge in ocean shipping. This is illustrated by the size of the American commercial ocean-going ship fleet compared to the British. In 1866, the British had 5,000,000 tons of shipping compared to the American total of 1,250,000 tons. The major problem with the American shipping and shipbuilding industries was high wages.

Still, American shipbuilding increased; first, the Navy ordered ships from U.S. shipyards, and second, the United States built a large fleet of commercial ships on the Great Lakes. The Navy business led to the development of an important product – steel plate. Since much of the demand for shipping on the Great Lakes came from the steel industry, here is another example of the growth of the steel industry feeding on itself.

Agriculture was also a major source of steel demand. There were many new and improved agricultural machines. Among them was a new version of the reaper and the mechanical thresher which separates the grain from its chaff and straw. The plow was also greatly improved during this period. John Deere developed the caste steel plow. F. S. Davenport invented a plow which could do more than one row. John L. Lane Jr. developed a plow made of laminated or layered steel. The layers consisted of different types of steel or iron. The outside laminated layer consists of hard steel, and the inside layer consists of either soft steel or iron. The hard steel outside layer makes for the easy cutting of the soil, while the soft pliant inner layers absorb the shocks from rocks and different soil consistencies.

Barbed wire became an important source of steel demand. Invented by Joseph Glidden of DeKalb Illinois, it solved a major problem faced by farmers – the high cost of fencing (Webb, 1959, pp. 280–318). Used to keep animals out of the crop land and inside the pasture land, fences were one of the most valuable capital assets in the country. Most fences were made of wooden rails. These fences were quite expensive because it took much labor to construct them. This cost was even larger in the highly fertile prairie lands where there were relatively few trees.

Many attempts were made to find low-cost fencing; among them were experiments with materials such as wire and hedges. Barbed wire was the most successful of these materials. With its barbs, it could keep animals either out of or in the enclosed field as the case may be.

Economically, barbed wire had two major impacts. First, it lowered the costs of farming in all locations. Second, it made the especially fertile but treeless western plains and prairies economical to farm, greatly increasing the country's agricultural productivity. In 1901, 248,000 tons of barbed wire were produced.

Non-agricultural machinery was becoming an important source of demand for steel in this period. It helped shift demand from Bessemer to OH steel. Machine tools, a major component of this machinery demand, often required many types of steel. Many operations were performed with these machines, among them drilling, turning, milling, planing, grinding, and forming. The machines were used not only for shaping steel objects but also for shaping other materials.

Improvements in machine tools increased the demand for steel in two ways. First, with the increase in the number of machine tools themselves, there was a greater direct demand, and, second, improvements in these machines increased the number of objects that could be made of steel. Improved machine tools made it easier to use steel in other objects.

After the 1880s, internal combustion engines and electric motors started to be used in places where steam and water power had been used earlier. This increased the demand for steel in two ways; first, the engines and motors themselves were made of steel. Second, the high speeds at which these motors operated increased the need for more hard metal fittings, cogs, and wheels.

With these machines, metallurgy became more important. There was a search for just the right steel to use for these various machines. Crucible steel was still used for many cogs and wheels in the 1860s and 1870s; this accounted for the increase in the use of that metal. After 1880, however, it was found that many of these items could be made of OH process steel.

The construction industry continued to be a major user of iron and steel in this period. First, large construction and mining machines such as steam shovels and steam bulldozers came into use. Then, two developments in the nail industry affected the steel sector. First, the major material for nails changed from iron to steel. Second, while at first the steel nails like the iron ones were stamped out of sheets, a process was developed for making nails out of wire.

Also, in this period, iron and steel bridges came into use; some were spectacular, gaining much publicity for the steel and construction industries. Examples were the Eads Bridge built over the Mississippi River at St. Louis in 1874 and the Brooklyn Bridge in New York City built in 1883.

Another construction development impacting upon the steel industry was the appearance of the large urban office buildings called skyscrapers. The steel industry itself contributed to this change. From it came the I-Beam, a structural piece of iron or steel that could be used as the major support for a building. Other factors increased the efficacy of these large steel buildings. Among them were elevators, fire-proof hollow bricks, and electric and gas lighting. The pioneering city for these buildings was Chicago, but New York soon followed. (For the special role of Chicago, see Hogan, 1971, pp. 324–327.)

In this period the oil industry became a source of the demand for iron and steel. The industry started with the discovery of commercially feasible oil in 1859. Three objects were used in the oil industry: pipes, tanks, and ships. There were two types of pipe used in the oil industry: skelp and seamless tubes. The former items were made from pieces of sheet steel that were bent into tubes and welded along seams. The seamless tubes were extruded into a hollow tube from a bloom or billet. Different circumstances required different pipes. The steel pipes were used for oil wells for extracting the oil from the ground and for pipelines for moving the oil from well to refinery to customers. The second major use for steel in the oil industry was for tanks. Initially, tanks were used on railroad cars for moving oil. Also, tanks were used in refineries both for processing and storage.

The third major use of steel in oil was for the ships, called tankers. The Russians first used oil tankers for moving oil from their main oil field on the Caspian Sea up the Volga River to the oil customers in Russia. Shortly thereafter, Americans began to build and use tankers.

Containers became a major source of demand for steel, the major component of it at this time being canning. The canning process consists of sealing the produce in a container and then heating it until the organisms that would spoil the material have died. The process was invented in 1809, and from 1809 until the 1840s, glass jars were used for canning. In the 1840s, a shortage of jars led to the use of tin-plated iron and steel. At first, it was a small industry geared to special uses. The demand for canned food brought about by the Civil War led to a great boom in canning and tin-plated iron, but it was the 1890s before the United States built a successful tin-plate facility.

A small but important new source of demand for steel was the bicycle industry. It used seamless tubes for the frame and hard types of steel for the gears and chains. The problems with finding metals for gears and chains were similar to those that later faced the auto industry.

The firms in the industry: the business cycle, consolidation, and innovations

In this period, the major problems faced by iron and steel firms were technological change, growth, and the business cycle. There were also organizational and internal firm governance issues. We examine each of these problems in turn.

During this period, technological change led to a great increase in the minimum efficient size (MES) of the iron-processing plant. (The minimum efficient scale is the smallest plant size at which an increase in plant capacity does not result in a significant decrease in average unit cost.) To illustrate the problem, we examine the change in the minimum efficient scale of various parts of the iron and steel process. For the BF, the best estimate of that size rose from an output of 1,000 tons in 1860 to about 100,000 tons in 1900.

In 1860, the next step in the process for most iron was the puddling furnace. For this process, the minimum efficient size in yearly output was between 1,000 and 2,500 tons in 1860. By 1900, most pig iron was made into steel, and the minimum efficient size plant was about 100,000 tons for the Bessemer process and 10,000 tons for the OH furnace. The efficient size for the rolling mills depended on the particular product, and often they were larger than that of the steel furnace.

With the growth of the industry, many firms entered when times were good but got into financial trouble when times were bad. The periods of booms and depressions were as follows: a boom period, 1862–1871, a depression, 1872–1879, a boom period, 1880–1891, a depression, 1892–1897, and a boom period, 1897–1900. The alternating periods of good and bad times combined with increasing efficient sizes of the plants created an unstable environment. In the boom periods, many companies came into the market. When the depressions arrived and prices fell, many firms found themselves in unprofitable positions. The increasing size of the efficient plants magnified the problems of the older plants.

Table 3.5, showing the changes in the number of blast furnaces over time, gives one an idea of what happened with the firms in the iron and steel sector. Between 1880 and 1900, the number of BFs fell. While the number of furnaces was not equal to the number of firms, most of these furnaces each represented a firm. Since a

Table 3.5. The number of blast furnaces in the United States, 1880–1900

Year	Number of blast furnaces	Iron production	Average size
1880	681	4,295,414	6,308
1890	559	10,307,027	18,438
1900	399	15,443,951	38,707

Source: Hogan, 1971, pp. 14, 184, 185, and 211.

minimum efficient furnace could produce 100,000 tons, there was room for only 154 furnaces instead of the 339 that were in operation. However, transportation costs and specialized demands counteracted somewhat the effect of scale economies. In this situation, firms with seemingly safe geographic and product niches often became vulnerable to competition. Consequently, the number of firms fell off.

Nevertheless, some high-cost firms stayed in the industry or returned to the market when price went back up. This occurred because of the very high fixed cost structure of these firms. If fixed costs were high, variable costs were a small part of the total. Firms remained in business in the short run as long as revenues were greater than variable costs. This means that prices had to drop to a very low level before many firms left the market. This situation only accentuated the downward tendency of prices in a bad market.

Hence, as long as prices are above average variable costs, a firm will keep its mill running, even though it is losing money. Sometimes, a firm's owner would leave the industry, but its capacity would remain in production under a new firm. Many new firms messed up their plants, but the next firm revamped the capacity. Two examples of this sequence were the Pennsylvania Steel Company of Steelton, Pennsylvania and the Maryland Steel Company of Sparrows Point, Maryland. A firm operating one of the plants might go broke, but within a short time another firm began to use the capacity again.

The ability of firms to stay in operation even in times of low prices increased the instability of the environment. As stated above, the firms had two reactions to the problem: price-fixing and consolidation. It was thought that firms could be put in a more secure position if the competitors in particular cooperated on fixing prices. This impulse led to the formation of pools. (The Sherman Antitrust bill forbidding such activity was passed only in 1890, but even after it passed it was not always enforced.)

In order to keep the product prices high, the firms had to control either the amount of product or the price. By controlling the amount produced, the pool automatically controlled the price; the law of demand dictates that decreasing output will raise price and increasing output will decrease price. Conversely, if the pool controlled the price without any firm deviating, the output would automatically be controlled.

The pool organization controlled the behavior of its members through a financial incentive. To be in a price-fixing pool, a firm had to deposit a fund of money in the organization's bank account or "pool" when it first joined and replenished it periodically. If the member firm lowered price or produced beyond its quota, it was fined, and the fine was taken out of its deposit in the pool.

Two problems existed with pools; entry of non-pool firms, and violation of the rules by pool firms forfeiting their fines. The most successful pool was that for Bessemer rails. It succeeded in controlling the amount of product produced, because of the difficulty of getting into the market.

Essentially, the patents held by the Pneumatic Steel Association patents kept most firms out of this market. The most relevant patent was that of Holley on the removable bottom to the Bessemer converter. Until 1875 the association allowed anyone who would pay a license fee to use the patents to make Bessemer steel. After 1875, it allowed no new firms to use the patents; by that time, the first three patents had expired, and the main patent controlled by the association was Holley's. Without it, a firm could not efficiently produce Bessemer steel.

Describing some of the details of this pool gives one an idea of how the pools worked. In addition to controlling the various patents on the converter technology, the Pneumatic Steel Association fixed the price of steel rails.

The Bessemer Pool not only kept firms out of the market but also controlled companies on its fringes. Two episodes demonstrate the pool's policy. The first concerned the Vulcan Works which was started in 1873 but then went bankrupt in the subsequent bad times. The other companies in the pool took over the debt of the Vulcan Works in return for control over the production decisions of the firm. They kept the company's steel production off the market in bad times but allowed it to operate in good times. In that way, they used the Vulcan Works to help keep prices up.

The failure of the Pittsburgh Steel Company of Homestead, Pennsylvania illustrated the role of patents in preventing entry into the rail market. When the firm set up its business, the Pneumatic Steel Association did not allow it to use the Holley patent. Without this patent, the firm could not produce steel at a low enough cost to stay in business during the hard times. The firm soon went broke, and its facilities were purchased by a member of the association, the Carnegie Steel Company.

A third reason for the success of the rail pool was the simplicity of the product. If the products were complicated, then the pool organization had to not only adjust price but also prevent firms from changing effective price by changing quality. If there were many grades of steel, then the pool would have to keep track of not only price but also of the exact characteristics of all these grades. Rails, being a simple product with few grades, did not require a great deal of quality monitoring. Therefore, it was easy to keep track of the real prices of this product.

There were pools in other products, but they usually failed due to one of the three problems – preventing entry, controlling the behavior of the established firms, and/or adjusting quality. Among the products with pools were various kinds of wire, nails, and iron ore. The failure of pools in these and other products increased the pressure for consolidation, but this solution led to the problems of firm governance.

To analyze the governance problems, some particular companies are examined. One problem faced by firms was the control of inputs; it was illustrated by the experience of John Fritz, a technological pioneer who was the chief executive officer of the Bethlehem Iron Company. He had a major dispute on iron ore procurement with his board of directors. Fritz wanted to buy iron ore on long-term contracts, because he needed to control its chemical content in order to run Bessemer converters efficiently. The board of directors wanted to use the spot market to get the best price. The board did not realize that if the content of iron ore was bad, the cost of the converters not working right would more than offset the lower price of the ore.

Fritz won the dispute eventually not only by making long-term contracts but also by backwards integration; Bethlehem bought its own iron mines in Cuba.

The Carnegie Steel Company, the largest and most successful firm of this period, illustrated other governance problems. It was first a partnership of many people and then a collection of many corporations held in a confusing network of cross-ownership. The company's center of production was a group of mills, coking facilities, and coal mines southeast of Pittsburgh. The dominant personalities in building the company were Andrew Carnegie who controlled the iron and steel mills and Henry C. Frick who developed the Connellsville coal properties.

Carnegie and Frick had a dispute over the pricing of coke. The coal and the steel companies were still separate entities even though Frick, Carnegie, and the other partners each had shares of both, but Frick owned a larger share of the coal companies and Carnegie owned a larger share of the steel facilities. Essentially Frick's company sold coke to the steel company, and he wanted a higher price for the coke, while Carnegie wanted a lower price. Eventually the two companies merged together, each having an equal stake in the coke and the steel. The coke was now merely transferred within one organization.

Consolidation became one of the answers to the problems of the instability and the internal governance problems. There were three ways in which steel firms could consolidate. The first was backwards vertical integration where the iron and steel companies would buy the firms supplying coal and iron ore. An example was the purchase by Bethlehem of the iron ore mine in Cuba. The second was forward vertical integration where the iron and steel makers would be companies making the steel products such as bridges, hoops, and pipes.

The third method of consolidation was the horizontal merger of competitors, firms making the same product. Many steel firms, then, started to buy out their rivals. A good example was the purchase of Pittsburgh Steel of Homestead, Pennsylvania by the Carnegie company.

There were two focuses of these horizontal mergers. One focus was consolidating the rival firms producing given steel products such as pipes, hoops, and tin-plate sheet. Examples of these product consolidations were the National Tube Company, the American Wire Company, the American Steel Hoop Company, and the American Tin Plate Company. The second focus of consolidation was basic steel manufacture around given geographic areas. For example, the Illinois Steel Company and later the Federal Steel Company consolidated the steel mills around the Chicago area. Carnegie consolidated the mills around the Pittsburgh area.

Here, two of these consolidations are examined in detail. The Carnegie Company has already been mentioned in regard to the transfer pricing of coke. The basic strategy of the Carnegie Company was to buy out as many of its rival firms in the Pittsburgh area as possible. The Carnegie Steel firm owned the Frick Coal Company with its coal fields and coke ovens. The coke from this part of the firm went to the three steelworks owned by the Carnegie group at Duquesne, Homestead, and Braddock, Pennsylvania. The company also owned some free-standing BFs. The firm owned limestone mines, steamship companies, and a railroad from Lake Erie to Pittsburgh.

By the late 1890s, the Carnegie Company had a very large capacity to produce iron and steel. It could produce 2.8 million tons of pig iron a year compared to a U.S. total 15.5 million tons in 1900. Its steel capacity was 3.5 million tons a year compared to a total national production of over 11 million tons. Thus, the Carnegie firm not only dominated the Pittsburgh area but also controlled a sizeable portion of the total capacity for the United States.

Jones & Laughlin demonstrated the limits of consolidation. It was an example of how firms like Carnegie were never able to totally control iron and steel production even within one area. Starting in the 1850s, Jones & Laughlin built a number of iron and steel mills in the Pittsburgh area, and it remained independent.

One group called the Moore Group set up both geographical and product consolidations. Its National Steel Company had plants in Youngstown, Ohio and Sharon, Pennsylvania. This firm did for eastern Ohio and far western Pennsylvania what Carnegie Steel had done for the Pittsburgh area and Federal Steel for the Chicago area. The Moore group also owned the American Tin Plate Company which produced tin-plate, the American Steel Sheet Companies which made sheet, and the American Steel Hoop Company which made hoops.

In 1901, the above groups were later consolidated into the United States Steel Corporation. This consolidation is further discussed in Chapter 4. Thus, to alleviate the problem of market instability and deal with internal problems, a movement began toward industry consolidation.

Substitutes

In this period, the major modern substitute for steel was developed, but it did not significantly impinge on steel. A process was developed to smelt aluminum out of bauxite. The Pittsburgh Reduction Company was set up to smelt aluminum. The company eventually became Aluminum Company of America or Alcoa.

Input suppliers

This section focuses on events in the following inputs: iron ore, coal, and labor. During this period, there were four major changes to the iron ore industry. First, as indicated in Table 3.6, the iron ore deposits in Pennsylvania and Missouri were

Table 3.6. Sources of iron ore, 1860–1900 (1,000s of tons)

Year	Pennsylvania	Missouri	Michigan	Minnesota	Alabama	Imports
1860	1,351.0	35.0	114.4	*	3.7	*
1870	2,337.3	126.2	859.5	*	11.4	*
1880	1,951.5	344.8	1,948.3	*	171.1	493.4
1890	1,560.2	265.7	5,856.2	864.5	1,570.3	1,246.8
1900	877.7	41.4	9,926.7	9,834.4	2,759.2	897.8

Source: Hogan, 1971, pp. 20, 196, and 203.

* The information was not available.

depleted. Second, Alabama and Colorado developed iron and steel industries around their local sources of iron ore and coal. Third, the iron and steel firms on the East Coast such as Bethlehem, Pennsylvania Steel, and Maryland Steel began to look abroad for iron ore. Spain, Cuba, and Chile became the major sources of iron ore imports.

The fourth change, however, was the most important: the growth of iron ore production in the Lake Superior areas of Minnesota, Wisconsin, and Michigan. Two major difficulties had to be overcome for this area to be a major source of iron ore: lake transportation, and the chemical content of the ore. For the iron ore to be moved efficiently from the mines to the mills, a canal was needed to circumvent the cataracts on the Sault Ste Marie River which connected Lakes Superior and Huron. A canal was completed in 1858. The development of large steam ships on the lakes further increased the efficiency at which the ore was moved to the mills over the Great Lakes.

The second difficulty was the phosphorous content of the very large iron ore deposits in the Mesabi Range of Minnesota. The Bessemer converter and the early BFs could not effectively handle them. The OH furnaces with basic linings could handle these ores, and the introduction of that process made possible the use of these deposits. Accordingly, changes in the BF were made to accommodate this ore. With these developments, the major source of iron ore became the upper Great Lakes.

In this period, there was a great change in the fuel used for the iron and steel industry. As shown in Table 3.7, anthracite coal, which had earlier replaced charcoal as the primary fuel, was now replaced by bituminous coal. Even so, the amount of iron smelted with charcoal continued to grow until the 1890s. The demand for iron and steel grew so much that even very obsolete processes could continue to operate.

Two developments eventually stopped the growth of the charcoal furnaces: the depletion of the forests and the efficiency of the coal BFs. With the lack of forests and competition of the coal furnaces, the charcoal part of the industry started to decline in the 1890s.

In the 1850s and 1860s, anthracite coal was the most efficient fuel for iron smelting, but other developments led to its eventual demise. It became the best fuel to heat homes, factories, and offices. This greatly increased its price to the point where the bituminous coal BFs had lower costs.

Table 3.7 Types of fuel used by iron and steel, 1860–1900 (1,000s of tons of pig iron processed by each type of fuel)

Year	Anthracite	Charcoal	Bituminous coal
1860	519.2	278.3	122.2
1872	1,369.8	501.6	984.2
1880	1,807.7	537.6	1,950.2
1890	2,448.8	703.5	7,154.7
1900	1,879.3	380.7	13,134.9

Source: Hogan, 1971, pp. 25 and 205.

Table 3.8 Daily wages (US$) in the iron and steel industry, 1860–1900

Year	Founder	Keeper	Iron laborer	Manual laborer	Military officer[a]
1860	2.25	2.01	0.80	1.03	6.64 [1865]
1870	3.86	2.94	1.45	1.52	
1880	3.08	1.78	1.00	1.32	
1892	Heater[b]	5.65	1.68	2.44	
1900[c]	Heater	4.98	1.80	2.59	8.64 (1898)

Source: Hogan, 1971, p. 79, U.S. Bureau of the Census (1975), pp. 168 and 176, and Fitch, 1969, p. 157.

Notes
[a] A military officer is used for a comparison because the income of an officer gives one a good indication of the income needed to support the life style of a middle class person.
[b] The heater was a worker with a skill level comparable to the founder and keeper.
[c] This date is 1907 for the heater.

Several other events led to the rise of bituminous coal as the major fuel for the iron and steel industry. Starting with the Connellsville mines, many more deposits of coal useable for iron and steel were found in Pennsylvania, West Virginia, Alabama, Colorado, and Illinois. Furthermore, improvements in the coke ovens and BFs increased the number of coal types that could be used for smelting iron.

Two labor issues assumed importance during this period: wages and unions. Steel was often berated for being a low-wage industry by politicians and social reformers, and this claim led to public sympathy for the union movement in the steel industry. Table 3.8 gives an indication of the level of general wages in the steel industry. Steel workers' wages are compared with those of a military officer because the income of an officer is roughly the income needed to support a middle-class life style. The skilled workers had pay somewhat above the average for manufacturing labor, but they were not as high as that of the military officer.

Two large unions were active in the iron and steel industry during this period. The first one to be organized, the Sons of Vulcan, was centered around the old iron technology. The bulk of the member were puddlers, the people who worked in the puddling furnaces to produce wrought iron. This union went into a decline in the 1870s, but it was soon replaced.

Like its predecessor, the Amalgamated Association of Iron and Steel Workers was dominated by the iron puddlers. Its major problem was that it was organized around the old centers of production. Workers usually came to know each through the parts of the mill in which they worked. A union would attract workers by using the network of friends that develops around the various parts of a mill. The major parts of the mills in which the Amalgamated Association was organized were the puddling furnaces. They were becoming less important; consequently, these furnaces employed a smaller and smaller proportion of the work force compared to the new Bessemer and OH steel shops. Thus, being centered in the declining parts of the steel mills put the Amalgamated Association at a disadvantage.

The stake that the union had in the old technology also prevented it from adjusting to new situations. One issue was the eight-hour day; in the 1880s, many managements actually wanted it, especially in the rolling mills. It was found that a shift of eight hours fitted into the organization of the rolling mills better than the twelve-hour day. It was introduced in some areas in the 1880s. The union heads were willing to go along with the companies, but the rank and file did not like it because the pay for the eight-hour shift was less than for the twelve-hour shift.

Even with the conflicts with the new technology, the Amalgamated Association might have succeeded in organizing the production workers in the industry but for the opposition of certain companies. Most of the iron and steel workers in the Pittsburgh area were members of the Amalgamated Association of Iron and Steel Workers. The Carnegie Company, the largest company in the area, played an instrumental role in its decline. Andrew Carnegie had ostensibly been in favor of unions. In contrast, Henry C. Frick, his number two, opposed unions; Frick persuaded Carnegie to follow him in a number of conflicts with the unions. The result was a series of strikes the worst of which was at Homestead, Pennsylvania in 1891. Due to slack labor markets, the Carnegie Company could bring in strikebreakers. Violence resulted, and Frick was shot and wounded, but the union was broken. (The would-be assassin was a radical activist who was not connected to the Homestead union, but the act still militated against the workers.) By 1893, the Carnegie Company was totally non-union, and by 1897, the other Pittsburgh firms followed.

Three things destroyed the early steel unions. First, they were skill centered, and often that prevented them from uniting with the other workers in the plant. Second, the management opposition was fatal. Third, immigration from abroad and other parts of the nation provided alternative workers who made the strikes ineffective.

Government policy

Government policy helped the iron and steel firms in many ways. First, the local governments usually but not always supported the companies in strikes. They protected the mills from the strikers, and often helped strikebreakers to go through the picket lines. The state governments set up the general incorporation laws that made it easier for the firms to organize themselves. Additionally, the national government tariffs affected the iron and steel industry.

Between 1860 and 1883, the tariff-business cycle interaction described in Chapter 2 broke down. The high tariff of 1861 was followed by a boom which resulted from the Civil War. This war affected the industry more than any change in trade policy. Consistent with the earlier cycle, the low tariff of 1867 was followed with a slight lag by the depressed business conditions starting in 1869. After this recession, however, the older pattern did not reassert itself; tariffs were not raised on steel products. In the 1870s, the iron and steel industry did not re-raise steel and iron tariffs to the earlier levels.

Beginning in the 1880s, the position of the iron and steel industry toward tariffs began to change. First, the industry was divided on the issue. Different firms had different attitudes toward the tariffs. The East Coast firms such as Bethlehem, Maryland Steel, and Pennsylvania Steel wanted low tariffs because they used iron ore from abroad. In the lobbying efforts, these firms often allied themselves with interests wanting low tariffs such as farmers. In the rest of the industry, some firms made products for which there was strong import competition, and others made products for which there was little or no import competition.

Many iron and steel entrepreneurs felt that their industry had gotten so efficient that tariffs were no longer important. This attitude was reflected by the two generally protectionist tariff bills of the 1890s. The McKinley Tariff Bill of 1890 was famous for high tariffs on most goods, but it did not raise tariffs on most steel products. The Dingley Tariff Bill of 1897 raised the tariff on some steel products, but it had little impact because not that many steel products were imported in the subsequent periods.

The tin-plate industry was an interesting case study on the effect of tariffs on new markets. The McKinley Tariff did raise the tariff on this product. At the same time in 1890, the first tin-plate mills were built in the United States. The industry had become competitive, and by 1896, domestic tin-plate production surpassed imports.

The American tin-plate industry has been cited as a representative case of an infant industry argument where tariffs allow new industries to develop. A difficulty with this argument is that the tin-plate mills had been built shortly before the McKinley Tariff had passed. Nevertheless, one can argue that the builders of the mills could have anticipated the tariff. William McKinley was from Ohio, an iron and steel manufacturing state; consequently, the builders of tin-plate would very well have known that the tariff would be imposed. A plausible argument, however, can be made that, tariff or no tariff, they would have been built anyway. The introduction of the OH increased the supply of steel used for tin-plating. Furthermore, the demands for tin-plate increased. Consequently, the industry could very well have developed in America without the tariff. With the information presently available, one cannot make a definite conclusion on the subject.

Conclusion

In this period, the steel industry developed into a great sector with production rising from just over 13,000 tons to just less than 12,000,000 tons. Increases in both supply and demand accounted for this great boom. The great increase in supply was brought about by the new steel-making processes and the improvements in the blast furnaces and rolling mills. The rise in demand came from increases in the many steel-using industries. Even with its instability and governance problems, the industry did much to help change the United States into the world's leading industrial nation.

4   Growth and consolidation
1900 to 1920

Introduction

The first decades of the twentieth century saw an immense growth in steel production and the consolidation of the industry into a few large firms. Most attention has been given to the formation of the United States Steel Corporation (U.S. Steel), but smaller competitors such as Bethlehem, Republic, and Armco also grew significantly.

To examine these issues, we follow our standard taxonomy by first analyzing changes in the product and its production and the steel customers. Next, the activities of the competing steel companies are scrutinized. After that, we examine substitutes and the steel input markets (iron ore, coal, and labor). Finally, government actions toward steel are analyzed, and a conclusion follows.

Growth and the production process

In this section, innovations in the production process are described. Before going into the change in the process, however, we show the growth in total production to lend context. Table 4.1 shows that total steel production increased over four-fold from 11.41 million tons in 1900 to 47.19 million in 1920. Most of this addition resulted from the rise of the open hearth (OH) process which increased over ten-fold from 3.81 to 36.59 million tons, going from 33 percent to 77 percent of the total. This period also saw the advent of the new electric furnace (EF) that replaced

Table 4.1 Steel production in the United States broken down by process type 1900–1920, 1,000s of tons

Year	Total steel production	Open hearth	Bessemer	Crucible	Electric furnace
1900	11,410	3,810	7,490	110	0
1905	22,420	10,050	12,250	110	10
1910	29,230	18,490	10,540	140	60
1915	36,010	26,520	9,280	130	80
1920	47,190	36,590	9,950	80	570

Source: Hogan, 1971, pp. 413 and 420.

the crucible process in most specialty uses. Now, the technological innovations behind these changes are analyzed starting with the blast furnace (BF).

In this period, almost all the iron was smelted by BFs. By the early twentieth century, most iron was moved to the steel furnace in a molten form, but significant amounts were produced by merchant furnaces which sold the metal to other firms; in these plants, the iron was still cast into pigs.

Three major changes in BF technology occurred during this period. First, much more of the iron ore came from Minnesota where the iron and phosphorous content of the ore was much higher. Additionally, the ore came out of the mine in the form of fine dust. It was difficult to smelt this fine ore in the older plants, but changes in the shape of the newer BF vessel made it possible to use it efficiently.

Connected to this change was an overall increase in the size of the furnaces. This led to greater productivity. While the number of operating furnaces rose and fell with economic conditions, the average unit production rose from 59,435 tons in 1900 to 170,949 tons in 1920. There was also much idle capacity in the country; in 1920, 236 out of a total of 452 furnaces were idle.

The third development in the BF was in the auxiliary equipment connected to it. To improve the reactions within the furnaces, stoves (which looked like high towers similar to the furnace itself) were added to the plant to further heat the air going into the furnace. Additionally, the hoists that fed the materials into the furnace were becoming mechanized.

In the next part of the process, four types of steel furnaces converted pig iron into steel: the OH, the Bessemer converter, the crucible, and the EF. The major development in this part of the process in the period was the shift from Bessemer to the OH furnace. In the first two decades of the century, the production of OH steel rose over 800 percent, while Bessemer production only increased 32 percent.

There are three reasons for this change. First the OH furnaces did a better job at processing the iron ore from Minnesota. Second, the OH was better suited to use scrap steel than the Bessemer process. In the latter process, the dose of scrap used for each steel heat was relatively fixed, while it could be varied for the OH. With the OH, the steel companies could adjust their use of scrap to conditions in its market. With the greater use of steel, more scrap was becoming more available.

The third reason for the rise of the OH was the most important. With this furnace, the product specifications were easier to alter and control. The uses of steel became greater, and this wider patterns of demand increased the number of differing specifications. The greater time used in the OH enabled the steel firms to vary the types of steels more than in the Bessemer process.

While the Bessemer Process was eclipsed as the major source of steel, it did display signs of progress. The converters got larger – going from about 6 ton vessels to vessels of between 12 and 15 tons. Nonetheless, the efficiencies indicated by these greater sizes could not offset the advantages of the OH process for most products.

The old crucible process had been overshadowed by the Bessemer and open hearth methods in the late nineteenth century. There were, however, certain types of hard steel with tight specifications that were still most amenable to the crucible process. Examples were the steels used for machine tools, bearings, axles, and certain machinery parts. In the first two decades of the twentieth century, however, the crucible furnace was again eclipsed by another process in even these narrow product lines.

The EF became important with the increased availability of relatively low-cost sources of electricity. In 1878, William Siemens, who had also worked on the OH process, found that electric arcs could be used to heat iron charges and adjust the carbon content to make steel. With the EFs one could adjust the iron and carbon content more precisely than with either the OH or Bessemer process.

While the process was still relatively expensive, there were many uses including the products originally made from the crucible process. Four factors helped spread the process. First, electricity prices dropped during this period making the process more economical. Second, the furnace was very flexible in that it could fit into plants using other processes. Sometimes it was combined with the OH, Bessemer, and even crucible methods to further refine the product. Third, it was found that the EF could "produce a better steel" (Hogan, 1971, p. 418). Certain parts of the new machines such as cylinders, piston rings, and tappets required very strong and reliable metals.

In this period, rolling mills still consisted of the traditional two parts: the primary mills and secondary mills. Two changes characterized this sector in this period. First, the production of certain products was greatly increased. With development of the automobile and other similar machines, the demand for sheets increased greatly. Additionally, a new superior shape for large-scale steel construction was invented. It was called the Grey I-beam or H-beam after its inventor, Henry Grey. This beam could be used in many larger buildings than could the earlier types of steel shapes.

The second major development in the rolling mills was the advent of the electric motor as the source of propulsion for the rollers, hoists, and other moving parts of the plant. Previously, the power to move these parts was provided by steam. By 1920, it was obvious that in almost all applications electricity was more efficient (Hogan, 1971, pp. 431–441). One of the pioneer plants in using electricity was the new U.S. Steel plant in Gary, Indiana.

Growth in the uses of steel

Technological change and the introduction of new products led to a great increase in steel use throughout the economy. The following sectors were important in the period 1900 to 1920: transportation, construction, agriculture, machinery, oil, and containers.

In this period, the railroad industry reached maturity. In 1916, the point-to-point railroad mileage reached its peak, but due to the increase in double tracks, the actual total track mileage continued to increase, rising from 258,784 miles in 1900 to 406,579 miles in 1920 (Hogan, 1971, p. 652). Between 1900 and 1920, traffic on the road also rose with freight ton miles increasing from 141.6 billion to 255 billion tons, and passenger mileage increasing from 16 billion to 47.4 billion. Thus, while the rail system stopped expanding geographically, its use intensified.

Table 4.2 Statistics on steel use by railroads, 1900–1920

	Total production of iron and steel rails (1,000,000 of tons)	Number of locomotives	Number of freight cars	Number of passenger cars
1900	4.2	3,153	113,070	N/AVAL
1905	3.8	5,491	165,155	2,551
1910	4.1	4,755	180,945	4,412
1915	2.5	2,085	74,112	1,449
1919	2.5	3,272	163,185	511
1920	2.9	3,672	75,435	1,440

Source: Hogan, 1971, pp. 653, 655, 659, and 660.

Table 4.2 shows the trends in the use of steel in railroads. The sale of rails reached a peak of 4.4 million tons in 1906. After that it dropped to 2.9 million in 1920. Two things led to this change, first, the expansion of the system stopped, and, second, the quality of the rail rose, attenuating the replacement demand.

The drop in demand for rail steel was partly offset by an increase in steel use among rolling stock. The rather flat statistics of the rolling stock in Table 4.2 hide the increase in steel use in this sector. Both the proportion of all steel freight cars and the amount of steel used in the rest rose during these two decades. Steel was also rapidly adopted for passenger cars during this period. To sum up, even though the demand for steel from railroads was starting to attenuate, it still was the largest user of steel, with rails accounting for about 6 percent of the total production in 1920.

The manufacture of automobiles emerged during this period, and by 1920, it was well on its way to becoming America's largest industry. The number of autos produced rose from only 4,152 in 1900 to over 1,600,000 in 1920, and the total automotive use of steel also increased from insignificant in 1900 to over 1,000,000 tons in 1919.

This rise in demand led to changes in the composition of the steel product. Certain parts of the automobile required special types of metal. The engine blocks, cylinders, pistons, and many gears required hard heat-resistant types of specialty steels. For the frames and bodies of cars, a steel able to take rough jolts from the road was needed. By 1920, it became apparent that the outside body of the car was best made of sheet steel.

At first, the steel industry was hesitant to develop and supply these products. The larger companies faced growing demand from other sectors. As a result, the development of the new alloys fell to small firms such as Armco of Middletown, Ohio and United Steel of Canton, Ohio.

By the second decade of the century, however, most steel companies came to recognize the promise of the auto industry, and they began to address its problems. The industry developed chromium, vanadium, and nickel steel alloys which could be used in the parts of the automobile with special heat and stress problems. Sheet steel was also improved during this period in ways that made it more suited to the automobile. The demands of the auto industry also influenced the development of machine tools. The increased demand for these specialty steels by autos and the machine tools used in their manufacture hastened the adoption of the EF.

The third transportation industry that used much steel was shipbuilding. This was a period of great technological change in ships. Two new sources of propulsion were introduced: steam turbines for larger ships and diesel engines for smaller boats. The already growing advantage of power ships, usually made of steel, over the old sailing ships, usually but not always made of wood, increased.

Even with these improvements, the American shipbuilding industry was troubled in this period. In ocean shipping, the United States was left behind by the lower-cost British and German industries. Even government subsidy programs did not change this situation.

Several things, however, lessened this problem. First, there was considerable shipbuilding activity on the Great Lakes which were sheltered from international competition by the long St Lawrence River. Second, the American maritime law dictated that shipping along the American coast be done only in U.S.-built ships. Third, America developed a lead in building oil tankers which counteracted industry problems in building other ships.

The military situation of the country also helped U.S. shipbuilding. Between 1900 and 1915, the United States enlarged its Navy. World War I increased the demand for American-built ships. Later, this country's entry into the war led to a large shipbuilding program to answer the need for moving troops and supplies to Europe.

Construction was also a large steel-using sector; the production of structural shapes, this mainstay of construction steel, increased from 913,000 tons in 1900 to 2,553,800 tons in 1920. Many innovations occurred with steel construction materials.

In this period, the demand for large office buildings increased, and the modern skyscraper was further developed. The center of skyscraper construction moved from Chicago to New York. Many famous buildings such as the Woolworth, Metropolitan Insurance, and Flatiron Buildings were put up during this period.

Facilitating the construction of these buildings was the Grey I-beam or H-beam which had 30-inch flanges. Henry Grey invented this type of steel shape at his mill in Wisconsin near Duluth. The first mill to make these beams was in Germany. Finally, in 1906, Bethlehem Steel adopted the Grey beam, and its production began in earnest. Additionally, plates used in walls and floors were also part of the structure of many buildings. Other construction uses for steel were for bridge towers, subway walls and supports, and factories. Reinforced concrete also became popular with construction engineers during this period. This increased the demand for bars. Many large edifices such as the Warton and Montgomery Ward buildings used reinforced concrete.

In this period, the steel sector supplying machinery underwent important changes. The steels used for machines and machine tools vastly improved. Prior to this period, the metal used for these wheels, gears, and cogs was steel that went though a "hardening" process at the point of fabrication. This process was a hit-and-miss proposition where sometimes the metal would come out right and sometimes not.

Metal processed this way was replaced by special use alloys which were usually mixtures of iron, carbon, and other metals such as tungsten, manganese, and vanadium. The introduction of the EF also increased the ability of the steel firms to provide low-cost reliable specialty metals. Before this, much of the steel for these uses was made by the crucible process which was slow and idiosyncratic in its output.

The second factor increasing the use of steel by machinery was the increase in the uses of many types of machines such as bulldozers, steam shovels, conveyors, fork-lift trucks, industrial tractors, and hoists. Additionally, the paper industry provided a market for steel in its rolling machines and pulp mixers.

One steel-using industry that increased greatly was electrical machinery. First conceived in the 1880s, the electrical industry used steel of two types. First, the large structures such as power plants and line towers called for conventional con-struction steel. Certain types of electrical equipment called for new specialty steels. For instance, the turbines used to generate electricity called for special carbon steel that allowed for high temperatures and speeds. Transformers vital in the transmis-sion and distribution of alternating current used cores made of special silicon steel.

Two types of steel containers became more important in the first two decades in the twentieth century: tin-plated cans and steel drums. The growth of cans and can-ning is reflected in the great increase in tin-plate steel production from 353,000 tons in 1900 to 1,500,000 tons in 1920. The safety of canned goods greatly increased. This development brought about the increase in the food products amenable to canning. Examples were pineapples from Dole and soups from Campbell's.

This period saw the manufacture of cans become a separate sector. This resulted from the invention of mechanized can-fabricating machines. Two companies, American Can and Continental Can, emerged as the dominant firms in this sector.

At this time, then, the tin can sector emerged with three separate sets of firms: the steel firms making the tin-plated steel, the can-makers fabricating the cans them-selves, and the food firms canning the food. The steel firms used furnaces and rolling mills, while the can-makers had the complicated machinery for making cans and a knowledge of the canner customers. Lastly the canners employed knowledge of the canning and marketing of the food.

Steel barrels were used in this period primarily to move and store petroleum products. A major developer of the product was Mrs Elizabeth Cochrane Seaman, who was also known as the journalist Nellie Bly. She invented a new straight-sided barrel that fit the needs of the user. Then, she ran the company that marketed the barrels, but she lost the company in 1914, ironically right before the war boom in barrels.

In this period, the agricultural use of steel did not change a lot. There was still the demand for steel in reapers and plows. The mechanical tractor and farm trucks had not yet been adopted on a large scale. As of 1918, there were 85,000 tractors and 80,000 trucks on the American farms, as opposed to 26,500,000 mules and horses. Thus, animal power was still the major source of energy in the farm sector.

An indirect effect on steel of developments in agriculture was the increase in the use of automobiles by farmers. Farmers used cars for many purposes other than transportation. The engine of a Ford Model T car could be disconnected from the power train so that it could be used for power on various farm tasks. As of 1918, a low estimate of the number of farmers with cars was 950,000. This figure was to increase greatly in the next decade.

In this period, the oil industry grew greatly, rising 600 percent from a production of 63.6 million barrels in 1900 to 442.9 million barrels in 1920. The supply of oil increased massively with the discoveries in Louisiana, Texas, and Oklahoma. This all led to a great increase in the demand for steel pipes of almost any type.

All in all, technological change in a wide set of industries and the introduction of new products greatly increased the demand for steel during the first two decades of the twentieth century.

Competitors

In this section, the structures and changes in the pivotal steel companies are described. The major event was the formation of U.S. Steel. Although this corporation dominated the market, the activity of other companies cannot be ignored. Below, the activities of four other companies are also described. Each of these latter firms illustrates an important aspect of the competition that developed in response to U.S. Steel.

U.S. Steel

In 1901, the United States Steel Corporation was founded; it was a merger of a number of major iron, steel, iron ore, metal fabricating, support and input firms. It had a capitalization of $1.4 billion ($32.9 billion in 2007 dollars). The two biggest components were Carnegie Steel and Federal Steel.

The formation of this firm has raised many questions about not only the American iron and steel industry but also the whole business sector. To understand why U.S. Steel was founded and why it behaved in the manner in which it did, we examine the environment of American business in the late nineteenth and early twentieth centuries. Between American businessmen and bankers, a strategy called the Trust Movement developed. The Trust Movement posited that if one firm or group had a large market share, then it could earn higher profits by charging high prices. Often in the newly created national markets, prices were unstable. In periods of low prices, many firms would face bankruptcy. Chapter 3 describes many of these episodes in the iron and steel markets. Lamoreaux (1985) develops a model of the price fluctuations that describes these situations. Firms used price-fixing agreements to keep prices high, but usually these schemes did not work. Consolidating the industry into a large dominant firm was viewed as a way to prevent this instability. These consolidations were often organized as trusts, and even when they were set up as some other legal entity, they were still often called "trusts."

The founders of these consolidated firms also believed they could achieve lower costs. First, these entrepreneurs believed in the adage that "large is efficient." Large firms could produce at lower costs than the smaller firms. This concept is called scale economies. Costs also could be lowered by gaining control of their raw materials, thereby obtaining them at a lower price.

Whether the goal was raising price or alleviating price instability, the founders and managers of the trusts faced serious problems, including the threat of entry and competition from established firms outside of its control. Often the question was how fast entry could take place. Some trusts would make a great deal of money before the entry took place. Others did not earn high profits before entry occurred. In some situations, the dominant firm could use its control of inputs to slow entry or rival expansion. In many cases, entry or the enlargement of rivals could not be prevented. Nevertheless, during the time when entry or rival enlargement was being affected, there could be a period in which the dominant firm could still make high profits. (See Gaskins, 1971 and Stigler, 1965 for models of this theory.)

This problem did not prevent many people from attempting to form dominant firms or trusts. Examples include the American Tobacco Trust founded by James B. Duke, the famous Standard Oil Trust (Standard Oil Company) of John D. Rockefeller, and General Electric in electrical equipment.

In general, most companies were not able to take control of a whole industry because of entry. Often, scale economies were less than anticipated. Furthermore, industry growth may have, on occasion, overtaken any plans to monopolize.

These problems were complicated by the attitude of the government. Antitrust had developed in response to a fear of the power of these large consolidations. While the Sherman Antitrust Act had been passed in 1890, the case law had not been developed. Thus, what was legal was not always clear, and companies, including U.S. Steel, followed certain practices that were later ruled as illegal. The courts had not yet determined how much market shares constituted legal "monopolization." It was only by 1913 that the Standard Oil and American Tobacco cases set the precedent of the government breaking up firms who had (1) too much market share and (2) participated in certain "anti-competitive practices."

This situation did not stop businessmen from trying to consolidate the steel industry. In fairness, a motivation other than the desire for exorbitant profits may have impelled these consolidations. It derived from the situations described in Lamoreaux (1985) and in Chapter 3. Typically, capital goods markets, such as iron and steel, experienced price instability resulting from wide swings in demand.

This instability could be accentuated by the extremely competitive policies of some firms. Andrew Carnegie had the largest firm in the market with a concentration of capacity in the Pittsburgh area, a center of both demand and supply. Carnegie's strategy was to develop plants with very low costs and take on as much business as possible by charging prices lower than the competition.

In the iron and steel sector, there was a feeling of unease in the steel industry which led to consolidations in basic steel and in specialized products. In the 1890s, the cyclical nature of iron and steel seemed especially acute. From 1890 to 1896, there was a major depression. By 1896, prosperity had returned, but the economy slowed up a little in 1899 and 1900.

By 1899, this movement had resulted in the development of several mega-firms. In basic steel, three large firms had emerged; one, Carnegie Steel, operated in the Pittsburgh area. The second, Federal Steel, was a consolidation of the major steel and iron works in the Chicago area. Backed by the banker J. P. Morgan, Federal

Steel was created by a merger of Illinois Steel, Lorain Steel in western Ohio, and the specialist firm, American Bridge. The third firm was the National Steel Company, a basic steel producer centered around Youngstown, Ohio. It had been organized by William H. Moore who headed the Moore Group.

The second group of new firms specialized in particular final products. One of the new consolidated firms, National Tube Company, specialized in pipes and tubes. Aside from National Steel, the Moore Group also included the specialist firms American Steel Sheet Company, American Steel Hoop Company, and the American Tin Plate Company. The American Steel & Wire Company headed by the colorful John W. "Bet a Million" Gates had similarly merged together the bulk of the plants making steel wire.

Precipitated by the hyper-competitive strategy of Carnegie, there was considerable talk about merging all these groups together. The basic steel producers such as National and Federal Steel felt threatened by Carnegie's philosophy of low prices and full capacity. The people associated with Morgan in Federal Steel and Moore and Gates in their companies believed that the larger firms were better served by cooperating to raise price. Affecting the product specialists was the possibility of the Carnegie company integrating forward into the products such as tube, wire, and hoops. This firm could not only compete with them but also threaten their source of raw materials through its strength in basic steel and its control of iron ore and transportation. Still, by late 1900, Morgan and the other bankers were planning to merge the large steel firms other than Carnegie into one company.

In December of that year, Charles M. Schwab, the president of Carnegie Steel, made a speech to a group of businessmen in New York City. In the speech, he outlined his ideal big efficient steel company. He first emphasized backwards integration to the ore and coal mines. His company would also have large efficient mills specializing in particular end products such as tin-plate, hoops, tubes, and wire. He did not state that any company had plans to develop this system; he seemed to imply that it would be the logical way for any steel company to proceed. Among the guests were J. P. Morgan and his banking associates along with Elbert Gary, head of Federal Steel. After the speech, Morgan had a long conversation with Schwab.

How the speech was interpreted by Morgan and Gary is not clear. Two possibilities exist; first, they may have seen it as the Schwab plan for Carnegie Steel, or it could have been a proposal for a merger of the Carnegie and Morgan interests. In the former case, Carnegie represented a threat to the Gary-Morgan plans for combining some basic steel producers with product specialists. The message seemed to be that Carnegie would integrate forward. Additionally, the speech could very well have been a bargaining tool whereby Schwab was showing what his company might do, if Morgan and Gary did not buy it off.

Whatever Schwab's intentions, Morgan approached Carnegie with the goal of buying his company. He had reason for confidence even allowing for Schwab's speech. Aside from his apparent friendliness, he knew Carnegie was tired of the business. Morgan, thus, bought out Carnegie for $450 million ($10.5 billion in 2007 dollars). Schwab was made president of the new company, the United States

Table 4.3. The major steel producing and special products companies merged into United States Steel Corporation in 1901.

Name of firm	Product	Major previous owner
Carnegie Steel Company	Basic steel	Andrew Carnegie
Federal Steel Company	Basic steel	The Morgan interests
National Steel Company	Basic steel	The Moore Group
National Tube Company	Specialty product	The Morgan interests
American Steel Sheet Company	Specialty product	The Moore Group
American Steel Hoop Company	Specialty product	The Moore Group
American Tin Plate Company	Specialty product	The Moore Group
American Steel & Wire Company	Specialty product	John W. Gates

Source: Hogan, 1971, p. 474.

Steel Corporation (U.S. Steel), while Gary became the chairman of the executive committee.

U.S. Steel was a merger of, among others, the steel production and specialist product companies listed in Table 4.3. Three companies were basic steel manufacturers with some end products. The other firms made special end products. There were other important companies in the merger: the iron mines, coal mines, and steamship companies. In total, the new company had 65 percent of that basic steel market.

The reaction of society to U.S. Steel was problematic. The public had a great fear of large companies and "Trusts." This environment had a profound effect on the policies of U.S. Steel. Given the large initial market share, it seemed possible that the firm could raise prices. Furthermore, the company's great financial assets and large employment – in 1902 having more than 168,000 employees in 200 plants – raised questions about the concentration of political power in private hands. To make some comparisons, the company's capitalization was $1.4 billion at a time when the GDP of the whole United States was $20.7 billion, and the federal government budget was around $1 billion.

At this time, two conflicting philosophies dominated U.S. Steel. One emphasized lowering costs, and the other focused on raising and stabilizing prices. These two conflicting philosophies were represented by the two major personalities in the company, Charles Schwab and Elbert Gary. Schwab represented the first philosophy, the Carnegie strategy of lowering costs and increasing efficiency by rationalizing the flow of product among plants. Elbert Gary stood for the second idea. He wanted to use the company's large market share to increase or at least stabilize prices. Both of these ideas had antitrust implications. On the one hand, if the Carnegie philosophy prevailed, U.S. Steel might drive its competitors out of business, leading to pressure from the public to break up the company. On the other hand, Gary's idea of high and stable prices through cooperation with competitors could also violate section 1 of the Sherman Antitrust Act which forbade price-fixing.

Within two years, the Gary faction had become dominant partly because financial and personal scandals had forced Schwab out of the company. With this ouster, Gary (with Morgan's backing) became chairman of the board of directors, in essence the chief executive officer.

It is important here to understand the Gary strategy. While he wanted the company to have high and stable prices, he also feared that the very size of the company would lead to its breakup by the government. Indeed, his conflict with Schwab had been motivated by a fear that the hard-driving typical of the Carnegie company would turn the public (and competitors) against the company. Apparently, Gary felt that price-fixing would not make as bad an impression as the Carnegie strategy, even though it may have been just as illegal. Gary had one characteristic that Schwab lacked, a feel for the political system. The government and the public would tolerate somewhat higher steel prices but not the demise of small iron firms.

Gary then embarked on the strategy of keeping prices high while preventing the government from breaking up the company. At first, he tried to cooperate with other companies in a series of meeting called the "Gary Dinners." At these occasions, the company executive discussed prices and other policies with the idea of revealing their plans to competitors and coordinating their actions. To Gary's precise legal mind (he was a lawyer), these actions did not violate the Sherman Antitrust Act because they did not result in agreements. On finding that the government disagreed with this assessment, Gary terminated the meetings.

Even though this scheme did not work out, it did achieve two desirable outcomes for Gary and U.S. Steel. First, in subsequent years, U.S. Steel kept prices high by a policy of price leadership whereby the rivals merely followed the large company's price changes (Lamoreaux, 1985, pp. 118–158). Second, the policy gained the goodwill of the company's competitors. When the antitrust authorities moved against U.S. Steel, executives of the smaller firms supported the company in court. Among them was even the ousted Charles Schwab who had become the head of Bethlehem Steel.

Gary's feel for the political system is illustrated by some of his actions. The first was his handling of U.S. Steel's acquisition of the Tennessee Coal and Iron Company, a large steel and iron firm operating in the South. Even though arguably the company was a good fit for U.S. Steel and the merger helped the Morgan interests in other areas, Gary would not go through with the merger without checking with not only the attorney-general but also the president of the United States.

The second Gary policy that showed his astuteness was the internal initiatives that he undertook such as a safety program and stock options for the company work force. While these policies may have increased efficiency, they certainly enhanced the company's public image (Rees, 2004).

Even so, Gary's public relations initiatives did not prevent the government from bringing an antitrust case. However, it was not able to persuade the courts to dissolve U.S. Steel into smaller companies as it had with Standard Oil and American Tobacco. It is very likely that Gary's political strategy had much to do with this outcome. One historian stated, "The Gary policies, however, did permit Gary to achieve his goal of preventing the company from being broken up for violation of the Sherman Antitrust Act" (Chandler, 1990, p. 136). Ironically, the relatively high steel prices that Gary was able to maintain in this period probably may have hurt the public more than the competitive policy proposed by Schwab. The latter may have led to lower costs and perhaps greater innovation (Comanor and Scherer, 1995).

As for the position of U.S. Steel itself, there were two possible downsides to the Gary policy. First, the company lost market share dropping from 65 percent in 1902 to 46 percent in 1920. For U.S. Steel, however, this may have not been such a bad result. It reaped high profits by setting prices above cost and allowed smaller firms to gain market share. As the company's market share declined, the value of an original stockholder's holdings rose seven-fold, far better than the stock market average (Stigler, 1965).

The second possible downside to the Gary policy was technological. While U.S. Steel did build a new efficient plant in Gary, Indiana, it was relatively slow in both product and process innovation. In some cases, the old plants were retained in response to political pressure that overrode efficiency concerns. Gary failed to reorganize the company in order to rationalize its production. Essentially he kept the old firm organizations intact, using the overall corporation as a mere holding company. This policy probably led to the departure of many very good executives, among them Charles Schwab, E. T. Weir, and W. B. Dickson who went on to head other companies.

While Gary's actions may have to led high prices in the short run and technological inertia in the long run, it is clearly served the company stockholders well. Perhaps, the breakup of the company would have led to a more efficient industry in the late twentieth century as Comanor and Scherer (1995) speculated. All in all, while Elbert Gary was very successful at enhancing the stockholders' wealth, his strength was more in manipulating the political system than in developing an efficient steel company.

Little Steel

Here we describe the activities of the firms making up "Little Steel." Generally, these firms responded to U.S. Steel by using their niche advantages to grow. The Bethlehem Steel Corporation was a good example of a firm that took advantage of the "umbrella" offered by U.S. Steel's strategy of keeping prices high. Capitalizing on its position in marine steel products and its eastern location, the company emphasized production efficiency and product innovation.

In the late 1800s, Bethlehem, run by the pioneer technologist John Fritz, and owning at the time a number of shipyards, specialized in steel for other ships. Charles M. Schwab then bought Bethlehem in 1901 but was not active at first. After his ouster from U.S. Steel, Schwab immersed himself in Bethlehem Steel and developed the company by expanding its product line and increasing its efficiency. His main focus was on steel and its end products. Consistent with its interest in ships, Bethlehem developed a specialty in armored naval plate. Schwab also pushed the company into a new construction product, the Grey H- or I-beam, making Bethlehem a leading producer of construction steel products, especially on the East Coast. The company also made steel rails using the OH process. It secured a very large order from the Trans-Siberian Railroad.

On the production side, Bethlehem followed the old Carnegie strategy of improving the plants and operating at a high capacity. In a fashion similar to

Carnegie, Schwab developed and recruited very good executives. High compensation was one of his chief means. He offered to pay off one man's mortgage if the BF which he ran hit a certain production level. He paid a bonus of over $1,000,000 to Eugene Grace, the chief operating officer (about $18.4 million in 2007 dollars). In the same vein, Bethlehem modernized its plants and rationalized its processes and organization. The company also became more fully integrated by buying iron ore mines in Cuba and Chile and by increasing its coal holdings.

Aside from buying some shipyards, coal mines, and other input firms, the major acquisition of Bethlehem in these decades was Pennsylvania Steel. That company's Steelton plant was one of the oldest steel rail producers in the country. More important was the acquiree's large new mill at Sparrows Point, Maryland. Having a seaside location handy to foreign ore, it later became the largest plant in the country.

To sum up, Bethlehem prospered, becoming the dominant steel firm on the East Coast. By 1920, its capacity had grown to about 3.3 million tons, 8 percent of the market. Stigler (1965) finds that Bethlehem was the one other steel company that was more profitable than U.S. Steel.

Republic Steel Corporation was founded in 1899. It is important because it illustrated one way a firm could become important in steel. It was by combining a large number of small plants that have either a specialty product or geographic niche. Altogether, Republic bought 34 companies with locations in Ohio, Alabama, Pennsylvania, and Indiana, including coal and iron ore mines. Emphasizing specialty product markets, Republic's steel mills were generally smaller than the others, but the higher product prices made up for these lacks. So, the specialty emphasis outweighed the higher costs of the smaller mills.

Before Republic fully developed this strategy, an alternative plan, a southern strategy, was attempted between 1904 and 1907. John W. "Bet a Million" Gates obtained control of the company after selling American Steel & Wire Company to U.S. Steel. He planned to set up Republic as the dominant steel firm in the South. There was a local demand for the most steel and good local sources of iron ore and coal. To accomplish this goal, Gates planned to merge Republic with Tennessee Coal & Iron (TCI). With this merger most of the southern capacity would be in one company.

Gates, however, was unable to obtain the necessary financing. Tennessee Coal & Iron was sold to U.S. Steel in 1907 – supposedly to bail out one of Gates's brokers. Republic, then, maintained and expanded its southern mills, but it did not become the dominant firm in that part of the country. This left Republic a confederation of small specialty product mills with some southern capacity.

The other members of Little Steel can be classified in two categories. The first group developed geographic niches in the usual large-scale steel products. For example, Jones & Laughlin essentially operated out of the western Pennsylvania-Pittsburgh area. Youngstown Sheet & Tube was concentrated in eastern Ohio. Colorado Fuel and Iron sold its products, mostly rails, in the western part of the United States.

In contrast, the second group essentially integrated backwards into raw steel production from the fabrication of steel products; they included Phillips (later called

National Steel), Armco, and Crucible. Phillips integrated into primary steel from a position in tin-plated sheet by building a new plant in West Virginia. Armco started as a rolling mill for sheets and integrated backwards. Crucible interestingly stuck to making specialty items by the old crucible process, but when the EF became viable it started to use it to make the product. To give the reader a feel for how the small companies developed, we will examine two of them, Jones & Laughlin and Armco. (For information on the other companies, see Hogan, 1971, pp. 575–643, Schroeder, 1953, and Seely, 1994.)

As of 1902, Jones & Laughlin was the second largest steel company in the country. Its main mill was in Pittsburgh making basic steel and simple products, but later it built a mill in Aliquippa, just west of Pittsburgh. The company was noted for production process innovations, some of which worked and some did not. The company was one of the first to use the Jones mixer for carrying pig iron from the BF to the steel converter. This saved the cost of remelting of the metal for the converter. It was almost universally adopted by other firms. The company also experimented with the Talbot process, a method by which OH steel could be made with tighter specifications. The furnaces did not work that well, and the company supplemented them with OH and Bessemer converters. To sum up, Jones & Laughlin was a traditional iron manufacturer which successfully made the transition to steel and challenged U.S. Steel in the Pittsburgh area.

Armco was an example of a company that originally specialized in steel products and then integrated backwards into steel and iron smelting and refining. In the late 1880s, George Verity founded the American Steel Roofing Company in Cincinnati, Ohio. This company made a line of iron and steel building products. In 1900, the company was reorganized into the American Rolling Mill Company.

The company decided to build its main mill in Middletown, Ohio. This plant had a BF, steel furnaces, and rolling mills. The company chiefly made specialty products especially sheets. Among them were two types of sheets: silicon steel sheets and non-silicon electrical sheets. Armco also made pure iron-coated galvanized metal products. In 1911, the company went into automobile sheets. It was also among the first to develop research laboratories. Essentially, this company moved into steel production from fabricating products.

In summary, most of the companies making up Little Steel started as either traditional iron manufacturers or product fabricators. They seemed not to worry about U.S. Steel underselling them, even at first when the company's intentions were not known. There were other smaller firms who were able to grow and widen their product lines during this period; among them were Wheeling Steel, Pittsburgh Steel, and Portsmouth Steel.

Product innovation seemed to be centered in Little Steel more than at U.S. Steel. Armco developed various types of sheets and electrical steels; Youngstown developed special types of tubes. Phillips emphasized tin-plated sheets for canning, and Crucible developed hard specialty steel made with the EF process.

In contrast, U.S. Steel left the major innovations to others, and it did not expand as fast as others. As stated above, Gary's strategy of placating the government may have been partly responsible for this result. Additionally, the market probably was growing faster than even a very efficient dominant firm – let alone U.S. Steel – could accommodate.

Substitutes

In this period, aluminum became a major substitute for steel. The Pittsburgh Reduction Company was founded to devise ways of making and selling this metal. It was backed and financed by Charles M. Hall, the inventor of the aluminum smelting process, and the famous Pittsburgh banker, Andrew Mellon. In 1907 the company took on the name, Aluminum Company of America (Alcoa). Ironically, much of the expertise it took to develop this metal came from the iron and steel sectors. Processes such as metal rolling, extruding tubes, and making wire were applied to aluminum by men who had worked in steel. Early in the history of the auto industry, there were often decisions on whether to use aluminum or steel (Smith, 1988, pp. 91–93).

Resource suppliers: iron ore, coal, and labor

The market for iron ore was characterized by a further shift toward Minnesota as shown in Table 4.4. It became the dominant supplier. First, Minnesota had a great deal of rich ore. Second, BF engineers developed techniques for using it (discussed above). Third, the now dominant steelmaking process, OH, worked especially well with the Minnesota ores.

Michigan remained the second largest American supplier of ore. Its ore was especially amenable to the Bessemer process.

Alabama continued to be the third largest supplier of ore. Its production more than doubled from 2,800,000 tons in 1900 to 5,900,000 tons in 1920. This ore supply, combined with the presence of coal, led to the development of the southern steel industry.

The eastern companies such as Bethlehem continued to import most of their iron ore, but in the second decade of the century, imports declined. The ores from Minnesota were better for OH production than the foreign ores.

The major development in the coal part of the industry was a new coke oven. The geographical sources of coal remained the same during this period as in the later part of the nineteenth century: Pennsylvania, West Virginia, Illinois, Alabama, and

Table 4.4 United States production and imports of iron ore, 1900, 1910, and 1920

| Year | Total U.S. production (millions of tons) | Production in the states of | | | | Imports | |
		Minnesota	Michigan	Alabama	Pennsylvania	Total	From Cuba
1900	27.5	9.8	9.9	2.8	0.9	0.9	0.4
1910	56.9	32.0	13.3	4.8	0.7	2.6	1.4
1920	67.6	39.5	17.5	5.9	0.7	1.3	0.9

Source: Hogan, 1971, pp. 366 and 375.

Colorado. In order to work well in the BFs and steel converters, bituminous coal had to be transformed into coke. The new by-product coke ovens began to replace the older beehive ovens. The latter were usually located near the coal mines. In spite of their loss of market share, these units increased their efficiency. Their coke to original coal yields rose from 33 percent in 1900 to 56 percent in 1920. The smaller capacity of the beehive oven resulted in more flexibility in that capacity could be more easily added and deleted when needed.

The by-product ovens were physically somewhat larger, and they were located near the BF rather than at the coal mine mouth. These ovens were more efficient than the beehive with a yield of 75 percent as opposed to 56 percent for the beehive in 1920. However, they were more expensive to build than the beehive oven. As the name implies, they produced by-products. Among them were tar, benzol, ammonium sulfate, and sulfur. At first, these by-products worked to the disadvantage of these ovens because there were no markets. Later demand for the products developed, and that handicap became an asset. Accordingly, the share of the by-product ovens rose from 5 percent of the total in 1900 to 60 percent in 1920.

Resource suppliers: labor

The events concerning steel industry labor are now described. At this time, the labor market for steel workers could be divided into two segments. The first was that for unskilled workers. Generally, the people in this part of the market were young bachelors who migrated from a rural area to the steel mill cities and towns. These people were often immigrants from Eastern and Southern Europe – Slovaks, Poles, and Italians. Later in this period, the companies recruited men from the southern part of the United States – usually southern whites but more and more often blacks and, in some cases, Mexicans.

Turnover within the mills tended to be high. The companies varied the production rates greatly within given years, and in the down times, they laid people off. Even without the employment variation, there was much turnover. According to one congressional committee, only 20 percent of the employees in the iron and steel industry held their jobs for the full 12 months of the year (Rees, 2004, p. 89). In 1909, one large steel mill dismissed at one time or another 64 percent of its workers, hiring back only 26 percent (Rees, 2004, p. 90).

The second segment of the steel labor market was that for the skilled workers. They were used to tend certain complex metallurgical processes and to operate the complicated equipment. In this market segment, two trends appeared. First, there was a move away from the first types of jobs as the steel process became more mechanical and moved toward more emphasis on tending and maintaining machinery. This led to a convergence between the skill levels of the skilled and unskilled workers. Second the ethnic composition of the skilled workers began to change. Early in this period, these workers tended to be natives from the English, Welsh, Scots-Irish, and German backgrounds. Later in this period, these workers started to come from the Eastern European immigrant backgrounds with a small scattering of white and black southerners.

With the move from process skills to mechanical skills, there was a convergence between the wages of skilled and unskilled workers. Comparatively, skilled workers' wages tended to drop. In the early twentieth century, the steel plants started to simplify these jobs, which led to a decline in their pay. The pay of the other less skilled workers rose. By 1910, they were paid, on the average, $2.25 a day as compared to $2.10 a day in other manufacturing.

The shift to eight hours in the 1880s had been reversed in the 1890s. The longer hours continued into the twentieth century with the 12-hour day becoming standard. In many cases, the workers also had to work on Sunday nights. Some workers had to do a 24-hour shift, when they switched from day to night work. When asked about this situation, steel firms asserted that the work had become somewhat lighter than in the past, and thus, the work was safe even with the long hours.

Steel and iron mills had always been dangerous places to work. In addition to the usual occurrences with physical labor, injuries could occur due to the splattering of molten iron or steel. Furthermore, the dust that accumulated in these mills had adverse effects on the workers' health. Deaths came not only from horrendous accidents but also from diseases due to dust and heat. Because of both humane and insurance considerations, companies came to emphasize safety in these two decades.

They exhibited a sense of paternalism. Companies often had their own stores for workers that were frequently cheaper than others. Many mills were located in company towns. In many cases, the companies provided low-cost housing for their workers. This occurred because the mills were built in comparatively isolated places, and because they were often very large employers. Some companies, notably U.S. Steel, provided stock options and pensions for workers with long tenure. However, the tenure was usually hard to get due to layoffs from cyclical market conditions.

There is still controversy as to the importance of these measures in improving the welfare of the working men. Many writers thought that the programs were window-dressing to get the companies favorable publicity. Others felt that this "welfare capitalism" was designed to prevent unions from coming into the plants. The programs seemed very expensive to be mere public relations. The low rates of coverage and participation for many of the programs conflicted with the second hypothesis.

A third possibility was that the mills often depended upon a small group of workers who stayed when others were laid off. Perhaps they constituted a highly productive core around which the rest of the labor worked. This group might be compared to noncommissioned officers in the armed forces. From these, companies often recruited their foreman and some of their executives. Since one needed a quite long tenure at the mills to obtain the benefits of the stock options and the pension plans, it may have been these workers at whom the welfare measures were targeted.

For most of the first two decades of the twentieth century, steel workers acquiesced in the policies of the companies. The general lowering of the skills needed to operate the plants and the huge flow of immigrants into the steel centers put the workers in very vulnerable positions. The companies generally had little difficulty finding other workers, if their present employees were not satisfied.

In spite of this situation, there still were a number of strikes during this period. In 1901, the Amalgamated Association of Iron, Steel, and Tin Workers struck many of the plants of the new U.S. Steel Corporation. They felt that the new management's need for good public relations might lead to a more conciliatory attitude. Apparently, the union was mistaken, and the strike was broken.

In 1909, U.S. Steel itself precipitated a strike by declaring its tin-plate plants open shops. This action was directed at the Amalgamated Association of Iron, Steel, and Tin Workers. The strike centered around the tin-plate plant at McKees Rocks, Pennsylvania. U.S. Steel switched the orders for its products to other plants. The union lost the strike, and all the company's plants became open shops, meaning that workers did not have to belong to a union to work there.

Other strikes occurred in a wide scattering of areas. Colorado Fuel and Iron (CF&I) was struck in 1913. Much of the conflict centered on its coal mines, and one result was the Ludlow Massacre where the Colorado National Guard killed 18 people including two women and eleven children. Later, the workers went back to work. Bethlehem Steel was struck in 1910, but the company broke this strike. In 1916, there was a series of strikes in the Youngstown area, at, among others, U.S. Steel, Republic, and Youngstown Sheet & Tube which ended in the same way.

The failure of these strikes can be attributed to three circumstances. First, the governments, local, state, and federal, usually sided with management. In the name of law and order, police, national guard, and sometimes federal troops prevented the workers from meeting and picketing, making it difficult for them to carry out their strikes. The second factor was the labor market. There were just too many immigrants coming into the steel towns wanting jobs. Consequently, the companies could depend on a steady stream of people willing to work under almost any conditions.

The third factor was the nature of the union organization. The major union in the iron and steel industry, the Amalgamated Association of Iron, Steel, and Tin Workers, consisted mainly of skilled process workers. As stated above, many process skills were becoming obsolete. (One interesting hypothesis was that the companies were intentionally getting rid of these skills in order to gain control of the plants. See Stone, 1974.) Thus, the base for this union was diminishing. Furthermore, the union was slow at recruiting the new workers. This was partly due to ethnic differences. The Amalgamated men tended to be native-born of English and Welsh descent, while most of the unskilled workers were immigrants. As a result, it was relatively easy for the steel firms to break strikes.

World War I brought a great increase in demand for steel and a decrease in immigration. This resulted in labor shortfalls. In response, both the government and the steel companies went to great lengths to secure the cooperation of labor. Vague promises were made. The government seems to have promised to help the workers organize unions.

The American Federation of Labor (AFL) saw the war as an opportunity to organize the steel industry, but like the Amalgamated Association of Iron, Steel, and Tin Workers, the unions in this organization were based on crafts not industries. In a given industry, there were apt to be several unions, each representing a different craft. In the steel industry, the major craft union was, of course, the Amalgamated. The AFL persuaded this and other unions to put aside their jurisdictional disputes and cooperate to organize the whole industry – deciding later into which union to put the newly organized workers. The National Committee for Organizing Iron and Steel Workers was formed and led by William Z. Foster. In September 1919, over 100,000 workers struck basically for the things that were promised during World War I. Unlike in previous times, large numbers of the European immigrants joined the unions and the strike.

This strike, however, was broken. The fall in steel orders at the end of the war led to a surplus of labor. The companies used blacks and other rural-born men as strikebreakers in the same way they had earlier used European immigrants. Additionally, the Red Scare resulting from the Communist takeover of Russia turned many in the public against the strikers. William Z. Foster's radical background was publicized by the companies and media. Furthermore, the proportion of foreigners among the strikers alienated many parts of the public. This is ironic because until World War I immigrants and unions had not been that close to each other. Furthermore, the local, state, and federal governments played the same roles as they had in the past, preventing the union from going about its business. Thus, the 1919 strike was broken mainly due to the same conditions that militated against labor in earlier years: a labor surplus, uncooperative management, and a hostile government.

By 1920, the steel companies had established open shops. Consequently, unions became a very minor influence in the steel industry in the subsequent decade.

Government policy

The government was involved in the steel industry in three major areas: the antitrust case against U.S. Steel, labor relations, and tariffs. The antitrust case is described on pages 40– 44. Under the guise of law and order, the governments often intervened in labor disputes on the side of management as described on page 50.

In this period, the government made a slow retreat from protective tariffs. This change was in response to the new international position of the steel industry. In this period, the United States became a continuous exporter of steel. Accordingly, major companies became more concerned with opening up markets than with keeping foreign steel out of the country. Even in 1900, exports exceeded imports by a large margin (1,154,000 tons for exports and 209,955 for imports). By 1920 exports were about ten times higher than imports (4,935,137 tons for exports and 410,857 for imports). This favorable balance in trade can be accounted for by the lowering of production costs in the United States. This situation was supplemented by special efforts from the large steel companies, especially U.S. Steel and Bethlehem. The former company organized its own export division, the U.S. Steel Export Products Company. Bethlehem was especially active in the export of rails and construction material.

In general, tariffs on steel experienced a downward trend in this period. This was the result of a consensus across the political spectrum. In 1901, President William McKinley proposed a philosophy of lower tariffs. It recognized that the United States was becoming a leading manufacturing country with a need for foreign outlets for its products. His Republican successors, Theodore Roosevelt and William H. Taft, followed this course. The result was the Payne-Aldrich Tariff of 1909 which, while raising many tariffs, lowered tariffs on most steel items from the earlier Dingley and McKinley bills. The particular configuration of tariff rates resulted from an alliance of steel companies and users who raised the rates on some items, but did not push higher tariffs.

In 1913, the Democrats under Woodrow Wilson came into power. The result was the Underwood Bill of 1913 which lowered tariffs on steel and many other products. In 1916, Frank Taussig, an economist critical of iron and steel tariffs, became chairman of the Tariff Commission which supervised the setting of most rates. Given its exporting ability, the steel industry felt that it did not need tariffs.

Conclusion

In this period, the steel sector grew into one of America's largest industries with production rising from 11,410,000 tons in 1900 to 47,190,000 tons in 1920. The industry became more concentrated in this period with the formation of U.S. Steel and the rise of the smaller but still large companies, such as Bethlehem, Republic, and Jones & Laughlin. The companies also increased their control of the production process by integrating backwards into coal and iron ore and by breaking the unions in their plants. Thus, by 1920, the large American steel companies had risen to positions of strength that they had not occupied before.

5   The 1920s

Introduction

For the steel industry, the 1920s was a period of stability with four major changes. First, growth continued with total production rising by 34 percent between 1920 and 1929. Second, a much more efficient method of rolling sheet steel was developed. It was facilitated by the growth of the automobile, appliance, and container industries. Third, some of the smaller firms began to threaten the dominance of U.S. Steel. Fourth, a Federal Trade Commission action ended the basing point pricing system which may have led to more competitive pricing.

In this chapter, we will follow the taxonomy used in the earlier chapters. First, we examine changes in the product and its production, the steel customers, and competition among steel companies. Then, we examine substitutes, input and labor markets. Next, government actions toward steel are reviewed. Finally, a conclusion ends the chapter.

Growth and the production process

Steel production rose 34 percent between 1920 and 1929, but as Table 5.1 indicates, there were wide fluctuations. As a result of the 1921 depression, steel production dropped by over 50 percent – from 47.19 million to 22.16 million tons in 1921. After that, steel production recovered and rose to new heights. Finally the drop in 1930 reflected the beginning of the Great Depression. (Henceforth, when making comparisons to assess the changes during the decade, this chapter contrasts 1920 with 1929 instead of 1930 because by then, the Great Depression had started thereby distorting the data.)

Except for the sheet rolling mills, the 1920s brought only incremental change in the steelmaking process. In 1920, there were 216 active blast furnaces, while in 1929 there were only 165 furnaces. The average blast furnace (BF) production rose from 170,954 tons in 1920 to 258,267 tons in 1929. BF equipment such as ladles and blowers increased in size and efficiency.

In the 1920s, earlier trends in steel technology continued. The open hearth (OH) furnace continued to gain, with its production rising 48 percent, its market share going from 77.5 to 85.7 percent between 1920 and 1929. Facilitating this trend

Table 5.1 Yearly steel production with four years broken down by type of furnace (millions of tons)

| Year | Total steel production | Type of steel melting furnace | | | |
		Open hearth	Bessemer	Electric furnace	Crucible
1920	47.19	36.59	9.95	0.57	0.08
1921	22.16				
1922	39.88				
1923	50.34				
1924	42.48				
1925	50.84	42.60	7.53	0.69	0.02
1926	54.09				
1927	50.33				
1928	57.73				
1929	63.21	54.16	7.98	1.10	0.01
1930	45.58	39.26	5.64	0.69	0.002

Source: Hogan, 1971, p. 837.

were several technological developments. First, it was found that using a sloping back wall increased the life of the furnace, thereby lowering its capital costs. Additionally, mechanical devices were developed that automatically fed materials into the OH furnace. Last, the new chrome-magnesite bricks also prolonged the life of the furnace.

Bessemer steel production declined both absolutely and relatively as indicated by Table 5.1. Its share of the whole fell from 21 percent in 1920 to 12.6 percent in 1929.

In contrast, the electric furnace (EF) increased its role in the industry, its production nearly doubling from 570,000 in 1920 to 1,100,000 tons in 1929. This steel continued to replace crucible metal; this trend was accentuated by the increased use of machinery, concomitant with the rise of the automobile and appliances industries.

Two other innovations increased the attractiveness of EFs. The first was a change in where the pig iron, scrap, and other materials were fed into the vessel. Before the 1920s, most furnaces had been fed their input from the side, but it was found that loading the furnace from the top lowered costs and raised quality. Second, new electrodes lowered cost and increased the ability of firms to tailor products to customer requirements. Thus, the EF became the preferred method of making high-quality speciality metal.

With rolling mills, the 1920s saw an incremental innovation in most product lines but a major change in sheet production. The rolling mill sector was divided into two parts: the primary mills and the secondary mills. There was little change in the primary mills in the 1920s except for marginal enlargement and the further introduction of electric motors for turning the rollers.

In the secondary mills, the diffusion of electric motors continued. For most products, the rolling process got more efficient, especially the pipe mills. In the sheet mills, however, major progress was made. Until the 1920s, sheet steel was made in what were called hand mills where slabs were run through a set of rollers again and again until they became sheets of the desired thickness and width. The procedure required very skilled workers. It was difficult to customize the product to the desired specifications. It often took guesswork to get the desired metal characteristics.

Many people dreamed of developing a continuous sheet (also called strip) mill which started with slabs at one end and came out with sheets at the other end. Unsuccessful experiments with such mills had been conducted by the American Tin Plate Division of U.S. Steel in 1902 and 1905.

In the 1920s, Armco Steel, using the knowledge and leadership of John B. Tytus, undertook a major effort to develop a continuous sheet mill. They bought the Ashland Iron and Mining Company in 1921 and used its plant to experiment with their designs. Armco succeeded in this endeavor, but it found that another company, Forged Steel Wheel, had a mill that had many advantages. So Armco bought Forged Steel Wheel, and incorporated the strong points of each design into both plants.

By 1927, it was obvious that Armco had a superior process, and its continuous mill became the standard way to make sheets. While some companies persisted in using the hand mill, Armco had many imitators, and it licensed its patents to many companies.

The customer industries

Table 5.2 shows the breakdown of steel uses in 1926, a fairly typical year. The railroad and construction industries were still the largest users of steel, but the automobile sector was gaining.

The railroad industry's growth had leveled off. Freight continued to grow from 413.7 billion revenue miles in 1920 to 450.2 billion revenue miles in 1929, but passenger revenue miles dropped from 47.4 million to 26.9 million. The purchase of rails fell off; it was 2.9 million tons in 1920 and 3.0 million tons in 1929 in contrast to the record 4.46 million height in 1906.

With rolling stock, freight car production increased from 75,000 in 1920 to 116,000 in 1924, but it fell off to 93,965 in 1929. Passenger car production followed the same pattern, going from 1,440 in 1920 to 2,571 in 1924, and then back to 1,436

Table 5.2. The breakdown of economic sectors using steel by percentage, 1926

Sector	Percentage
Railroads	23.5
Automotive	14.5
Building and construction	19.5
Machinery	4.0
Oil, gas, water, and mining	9.5
Containers (Tin-plate and drums)	4.0
Agriculture	4.0
Others	16.0
Exports	5.0

Source: *Iron Age*, January 1, 1931

Table 5.3 Production and steel use in motor vehicles, 1920–1930

Year	Total unit sales of motor vehicles	Total automotive steel consumption (tons)
1920	2,227,349	2,755,000
1925	4,265,831	4,736,000
1929	5,337,087	6,012,000

Source: Hogan, 1971, p. 1001.

in 1930. The production of locomotives likewise increased in the earlier part of the period and then fell off, going from 3,672 in 1920 to 3,785 in 1923 and then dropping to 1,161 in 1929.

The total amount of hot-rolled steel used by the railroad sector went from 9,435,000 tons in 1920 to 8,663,000 tons in 1929 because flat demand and technological improvements lessened the use of steel. Thus, while the railroads remained the largest customers of steel, their share declined.

In the 1920s, the automobile and truck industry became a major user of steel. By 1926, it accounted for almost 15 percent of steel consumption. Table 5.3 shows the growth in motor vehicle production and automotive steel usage in this decade. Both vehicle production and steel usage in the industry more than doubled.

The increase in the demand from this sector had implications for particular steel products. For instance, as the auto companies lessened their use of wood and increased the proportion of closed body cars, sheets became very important. This increase in demand was a major impetus for the development of the continuous sheet or strip mill.

The automobile industry use of alloy steels declined. Steel and car company metallurgists found ways of treating ordinary carbon steel that made it work like alloys in hot places such as the motor cylinders. This same line of research also led to steel replacing aluminum in many uses.

Given the great increase in motor vehicle use, it was not surprising that steel companies paid much more attention to the industry. Even with this attention, one auto company, Ford, was not totally satisfied; so, it integrated backwards into steel, building its own mill at Rouge, Michigan. The motor vehicle industry was on its way to becoming steel's largest customer.

The use of steel in construction rose from 3,306,748 tons in 1920 to 4,778,020 tons in 1929, an increase of 44.5 percent. In 1926, it used almost 20 percent of the American steel output. Most of the construction industry was prosperous during the 1920s, but the residential sector fell off during the latter part of the decade.

In this decade, the American Institute of Steel Construction was founded. It encouraged the invention and diffusion of many new techniques for using steel. A new alloy steel called stainless steel was developed that could be used for outside decoration. This enabled architects to use the Art Deco ornaments for which the era is noted.

A product called battledeck floors was introduced which considerably lightened the structures of buildings and bridges. The product was a one piece item that consisted of a steel plate welded to I-beams. Besides being light, it provided some of the support for total structure of the edifice.

Some notable steel buildings were erected in this decade. Among them were a number of large skyscrapers, the tallest being the 73-storey Chrysler Building. Of the lower but very massive buildings of the period, most notable were Marshall-Field Mart in Chicago and the Cleveland Union project. Many interesting bridges and tunnels were built during this decade. Examples were the George Washington between New Jersey and New York City, the Camden-Philadelphia over the Delaware River, and the Mount Hope in Bristol, Rhode Island. The growth of the automobile indirectly contributed to the use of construction steel because the concomitant road-building led to not only the use of steel in roads but also a large number of new steel bridges.

The machinery and equipment sector was a large consumer of steel in the 1920s consuming 2,028,000 tons in 1929. Making the machine tools used in mass production factories, this sector demanded an inordinate amount of specialty steels. Construction and material-handling equipment used a wider selection of the steel produced in the country. The machines for pressing metal used in industries like automobiles and heavy equipment also used specialty metals.

Electrical machinery became a major user of steel. Between 1920 and 1929, electrical energy production more than doubled from 56 million kilowatt hours to 116.7 million kilowatt hours. Not only did this equipment use the ordinary carbon steel but also most of them had special requirements.

The growth of the oil and gas industry increased the use of steel. The production of oil rose from 442,929,000 barrels in 1920 to 1,007,323,000 barrels in 1929. The increase in the use of oil in automotive, heating, and industrial use accounted for most of this growth. Between 1920 and 1929, the amount of steel tubes used in the oil industry increased from 1,261,000 tons to 1,903,000 million tons. Additionally, the increase in the size and sophistication of oil refineries raised the demand for steel, as did the growth of the natural gas industry, a large user of pipes.

In the 1920s, the shipbuilding industry was depressed. The shipping boom of World War I led to a surplus of lake and ocean-going ships. In contrast with the 1919 production of 3,579,000 tons (of water displacement) of ship capacity, the 1925 production was 78,800 tons. Accentuating the problem, the Washington Naval Disarmament Treaty in 1921 cut the demand for Navy ships. The government had a subsidy program for shipbuilders, but it did little to counteract the slump.

In this period, there were two types of steel containers: tin cans and steel drums. The former items were made of tin-plated steel, the tin being needed because steel reacts with the contents to poison the food. Two developments were instrumental in the growth of the can industry. One was the scientific work on the coatings for the interior of the container. As a result, companies increased the canning of products like tomato juice, citrus fruits, and tuna. Hormel developed a new product, called luncheon meat. The second change increasing the canning sector was the growth of

Table 5.4 The number of tractors and motor vehicles on American farms in the 1920s

Year	Tractors	Trucks	Cars
1920	246,000	139,000	2,146,000
1925	549,000	459,000	3,283,000
1929	827,000	840,000	3,970,000
1930	920,000	900,000	4,135,000

Source: Hogan, 1971, p. 1065.

the Continental Can Company as a major competitor. This greater competition led to more uses and maybe lower prices for the cans. Production of tin-plated steel increased 32 percent from 1,539,977 tons in 1920 to 2,034,170 tons in 1930.

The production of barrels and drums rose from 4,000,000 units in 1920 to 11,552,000 units in 1929. This growth can be explained by lower costs, quality improvements, and new uses. Better coatings and paints made the drums more useful. A big factor in the increased use was the need to ship and distribute gasoline. Another was alcohol prohibition, because these containers could be used to transport and often hide illegal beverages.

For agriculture, the 1920s was a depressed period; while farm production actually grew, the farm acreage used dropped by over 31 million acres between 1920 and 1925. Due to low prices, farms were starting to go out of business. In spite of these troubles, the use of steel probably increased on the farm during this period. From Table 5.4, the growth in three types of farm machines is obvious. The number of tractors rose from 246,000 in 1920 to 920,000 in 1930. To put this in perspective, consider that there were still 17,612,000 non-food animals on the farm in 1930.

While the eight-fold increase in farm truck usage obviously was for production purposes, the increase in automobiles on the farm from 2.1 million to 4.1 million was not totally for leisure. Often car engines were used to power various machines like threshers. The increase in farm use of this equipment implied a big increment in the demand for steel.

The manufacture of appliances became a major source of steel demand in this decade. While the development and diffusion of electricity led to the invention and adoption of many new electric appliances, non-electrical appliances also contributed to this expansion. Among the electrical appliances were the refrigerator, the electric stove, and the washing machine. Additionally, the demand for ice boxes and gas and kerosene stoves played a role. Altogether, with the increases in the sales of these items, the amount of steel consumed by these industries rose from 216,000 tons in 1920 to 497,000 tons in 1929, a 130 percent increase.

Of this increase, refrigerators accounted for almost 40 percent of the change, but a third of this change was accounted for by increased steel use by non-electric ice boxes. However, in the period, electric refrigerators were becoming dominant. The production of electric stoves increased, but the growth rates in other stoves were more important in the increase in the use of steel. Of the increased steel use in appliances, 30.6 percent was accounted for by gas stove production, and 21 percent was accounted for by kerosene stoves. The production in washing machines and small appliances also expanded.

With the exception of rails and shipbuilding, most major uses of steel grew during this decade. This growth during a prosperous decade was consistent with the reputation of steel as a barometer for the whole economy.

The major competitors

During the 1920s, the major change among the steel companies was the growth of middle size firms. As indicated by Table 5.5, the market share of second through sixth largest firms rose from 17.2 percent in 1920 to 31.5 percent in 1930. This change can be mainly attributed to mergers. The market share of U.S. Steel declined from 45.8 in 1920 to 38.8 in 1929, but its production did not drop. The rest of the industry just grew faster. In addition, technological innovation increased the share of the second six firms.

To understand these changes, an examination of the largest firms is undertaken. After looking at U.S. Steel, the chapter analyzes the next seven firms: Bethlehem, Republic, National Steel, Armco, Youngstown Sheet & Tube, Jones & Laughlin, and Inland.

After the 1920 antitrust decree left U.S. Steel intact, the company was quite profitable, usually earning well over $100 million per year (roughly $1.1 billion in 2007 dollars). Even though it undertook some major investment programs, it began to lose its dominance. A look at this program gives some indication of the situation.

At least two of these investment initiatives, the wide-flange beams and sheets, were part of a strategy of catch up. U.S. Steel built a rolling mill for making wide-flange beams like the Grey beams of Bethlehem Steel. They got into this product almost 20 years after Bethlehem. A nasty patent fight resulted. In 1930, however, U.S. Steel gave up and settled, paying Bethlehem royalties (Hessen, 1975, pp. 266–269).

Like many other companies, U.S. Steel built a continuous sheet mill using the Armco patent. This did stop the firm from building more obsolete hand sheet mills. Additionally, U.S. Steel expanded in many areas without any particular focus.

It is not difficult to see why the company became so conservative. The management focused mainly on financial and legal issues. The lawyer, Elbert Gary, remained in charge of the company until his death in 1927. He was succeeded as chairman of the board by J. P. Morgan, Jr., a banker. Two other executives became influential, Myron C. Taylor, chairman of the finance committee and James Farrell, the company president, but they did not radically change Gary's policies.

The company divisions continued to operate more or less independently. This can be seen in two of the investment programs undertaken by the company, the expansion of the Tennessee Coal and Iron Division in the South and of the Chicago plants. It is not clear whether these expansions were coordinated with the activities of the rest of the company. Additionally, National Tube expanded its bar production at the same time as the Gary mill. There was no sharp focus on a particular product or geographic area. U.S. Steel tried to cover all areas, and did well in very

Table 5.5 Steel production for the leading firms and large concentration in the United States for selected years 1920–1930

Year	Total production	Company production U.S.Steel Quantity	Share	Bethlehem Quantity	Share	Republic Quantity	Share	National* Quantity	Share	J & L Quantity	Share	Armco Quantity	Share	Youngstown Quantity	Share	Inland Quantity	Share
1920	47,189	21,591	45.8	2,286	4.8	1,103	2.3	N/AVAL	N/AVAL	2,594	5.5	428	0.9	1,222	2.6	901	1.9
1925	50,841	21,167	41.6	5,986	11.8	1,127	2.2	N/AVAL	N/AVAL	2,772	5.5	698	1.4	2,251	4.4	1,590	3.1
1929	63,205	24,493	38.8	8,224	13.0	2,064	3.3	N/AVAL	N/AVAL	3,335	5.3	1,369	2.2	2,788	4.4	1,943	3.1
1930	45,583	18,762	41.2	5,954	13.1	2,620	5.7	980	2.1	2,426	5.3	880	1.9	1,821	4.0	1,544	3.4

Year	U.S. Steel share	Four firm concentration*	Six firm concentration*	Market share of six largest firms except for U.S. Steel*
1920	45.8	58.7	62.9	17.1
1925	41.6	63.3	68.6	27.0
1929	38.8	61.5	68.9	30.1
1930	41.2	65.3	72.7	31.5

Source: American Iron and Steel Institute and Moody's Industrial Manual. Data supplied by the companies: financial reports of individual companies, annual statistical reports of the American Iron and Steel Institute.

* National Steel, only came into existence in 1929, and thus, we only include the share of the other seven large firms in these figures in order to be consistent.

few. While the Depression would lead to some rethinking by the management, this had not happened as of the 1920s.

In contrast to the relatively flat production of U.S. Steel, Bethlehem's production grew by 260 percent from 2,286,000 tons in 1920 to 8,224,000 tons in 1929. Its market share rose from 4.8 percent to 13.1 percent.

Arguably, the main reason for this change was a corporate shopping spree including two major acquisitions. The first was the Lackawanna Steel Company in 1922. Founded by the famous Scranton family, this company originally had a mill in eastern Pennsylvania. It decided that the demand for steel was in the Midwest, and thus, in 1900, it built a plant on Lake Erie near Buffalo, New York. It prospered. Bethlehem saw this acquisition as a way to serve auto companies and other Midwestern customers. Furthermore, Lackawanna owned coal and domestic iron ore mines. The second major acquisition of Bethlehem was the Midvale Steel & Ordnance Company. Put together by W. E. Corey and W. B. Dickson, former Carnegie executives, this company consisted of a group of Pennsylvania steel and fabricating mills. The company ran into financial problems in the early 1920s and after contemplating a number of mergers, it decided Bethlehem offered the best deal. Midvale Steel & Ordnance's Johnstown plant gave Bethlehem access to the iron and steel markets in western Pennsylvania near Pittsburgh. Bethlehem also bought small steel plants on the Pacific Coast.

In technology, Bethlehem kept up with the industry better than U.S. Steel. It remained the leading firm in construction shapes. With the Lackawanna plant, it started to develop sheet production for the auto industry.

In summary, while Bethlehem remained the big steel power in the East, its acquisition of the Johnstown and Lackawanna plants gave it access to western Pennsylvania and the Midwest. Since the 1920s were a time of prosperity in the construction trade, Bethlehem did well with its base products. The major difficulty of the company was its position in the depressed shipbuilding industry, but the prosperity of the other products made up for this weakness.

Republic, the second company eroding U.S. Steel dominance, did not begin the decade auspiciously. For the first five years of the 1920s, Republic experienced hardly any production gains; steel tonnage rose from 1,103,000 in 1920 to only 1,127,000 in 1925.

In 1927, however, Cleveland financier Cyrus Eaton emerged as the largest stockholder, and he proceeded to acquire some strong companies. One was the Trumbull Steel Company which made tin-plate and specialty sheets. Another acquisition, Steel and Tubes, Inc., made tubular products and had a patent of the electric welding of tubes. The third company purchased by Republic was the Union Drawn Steel Company which made cold-drawn steel products.

In 1930, Republic was reorganized into the Republic Steel Corporation, and it purchased the Central Alloy Steel Corporation, the Bourne-Fuller Company, and the Donner Steel Company. Central Alloy Steel was the leading producer of important alloys such as stainless steel. Bourne-Fuller made many steel products such as nuts and bolts, while Donner Steel had a large plant in Buffalo, New York.

Through these mergers, Republic had developed a strong position in tubular products, alloys, and sheet. Cyrus Eaton assembled a very competent management team headed by Tom Girdler who had been lured away from Jones & Laughlin. Among the other leaders were Benjamin Fairless and Myron Wick. These mergers basically continued the company's policy of using geographically scattered plants to produce specialized products. By 1930, Republic was the third largest steel firm having plants in 19 cities in eight states and Canada with 13 blast furnaces, 68 open hearths, two Bessemer, and seven electric steel converters.

Like Bethlehem and Republic, three other firms grew mainly through mergers: National Steel, Armco, and Youngstown Sheet & Tube. As of 1920, the firm that would become National Steel was called Weirton Steel Company. Its specialty was tin-plate sheets. Its main plant in Weirton, West Virginia had recently become a fully integrated mill, having built a BF in 1919 and seven OH furnaces in 1921.

The tin-plate specialty protected the company from the fluctuations endemic to the steel sector which usually fed the volatile capital goods industries. In the early part of the twentieth century, tin-plate was mainly used in the canned food industry which was more stable than the capital goods sector. Even with this protected market, Weirton Steel did not lag in technology. In the late 1920s, it installed a continuous sheet mill for its tin-plate using the Armco patent.

The firm's position also did not prevent it from merger activity. In 1930, it joined two other major companies to form National Steel. One firm was the M. A. Hanna Company, a supplier of iron ore. Combined with its own sources of coal, this acquisition gave the firm good access to raw materials. Additionally, a third firm came into the merger, the Great Lakes Steel Company. Headed by George Fink, it originally had a small mill in Detroit servicing the auto industry. Fink, however, had big plans, and at the time of the merger, he was building a large modern fully integrated plant specializing in auto sheets. Located in Ecorse, Michigan near Detroit, its closeness to the auto firms gave it the ability to tailor its product as to the specification and the timing of orders. In summary, National Steel in 1930 had an important source of iron ore, a strong position in tin-plate, and a special connection to the auto industry.

Armco used its mergers to develop a strong technological position. The firm's steel production more than tripled from 428,000 tons in 1920 to 1,369,000 tons in 1930. Armco made two major acquisitions. In 1921, Armco bought the Ashland Iron & Mining Company of Ashland, Kentucky. John B. Tytus then used the Ashland mill to experiment with and finally perfect the new continuous hot strip mill.

The second Armco acquisition resulting from this innovation was the Forged Steel Wheel Company. At its Butler, Pennsylvania plant, Forged Steel Wheel had developed a continuous strip mill which infringed on Armco's patent. Armco found, however, that the Forged Steel Wheel design had many advantages over its own. Since it could not cheaply duplicate the Forged Steel Wheel techniques, Armco bought Forged Steel Wheel. Thus, Armco received the services of the acquired firm's skilled engineering staff, mainly the two technicians, H. M. Niagle and A. J. Townsend.

In 1930, Armco bought another firm, the Sheffield Steel Corporation of Kansas City, Missouri, but the motivation here was market extension rather than technological synergy. Taking advantage of its location, this plant produced tubes and pipes for the oil industry. Being far from good sources of iron ore, this firm totally depended on scrap steel as its raw material. (The furnace for the mill was open hearth which could use scrap exclusively.)

The company was quite prosperous in the 1920s. It had good management including George M. Verity, Charles Hook, and the technologist, John B. Tytus. Furthermore, the sheet mill patent provided royalties from most of the other major steel firms, including U. S. Steel, Republic, Weirton, Great Lakes, and Youngstown.

Another company that grew by merger was Youngstown Sheet & Tube. Starting with a production of 1,222,000 tons of steel in 1920, it more than doubled its output to 2,788,000 tons by 1929. In the early 1920s, it was involved in an attempt to merge seven of the major steel firms in the United States. The other companies were the Midvale Steel & Ordnance Company, the Lackawanna Steel Company, Republic, the Inland Steel Company, the Steel & Tube Company of America, and the Brier Hill Steel Company. The plan was opposed by the Federal Trade Commission, and it fell through when Bethlehem bought the first two companies.

Youngstown then bought the Brier Hill Steel Company and the Sheet & Tube Company of America. The first merger led to synergies between the Brier Hill mill in Youngstown and the original company mill. Brier Hill also had a strong position in tubular products plus coal and ore properties. The second acquisition, the Sheet & Tube Company of America, with a plant on Lake Michigan in Northern Indiana, gave Youngstown Sheet & Tube access to the Chicago markets. To sum up, Youngstown, through its mergers with Brier Hill and Sheet & Tube of America, fortified its position in eastern Ohio and gained a foothold in the Chicago area.

Two firms became important in this period through internal growth, Jones & Laughlin and Inland Steel. Jones & Laughlin's production grew 28 percent from 2,594,000 tons in 1920 to 3,335,000 in 1929. The company devoted many resources to research; among its discoveries was the reason that Bessemer steel was brittle. It was nitrogen that lodged in the metal when air was blown through it, but the company did little at this time to take advantage of this research. In 1923, Jones & Laughlin became a publicly traded company, and it did bring in some good managers including Tom Girdler, Benjamin Fairless, and George Crawford.

The other major company to develop through internal growth in this period was the Inland Steel Company. Its production increased 115 percent between 1920 and 1929. The company continued to concentrate on its one fully integrated plant at Indiana Harbor, Indiana on Lake Michigan. It added to the plant, and consolidated its control over its sources of iron ore, and coal mines.

The 1920s saw the emergence of a number of strong rivals to U.S. Steel, the largest being Bethlehem and Republic. Armco grew by developing the strip mill for sheet. Youngstown Sheet & Tube increased its size through mergers, and a new firm, National Steel, emerged with strong positions in the tin-plate and automobile sectors. In contrast, Jones & Laughlin and Inland continued to grow through internal expansion.

Substitutes

The major substitute for steel was aluminum. It was still too expensive to threaten most steel uses, but the main producer, Alcoa, was developing the technology that would eventually lead to its emergence as the major steel substitute.

As stated in Chapter 4, the Pittsburgh Reduction Company, later called Alcoa, used the Hall-Heroult process patent to develop a major industry. Under the guidance of the former University of Minnesota Professor Francis C. Frary, it developed a modern research program.

Essentially, Alcoa had a monopoly on aluminum sales for not just the United States but also the entire North American continent. Alcoa's general strategy was to integrate backward and forward. Alcoa had first bought deposits of bauxite, the ore for aluminum smelting. It also obtained either ownership of or contracts for the supplies of electricity, the major energy input into aluminum. As for forward integration, the company developed aluminum uses and bought production facilities for jewelry, pots and pans, wire, foils, and sheets.

Nonetheless, the metal did experience one setback in use. Irons and steels for the automobile engine blocks were developed that were superior to aluminum, and thus, in those uses, steel actually replaced aluminum.

Input supplies: ore, coal and labor

The major inputs into steel production were iron ore, coal, and labor. During the 1920s, there was not a great deal of change in these economic sectors. In iron ore, the mines in Minnesota and Michigan continued to dominate the industry, with the Great Lakes sources of ore constituting 85.59 percent of the total United States production in 1920 and 86.03 percent in 1929. Alabama in the South remained the second largest source of ore. Furthermore, improvements in loading and handling at ports on the Great Lakes increased the efficiency of the industry.

In the coal sector, the major change was the further increase in the share of by-product coke ovens. Its market share rose from 60 to 94.2 percent. It seemed that the beehive oven was a thing of the past, but one future development, the increase in demand caused by World War II, would delay its demise.

In the 1920s, the companies gained much more control over their labor force. This occurred because of a combination of intimidation and accommodation. Evidence of this change can be seen in the drop in the number of strikes from 25 in 1920 to two in 1928.

The companies, however, did make a number of moves to placate their labor force. Many firms provided some workers with pensions, company stores, and often low-cost housing. A major change was the institution of the eight-hour day in 1923. This came about due to political pressure from the public, churches, and government.

A number of companies instituted Employee Representation Plans. Among them were Bethlehem, Armco, and Colorado Fuel & Iron. Under most of these plans, each plant had a board of elected employees who presented individual and group grievances. Additionally, the boards presented to the companies worker opinion on wages, working conditions, and safety.

The impacts of these plans varied across companies. Many experts and workers found the plan at Colorado Fuel & Iron to be very effective. Some thought that the reason for this situation was the motivation of the chief owner of the company, John D. Rockefeller, Jr. He was a second-generation tycoon who spent most of his time on philanthropy rather than on business. In contrast, Bethlehem's Employee Representation Plan seems to have been a way to gain public acclaim and thwart unions with little impact on management practices (Rees, 2004).

The major situation that led the companies to accommodate the workers was a tight labor market for much of the decade resulting from general prosperity. Furthermore, the Immigration Bill of 1920 stopped the flow of workers from Europe. In reaction, the company started to recruit rural Americans (often blacks) and foreign people not covered by immigration laws – usually Mexicans. In 1925, 10.9 percent of the steel workers in Pennsylvania were blacks, and 11.7 percent of the steel workers in Illinois were Mexican.

Government policy

In the 1920s, the government impacted the steel industry in three places: labor supply, tariffs, and antitrust. In the area of labor, President Warren Harding prevailed upon the steel companies to institute the eight-hour day. This was effected mainly by direct contact between the President and Elbert Gary, chairman of the board of U.S. Steel. Thus, even a Republican pro-business administration would respond to humanitarian pressure.

Another initiative impacting steel labor supply was the Immigration Law of 1920. Essentially it cut off a major source of workers by grossly limiting the immigration of people from Europe. As stated above, this led the companies to hire more black and Mexican workers.

The second area where government had an important influence was international trade. Two major tariff bills passed during this decade. The first, the Fordney-McCumber Act of 1922, raised most duties, giving the steel industry an average tariff of 33.22 percent of sales. Apparently, this rate had a small effect on the steel trade. Total iron and steel imports rose from 123,615 tons in 1921 to 725,855 tons in 1922, but they did not fall in response to the tariff, fluctuating between 721,775 tons in 1927 and 1,084,342 tons in 1926 for the rest of the decade. The Smoot-Hawley Tariff of 1930 raised the tariffs on most goods, but it had only a modest effect on iron and steel items, raising the average tax to only 35 percent. Any positive effect this Act had on the steel industry was soon swamped by the Depression. One action that had portents for the future was the enhancement of the power of the United States Tariff Commission. The Fordney-McCumber Act gave the commission the power to recommend adjustments in the tariff (of 50 percent, either up or down) to the president.

The third area of government influence was antitrust. Two major cases affected the industry. The first was the United States Steel case in 1920 discussed above. The second antitrust issue of the period was basing point pricing, namely the system known as Pittsburgh Plus pricing. In cases where transportation cost is a significant portion of the total price of a good, the usual custom is to charge what is known as FOB (Free on Board) prices, the sums of the prices at the factory and unit transportation costs from the factory to the customer.

In contrast to FOB pricing, the steel industry for most of the period between 1900 and 1924 used the Pittsburgh Plus pricing system. Here, the price charged to a customer was usually the factory price at Pittsburgh plus transportation from Pittsburgh to the customer's location. Normally all firms would charge this price, even the firm just down the street from the customer.

There is a great deal of controversy on the reasons for basing point pricing. Some economists assert that it would occur mainly under competitive or non-collusive conditions (Haddock, 1982). Others see it as a way for oligopolistic firms to signal a mutually beneficial price for any given customer or area.

It was the latter assertion on which the Federal Trade Commission (FTC) based its case against Pittsburgh Plus pricing. This system was seen as a way for firms to ascertain the prices that others would charge. Using this easily computed price, companies could follow the signals of other firms. Thus, with Pittsburgh Plus, the steel industry could possibly set a supra-competitive price. The FTC used a number of contemporary economic experts to support its case. Among them were Frank Fetter of Princeton University, W. I. Ripley of Harvard University, and John R. Commons of the University of Wisconsin.

In a 1983 article, Dennis Carlton of the University of Chicago posited three conditions under which basing point pricing would keep prices up: (1) freight was hard to calculate; (2) firms had good, quick information on actual prices offered by rivals; and (3) certain locations had concentrations of competing firms. In the 1920s, each seller had a choice of several different ways of delivering the product, making for uncertainty on transportation costs. Discounts and prices were rapidly communicated through the industry. In several locales, major competing firms existed virtually side by side; among them were Pittsburgh, Chicago, Youngstown, and Cleveland. Thus, basing point pricing could be an efficient collusion device.

This theory was accepted by the FTC, and in 1924, they proscribed U.S. Steel from using the Pittsburgh Plus pricing. As a result of this decision, the industry went to a multiple basing point pricing system, Chicago and Pittsburgh being the first two basing points. Additional ones were later added at Birmingham, Alabama; Middletown, Ohio; and Sparrows Point, Maryland.

In summary, while the decade was characterized by a conservative pro-business government, there were many areas where regulation impinged the steel industry.

Conclusion

In the 1920s, even with its 34 percent increase, two circumstances indicated future change. The first was the growth of the automobile industry which would later become steel's main customer. To this change, the industry responded with the development of continuous sheet mills by Armco.

The second portent was the set of initiatives by the government that would eventually lead to limitations on the companies' ability to control their destiny. While U.S. Steel was able to avoid dissolution, the 1924 Basing Point Pricing case limited its pricing control. Furthermore, the eight-hour initiatives from President Harding indicated that their power over labor could be attenuated. Finally, while the enhancement of the Tariff Commission's power over rates would likely benefit the companies, it would involve them in increased governmental maneuvering and rent seeking.

6 The Depression

Introduction

The experience of the steel industry in the 1930s reflected the wretched state of the economy during the Great Depression. Between 1929 and 1932, real gross domestic product (GDP, in 2007 dollars) dropped 25.6 percent from $950.9 billion to $707.4 billion. This resulted in over a 75 percent drop of steel production. After 1932, both the economy and the steel sector recovered but only slowly, and with some setbacks.

Two other developments affected the steel industry. First, the government, especially at the federal level, became much more involved in the operation of the industry. Second, labor unions became an established part of the industry. These events directly and indirectly arose from the Depression.

To see the impact of these events, this chapter follows our taxonomy by first examining changes in the product and its production. Then it looks at steel customers. Third, competition among steel companies is analyzed. Next, the chapter looks at substitutes and input and labor markets. Then, the government actions toward steel in the 1930s are reviewed. Last, a conclusion ends the chapter.

Low production and the production process

Table 6.1 shows the relationship of the steel output sales to the indicators of the macroeconomy. Between 1929 and 1932, both steel production and GDP dropped precipitously, and the unemployment rate rose from 3.2 to 24.1 percent.

After this period, steel actually recovered faster than the economy as a whole. Steel intensive products such as electrical appliances and automobiles led the recovery. After 1932, steel production rose 300 percent to 56,637,000 tons in 1937, but a sharp recession in 1938 cut production. After that year, production recovered to 66,983,000 tons in 1940. While the steel industry often did better than the economy as a whole, it did not recover to the 1929 level until 1940, when the war demand came into play.

Different parts of the economy performed differently. While some sectors such as containers and appliances remained stable or actually grew during the 1930s, most of the economy remained depressed. These depressed areas

Table 6.1 Yearly steel production and indicators of the well-being of the economy as a whole, 1929–1940

Years	Steel production (thousands of tons)	Capacity Utilization rate	Gross Domestic Product (billions of 2007 dollars)	Unemployment rate
1929	63,205	90.8	950.9	3.2
1930	45,583	64.2	836.0	8.7
1931	29,059	38.6	813.2	15.9
1932	15,323	19.9	707.4	23.6
1933	26,020	33.9	698.4	24.9
1934	29,182	37.4	773.9	21.7
1935	38,184	48.7	842.8	20.1
1936	53,500	68.5	952.4	16.9
1937	56,637	72.5	1,001.3	14.3
1938	31,752	39.6	966.8	19.0
1939	52,799	64.5	1,044.8	17.2
1940	66,983	82.1	1,136.5	14.6

Source: American Iron and Steel Institute, 1930–1940 and U.S. Bureau of the Census, 1975.

included large steel users such as railroads, agriculture, and construction. To add some context to the narrative, we examine some of the theories on why the Depression occurred. (For a more thorough discussion, see Atack and Passell, 1994, pp. 583–624.)

There is still a great deal of controversy in regard to the Depression, but three theories have gained widespread acceptance. The first is the Demand Composition hypothesis. It hypothesizes that certain markets had been growing so fast in the 1920s that they ran out of customers; in other words, they became saturated. Examples of these markets were automobiles and household appliances. A new product or improved version of an old one would be developed, and people bought it. With people buying the good for the first time, the industry boomed. Then, when all the people who could afford it had bought it, the industry had to rely on replacement demand, and this meant a much smaller volume.

The demand composition theory has general support, but many experts felt that other developments turned a short recession like those in the years 1907, 1921, 1949, and 1958 into the Great Depression. Two other theories have gained prominence. One blames the Depression on high tariffs. This theory starts with the Smoot-Hawley Tariff of 1930, which raised most import duties. This increase in tariffs cut off imports, and subsequently it cut down on exports in industries such as farming and autos. The height of this tariff led other countries to increase their own tariffs, and thus exports were lowered even further. This type of policy is called "beggar thy neighbor." Two types of evidence support this theory. First, statistics show a disproportionate drop-off in international trade during the early 1930s. Second, stock market fluctuations have been shown to be negatively correlated with progress in Congress on the Smoot-Hawley bill (Wannski, 1978). The idea behind the analysis is that market players could foresee the disastrous effects of this bill, and therefore, they got out of the stocks.

The third hypothesis is that the fall in the money supply in the years 1930–1932 had a drastic effect on economic activity. When these banks went broke, the savings accounts of millions of people became worthless. Thus, people who had resources previously could no longer spend money, and a depression ensued. The chief culprit of this theory was the Federal Reserve System, or Fed. It did not lend money to banks in difficulties, and it did not allow banks to use required liquid reserves, which presumably had been put in place to cover such contingencies. (See Friedman and Schwartz, 1963.)

To operate at a high level, the economy needs at any given time a certain amount of money, and the combinations of runs and the Fed's tight policies led to a 40 percent decrease in the money supply. Almost all experts agree that this contributed to the Great Depression, though there is still much argument about the exact mechanism. Thus, it is generally agreed that changes in demand composition, high tariffs, and the fall in the money supply explain much if not the bulk of the economic trauma of the 1930s.

There were few major changes in the process of making steel in the 1930s. The number of existing blast furnaces dropped from 300 in 1930 to 231 in 1940. Through the 1930s, the number of furnaces in operation varied with the demand for metal. Between 1930 and 1932, the number of operating furnaces dropped from 157 in 1930 to 46 in mid-1932. It rose to 187 in 1937 and then declined to 70 in mid-1938. In the next two years, the number rose to 201 in December 1940. Only three new furnaces were built in this period.

While the basic technology did not change, the productivity per man-hour increased. (There were some minor innovations in the bricks used in the furnace and in the auxiliary equipment.) In 1931, it took 1.1 hours of labor to produce a ton of pig iron; this figure had dropped to 0.60 by 1939 and 0.56 in 1940. First, in the latter years, the furnaces were operating at a greater capacity. Second, over the decade, the companies abandoned the least productive units and worked to improve their best blast furnaces.

As with blast furnaces, there was not a great deal of change in the steel converters. Open hearth converters again accounted for the largest portion of steel production, 86.1 percent in 1930 and 91.7 percent in 1939. There were not many new furnaces built. National Steel built ten furnaces at the Great Lakes Works, and Inland Steel built nine furnaces at its Indiana Harbor plant. The other companies only increased the size of their old furnaces.

There were a number of minor improvements in the steel-making process. Better instrumentation was developed for controlling the process. The companies began to use by-product gases from the other parts of the iron and steel process instead of buying gas from outside. Furthermore, not much occurred with Bessemer converters (*Iron Age*, October 1, 1940, p. 52).

While few electric furnace (EFs) were built during the 1930s, some other changes occurred. Some specialty steel users integrated backward to EFs. Among them were Timken and Northwestern Steel & Wire. The latter company has a special importance because it was the first firm to use the EF to make ordinary carbon steel. When the company integrated backward into steel in 1936, it built two Bessemer converters and two EFs. It abandoned the Bessemer furnaces in 1939 and continued to use the EFs to make carbon steel. Others still furnished high-quality specialty steels. In fact, EFs almost totally drove out the old crucible process during this period.

In the 1930s, more and more companies adopted the continuous strip mill developed by Armco, but another problem arose in the sheet rolling sector. It was that companies found it difficult to roll the sheets thinner with the current technology. A number of firms went to the cold rolling of the sheets that came out of the Armco type mills. So cold rolling mills for especially thin sheets were built. A small company, Wheeling Steel, developed the best version of this mill. By 1939, many companies had cold rolling capacity; among them were U.S. Steel, Republic, Bethlehem, Armco, Youngstown, Jones & Laughlin, and Wheeling itself. Reflecting progress in this area, the price of sheet steel used by automobile fenders dropped from $135 a ton in 1923 to $59 a ton in 1939 (Hexner, 1941, p. 66).

The customer industries

Table 6.2 shows the proportions of steel taken by various large users in 1935 and compares them to the proportions in 1926. To get a feel for the customer situation, we look at each sector starting with railroads. Table 6.3 shows the changes in freight and passenger revenue miles for given years in the 1930s. The industry experienced a drop in volume with total freight revenue miles going from 385.8 billion to 235.3 billion between 1930 and 1932. Furthermore, between 1937 and 1938, revenue miles fell by 20 percent. At the end of the Depression, neither freight nor passenger revenue miles had recovered to their 1930 level.

Steel use by the railroads varied much more than proportionately with its activity. While freight revenue miles dropped 39 percent between 1930 and 1932, the amount of steel purchased by railroads dropped 77 percent. The 20 percent drop in

Table 6.2 The breakdown of economic sectors using steel by percentage, 1926 and 1935

Sector	1935 Percentage	1926 Percentage
Automotive	25.0	14.5
Building and Construction (including Highways)	14.5	19.5
Containers (Tin-Plate and Drums)	11.5	4.0
Agriculture	9.5	4.0
Railroads	6.5	23.5
Oil, Gas, Water, and Mining	5.5	9.5
Machinery	4.0	4.0
Others	20.0	16.0
Exports	3.5	5.0

Source: *Iron Age*, January 2, 1936 and January 1, 1931.

Table 6.3 The economic plight of the railroad industry during the Depression and its impact on steel usage (freight and passenger revenue miles and steel usage by the railroads)

Year	Freight Revenue Miles (billions)	Passenger Revenue Miles (billions)	Steel Used (tons)
1930	385.8	26.9	5,240,000
1932	235.3	17.0	1,176,000
1935	283.6	18.5	1,961,000
1937	362.8	24.7	4,686,000
1938	291.9	21.7	1,444,000
1940	375.4	23.8	3,777,000

Source: Hogan, 1971, pp. 1299 and 1298.

the freight business from the 1938 recession led to a 69 percent drop in the steel purchases. Rail purchases and rolling stock acquisition could be postponed in bad years. By the end of the 1930s, however, there was considerable talk of the railroads being in bad physical shape and the need for more capital expenditure (*Iron Age*, January 5, 1939).

Three other developments, however, served to reduce steel use by railroads. First, as in the 1920s, more powerful locomotives were developed, eventually leading to the adoption of the diesel engine. With the larger engines, fewer units could move the same amount of freight or passengers. The second factor lessening the railroad's demand for steel was the creation of lightweight alloys to be used in rail cars and locomotives. A third change lowering this usage was the diffusion of the major transportation substitutes, automobiles and trucks.

The Depression slowed the growth of the automobile and truck industry, but recovery came soon in this sector. Since steel was a component of the physical product, steel consumption by the auto industry followed total production more closely than with the railroads. Between 1930 and 1932, automobile production fell by 75 percent, and steel usage in the industry fell by 71 percent. In 1938, the 48 percent fallback in auto production resulted in a 52 percent decline in steel use.

The auto industry recovered faster than most sectors, with total production coming to 90 percent of 1929 levels by 1937. While the 1938 recession slowed the advance in automobile production, by 1940 it was over 4,000,000 units, a level reached only a few times in the 1920s.

Additionally, improved technology increased the automotive use of steel. It was found that the cold-rolled sheets gave smoothness to the metal surface that eased the painting of cars. Sheet steel became a larger component in car bodies. Auto companies began to make the car bodies totally of steel. Also in 1935, Fisher, the body manufacturer for General Motors, introduced the turret top, which required wide sheets.

Private construction was in the doldrums in the 1930s, but there were some bright spots. The Empire State Building was completed in 1931 and the Rockefeller Center in the late 1930s. In the public sector, however, construction took up some of the slack left from the moribund private sector. The federal government built many large dams. The Works Progress Administration (WPA) built a large number of highways and edifices that used steel. State and local governments spent much money on highway and transit constructions. This activity included a number of bridges and tunnels. The period experienced a great deal of highway construction, a good example being the Pennsylvania Turnpike.

One major technological innovation increased steel use in large buildings. This was the addition of sheet to the battledecks used in building floors. Furthermore, the battledecks were improved on by Cellular Hollow modules in which preset wiring could be placed before the units were installed on the buildings.

The machinery and machine tool sector was also hurt inordinately by the Depression, but recovery slowly came in the late 1930s. Helping this recovery were improvements in most machinery. As in the automotive sector, cast carbon steel in place of alloys came into use. Increases in other steel-using sectors such as automobiles, construction equipment, and electrical machinery also fed back to general machinery and machine tools.

Electricity did not decline as much as other sectors. In fact, by the late 1930s electricity use was greater than in the 1920s. Electricity was built into homes, and people did not cut back on it as much as other goods. Furthermore, there was a continued increase in the consumer use of electrical appliances.

Additionally, more people, especially in rural areas, were hooked into the electrical grid. The federal government helped this trend with several programs and projects such as the Rural Electrification Administration (REA), the Tennessee Valley Authority (TVA), and the Bonneville Power Administration in the northwest.

Just as important as the consumer rise in electricity demand was the application of the electric motor to industrial use. By the late 1930s, almost all sources of power within the typical factory were from electric motors. This trend had been apparent in the steel industry itself twenty years before, when these motors were applied to the rolling mills. This development, combined with the new sources of electricity from TVA and Bonneville, did much to industrialize the South and West.

The oil and gas industry dropped its production in the early 1930s but later recovered. Between 1929 and 1932, total crude oil production dropped by 21 percent, but by 1937 crude production was 28 percent ahead of 1929. First, product demand, especially for gasoline, did not fall as much as that of most products, and second, continued oil discoveries increased its supply. In the late 1930s, exploration returned to the industry, and this increased the demand for steel pipes and tubes. Pipelines were also expanded to provide the cities with piped-in gas in homes and factories.

In shipbuilding, the poor performance of the 1920s continued into the early years of the Depression. In the late 1930s, this industry picked up. First, the merchant fleet, which had been built mainly during the World War I period, had become old and obsolete. The average useful life of a ship was about twenty years. Second, the Merchant Marine Act of 1936 increased government subsidies. Third, the Navy started to increase its building program.

In containers, a small fallback in the 1930s was followed by increases in demand. Food canning was less sensitive to the Depression because people did not cut back on food as much as on other items. Three things increased tin-plate volume. The first was an improvement in technology. In the late 1930s, U.S. Steel found that they could use an electrical process to coat tin onto their steel sheets. The resulting product was called electrolytic tin. The costs of the tin-plate were lowered because the process used less tin. Also increasing the supply of tin-plate were the Armco continuous sheet mill and the cold reduction mill invented in the 1930s.

Increasing the demand for tin-plate were new uses of tin cans. The work on the chemistry of coatings increased the number of foods that could be canned, and two new uses of tin cans arose in the 1930s. The first was for beer cans on which American Can had worked in the 1920s even though prohibition was in effect. Thus, they had concluded that beer would come back, and they wanted to be prepared for it. One problem was a method of opening the cans. An American Can researcher invented such an opener. In this author's youth, it was called a church key.

The second new use of cans was automotive lubricating oil. Certain companies had developed a consumer franchise in their oil, and they wanted consumers to be confident that garages were using it when the car was repaired. Thus, they found labeled cans a way to gain the confidence of consumers. Ironically, garages found that these cans were a cheaper and safer way to store oil.

With the second major steel container, drums, the Depression at first lowered production, but increases in the oil industry led to increased drum demand in the latter part of the decade. Additionally, steel drums began to replace wooden barrels for uses such as soft drinks and beer.

In the 1930s, agriculture was especially hard hit by the Depression. Low prices forced many farmers out of the industry. After the fallback in the early 1930s, however, farm mechanization moved ahead, if only slowly. The number of tractors on farms rose from 900,000 in 1930 to 1,540,000 in 1940. With the number of farm households counted at 7,160,000, this meant that still only a minority of farms were mechanized (U.S. Bureau of the Census, 1961).

The Depression almost cut off the growth of appliances, but in the late 1930s demand started to pick up. One reason for this turnaround was the increased availability of electricity. Technology advanced in many areas. For example, the coolant, Freon, was developed for refrigerators. Methods were found to put enamel on the steel surfaces of stoves, refrigerators, and other appliances. Washing machines continued to improve.

The major competitors

The large steel companies went through a very bad time in the first part of the decade. Table 6.4 displays the production and profit data on which the below analysis is based. In the mid-1930s, however, these firms recovered faster than the economy as a whole, but almost all of them were adversely affected by the fallback in 1937 and 1938. Some firms fared better than others. Essentially, companies like National and Armco, who had gone into sheet products, did the best. In this section, the experiences of the eight largest companies are described.

During the Depression, U.S. Steel experienced losses in the early years but recovered later. Production fell from 24,493,000 tons in 1929 to 5,521,000 tons in

Table 6.4 Steel production and market share for the leading steel firms in the United States, 1929–1940

| | | Company Outcomes | | | | | | | | | | | | | | | |
| | | U.S.Steel | | Bethlehem | | Republic | | National[a] | | J & L | | Armco | | Youngstown | | Inland | |
Year	Total Production	Share	Profit[b]	Share	Profit[b]	Share	Profit[b]	Share	Profit[b]	Share	Profit[b]	Share	Profit[b]	Share	Profit[b]	Share	Profit[b]
1929	63,205,000	38.8	220.3	13.0	59.0	3.3	13.0			5.3	23.8	2.2	8.5	4.4	27.4	3.1	15.0
1930	45,583,000	41.2	112.7	13.1	32.8	5.7	0.1	2.2	10.3	5.3	10.7	1.9	2.2	4.0	11.3	3.4	8.9
1931	29,059,000	38.9	-0.7	12.8	7.6	6.7	-5.4	4.5	7.1	5.3	-1.7	2.9	-0.8	3.9	-2.7	3.4	3.3
1932	15,323,000	36.0	-5.4	11.8	-12.5	6.6	-7.9	6.4	3.9	4.9	-7.4	4.2	0.2	3.0	-9.5	3.3	0.7
1933	26,020,000	34.6	-30.0	11.3	-2.0	7.9	-0.9	5.5	5.0	5.0	-5.0	4.2	1.6	4.0	-3.9	3.6	2.1
1934	29,182,000	33.2	-12.1	12.5	7.8	7.7	-0.3	5.4	9.2	4.3	-3.3	4.1	3.5	4.3	1.8	4.1	6.2
1935	38,184,000	32.7	12.2	10.9	12.4	8.5	8.6	6.0	16.3	4.7	0.1	4.7	7.4	4.6	6.3	4.3	12.9
1936	53,500,000	35.4	66.7	12.6	24.0	9.0	18.1	4.5	18.2	5.0	5.7	4.0	9.7	4.6	14.8	4.0	16.8
1937	56,637,000	36.6	129.6	14.4	45.7	7.9	17.8	5.1	26.1	4.0	7.2	3.6	0.7	4.0	17.6	3.5	18.2
1938	31,752,000	33.1	3.5	15.4	13.6	8.8	-3.0	N/Aval	10.7	4.8	-3.6	3.6	-0.7	4.2	2.8	4.5	7.9
1939	52,799,000	33.4	63.4	15.1	40.3	9.1	18.0	N/Aval	16.6	4.6	6.0	3.7	5.0	4.3	9.6	4.6	15.3
1940	66,983,000	34.2	142.1	16.0	87.8	9.1	34.9	N/Aval	24.4	5.0	15.9	3.1	0.4	4.3	15.9	4.3	22.7

Source: Moody's *Industrial Manual* and Kanawaty, G. D. "Concentration of the Steel Industry," Ph.D. Dissertation, Urbana, Illinois: 1963.

Notes

[a] National Steel only came into existence in 1929, and thus we only include the share of the other seven large firms in these figures in order to be consistent.

[b] This profit is measured by operating income in millions of current dollars.

1932. The company lost money in 1931, 1932, 1933, and 1934, but it returned to profitability in 1935. U.S. Steel's position moved its product mix toward sheets and underwent an extensive reorganization. The company had been a holding company, which consisted of large operating units such as the Carnegie Steel Company, the Illinois Steel Company, the Lorain Steel Company, and the American Tin-Plate Company. This situation was an artifact of the management of Elbert Gary whose main emphasis had been the relationship of the firm to the government rather than organizational or technical efficiency. In 1932, Gary's successors, Myron Taylor and William A. Irvin, hired the consultant firm, Ford, Bacon, & Davis, Inc., "to make a complete study of the corporation's management setup and recommend changes in order to remedy difficulties" (Hogan, 1971, p. 1203). As a result of the study, U.S. Steel combined most of its steel operating companies into one organization, the Carnegie-Illinois Steel Company. Then, it organized the United States Steel Corporation of Delaware to oversee all the operations connected with steel and located it at Pittsburgh. Benjamin Fairless was brought from Republic Steel to run first the new Carnegie-Illinois operating company and then the whole corporation. In 1937, U.S. Steel was also the first big steel firm to recognize the industrial labor union that would later be named the United Steel Workers (USW). Thus, in the 1930s, U.S. Steel began the organizational changes that would allow it to compete in future decades.

Like most other steel companies, Bethlehem Steel lost money in two of the years between 1930 and 1935. Also, like other companies, it prospered in the late 1930s. By 1939, its shipbuilding divisions and its specialty in armor plate helped it capitalize on the war. Like other firms, it expanded into sheet metal with its Lackawanna plant, which was close to the auto industry. At its Sparrows Point plant, Bethlehem installed modern sheet capacity to take advantage of the parts of the auto assembly industry on the East Coast and the other eastern sheet users.

Early in the decade, Bethlehem attempted to buy Youngstown Sheet & Tube, but the acquisition was blocked by Cyrus Eaton of Republic Steel, who wanted Youngstown for his company. A law suit over stock proxies delayed the merger until the Depression was so bad that Bethlehem could not afford it.

The management at Bethlehem was quite stable. Eugene G. Grace was a strong and powerful President who took over the company from Charles M. Schwab. Schwab died in 1939.

The third largest firm in the 1930s was the Republic Steel Corporation. It lost money in 1931, 1932, 1933, and 1934. Having recently merged several firms into one, the company was highly leveraged. By 1935, however, it merged with another firm, Corrigan, McKinney and Company of Cleveland. This strengthened the company's position by giving it modern sheet capacity near the auto industry. This merger was opposed by the antitrust authorities. Their major problem was the concentrated nature of the industry, not the particular companies in the merger. Their figures indicated that Republic had 8.4 percent of the market and Corrigan-McKinney had 1.6 percent. Republic, however, won the case.

Republic also acquired two other companies, a building products firm called Truscon Steel Company, and Gulf States Steel Company of Gadsden, Alabama.

The latter had an integrated mill and extensive iron ore and coal mines in the South.

Of the large companies, the National Steel Corporation performed the best. It did not lose money in any year in the Depression. Its production grew from 1,316,000 tons in 1930 to 2,912,000 tons in 1937. In general, the firm had modern well-located plants. At Weirton, it was the first outside company to use the Armco continuous rolling mill. Its Great Lakes plant in Michigan was brand new, built in 1930.

It concentrated most of its capacity on two products. Tin-plate, the main specialty of its Weirton plant, was not all that vulnerable to the Depression, since it was fed by the non-cyclical canning industry. With National's second major product, its Michigan plant's proximity to Detroit gave it low transportation costs. Furthermore, this location also facilitated the firm's communications with the automobile firms. This helped National Steel especially during the early 1930s when the demand for autos was often intermittent.

The National Steel Corporation had a tendency to cut prices more than other firms. This policy did much to increase sales. Thus, National's modern plants and concentration on tin-plate and auto steel gave it the strength to act independently of other firms, and still remain profitable.

Jones & Laughlin, the fifth largest steel firm in the 1930s, lost money in 1931, 1932, 1933, and 1934, but, with the exception of the depressed year of 1938, it was profitable in the late 1930s. To improve its performance, the firm moved more into sheets and continued its strategy of experimentation and research, enlarging the laboratory it built in the 1920s. Also, the company began to develop specialties in reinforced concrete and drums. Last, it set up a steel warehouse and distribution company on the East Coast.

Armco, the old American Rolling Mills Company, came out of the Depression in a very strong position. The company lost money in only one year during the early period. Its production grew from 880,000 tons in 1930 to 1,797,000 tons in 1935, the latter surpassing the 1929 tonnage of 1,369,000. The company's innovative behavior in the 1920s stood it in good stead. Its relatively efficient up-to-date capacity in sheets helped it to do well in the 1930s.

While no new plants were built, Armco developed some new products, the major one being galvanized sheets, which could be used in places like roofs and water tanks where the metal was in contact with moisture. Its Sheffield Steel division in Kansas helped it capitalize on the growth in oil exploration in the late 1930s. Thus, Armco survived the Depression in very good shape.

The Youngstown Sheet & Tube Company had a very hard time. It lost money in 1931, 1932, and 1933. Its production declined from 2,788,000 tons in 1929 to 467,000 tons in 1932. As with other firms, it then recovered somewhat, making money in all years from 1934 onward. By 1940, it exceeded its 1929 production.

The company's specialty in pipes hurt it disproportionately in the early part of the period because of the cutbacks in oil exploration. In contrast, its position in sheets assisted its recovery in the later years with the expansion of the auto industry. Its adjustment to the new situation was held up by the proposed merger with

Bethlehem. While considering the merger, the company put off plans to build a continuous rolling mill for sheet. As it turned out, the company did have a continuous mill installed by 1935.

The merger with the Brier Hill Steel Company strengthened the company's position, giving it a wider product line. Additionally, in the late 1930s, the firm installed another continuous sheet mill at its Indiana Harbor plant. Through these investments, Youngstown Sheet & Tube increased the share of its product mix accounted for by sheet from 17 percent in 1929 to 28 percent in 1940. In spite of the move toward sheets, Youngstown Sheet & Tube did invest in up-to-date types of pipes and tubes which fortified its position in the late 1930s. Thus, the company was able to realign its product line, bringing prosperity in the latter part of the decade. Unlike some others, it did not lose money during the 1938 recession.

The Inland Steel Company for most of its existence was the smallest of the Big Eight, but its location and ability to produce efficiently gave it a strength lacking in some others. The company weathered the Depression far better than most. Inland's response to the bad times was to change its product mix. Until 1930, the company had most of its sales in construction items. Thereafter, Inland moved its product mix more to sheet products. In addition to the automobile industry, the firm saw that many small sheet-using manufacturers such as the makers of appliances and construction equipment were growing.

The company also bought a number of final products and distribution firms. A major purchase was the warehousing firm and steel distributor, Joseph T. Ryerson & Sons. The purchase was not so much an integration move as a diversification effort in that neither the bulk of Inland's products were sold through Ryerson nor were most of Ryerson's products obtained from the parent steel firm (Hale, 1970). Whatever the contribution of Ryerson to Inland's overall position, it did contribute to its parent in one area, management. Three members of the Ryerson family went onto the board of directors. In 1940, Edward L. Ryerson later became Inland's chairman of the Board (*Iron Age*, May 9, 1940, p. 89-B).

Thus, Inland was able to refocus its product line toward growing or noncyclical products such as auto sheet and tin-plate. The success of Inland can be seen in its capacity utilization rate which was 72.5 percent in 1935 as opposed to the total industry rate of 48.7 percent.

Substitutes

The two major substitutes for steel in the twentieth century were aluminum and plastics. Table 6.5 compares the production and prices of steel and aluminum in the early twentieth century. In the early 1900s, aluminum was a relatively new product that had not fully developed its process and marketing. On average, its price was about 16 times that of steel. The ratio does not necessarily have to be one-to-one for materials to be competitive (Smith, 1988, p. 89). Nevertheless, a fall in the ratio suggests that aluminum was becoming more competitive with steel. By 1920, the price ratio had dropped to about nine, but it did not materially change until the very

Table 6.5 Steel and aluminum production and prices in the United States, 1900–1940

Year	Total Production of Steel Tons	Aluminum Tons	Steel Price (Per Ton)	Aluminum Price Per Ton	Ratio Between the Two Prices
1900	11,410,000	23,000	41.2	654.4	15.88
1910	29,230,000	151,000	35.8	445.0	12.43
1920	47,190,000	521,000	72.6	654.4	9.01
1925	50,841,000	317,000	53.6	543.8	10.15
1929	63,205,000	366,000	50.8	478.0	9.41
1930	45,583,000	331,000	46.4	475.8	10.25
1932	15,323,000	96,000	43.0	466.0	10.84
1935	38,184,000	245,000	48.8	410.0	8.40
1940	66,983,000	439,000	53.0	373.8	7.05

Source: American Metal Market, 1974, U.S. Bureau of the Census, 1960, and Kanawaty, 1963.

late 1930s. As shown in Table 6.5, the aluminum price dropped marginally only from $654 per ton to $373 per ton between 1920 and 1940.

The aluminum industry in 1930 was still totally dominated by the Aluminum Company of America (Alcoa). By the late 1930s, however, two events took place that would lead to change. First, the government began a structural antitrust case against Alcoa, which would eventually lead to a de-concentration of the industry.

The second development was the increased demand for aluminum from the airplane industry due to the war. In the late 1930s, Germany greatly increased its aluminum production to supply its military. This led the United States and other countries to increase aluminum capacity to build more airplanes. In fact, the federal government directly financed much of this expansion.

In the 1920s and 1930s, the chemical industry was conducting extensive research that would lead to the development of the second major substitute for steel, plastics. A number of parallel lines of research in organic chemistry led to the discovery of a number of materials that could be synthesized from standard chemicals. Some research was done on the plastics polymers that could eventually be substituted for some steels. In 1937, the Census Bureau, which collected data on industrial performance, began to publish separate information on plastics (Backman, 1970, p. 322). Thus, a plastics industry was in place that would become a major source of competition with the steel industry in many products.

Input supplies: ore, coal and labor

Reflecting the economy as a whole, iron ore production fluctuated a great deal during the 1930s. Production dropped from 73.0 million tons in 1929 to 9.8 million in 1932. Production had almost totally recovered by 1937 when it was 72 million tons, but the 1938 recession caused a drop to 28.4 million tons. By 1940, it was at 73.6 million tons due to wartime demand. There was some increase in the beneficiation of the ore, but the change was not that important. The average iron content of the mined ore stayed about the same, changing only from 51.53 percent in 1931 to

51.45 in 1936. The Adirondacks region experienced a revival in its iron ore mining with production rising from 254,000 tons in 1931 to 2,713,141 tons in 1939. Iron ore mining in the South declined at first, but then revived with a net production change from 6,437,518 tons in 1929 to 7,140,612 tons in 1940.

Coke production dropped from 59.9 million tons in 1929 to 21.8 million tons in 1932. It then rose to 52.4 million tons in 1937 with a drop to 32.5 million in 1938. Recovering from the 1938 recession, it reached 57.1 million tons in 1940. In this period, the market share of by-product coke ovens rose from 94.2 in 1930 to 97.4 percent in 1938. There were two technological improvements in by-product coke ovens during this period. The first was a better arrangement of the components within the oven. The second was the practice of washing the coal before putting it in the oven; this improved the yield from the material.

In the 1930s, two events changed the position and attitudes of the steel industry workers. First, the Depression turned what were good times into very bad times. The fall in steel production led to layoffs. Moreover, the Depression meant part-time employment for many workers who were not laid off. In the past, the reactions of the workers to economic woe had usually been passive. In the 1930s, however, the improvement did not come as fast as in the past. Even when the economy improved in the middle 1930s, a setback occurred with the 1937–1938 recession.

Two other developments changed the situation of the workers. First, by the 1930s, most steel mill workers had become much more sophisticated than they had been earlier. In the early part of the century, a large portion if not the majority had migrated to the steel towns from Europe and the South. (See *Iron Age*, February 10, 1938, p. 68 for statistics on the origin of steel workers.) By the 1930s, these people had become inured to the ways of urban America, and thus, their views on the steel companies and their jobs were much more jaundiced than they had been in the past.

In spite of some concessions and some efforts to placate their employees, the steel companies continued to be domineering top-down organizations. The companies, however, still treated the workers, no matter what the skill level, as unknowing automatons. This led the workers to take a much more militant stance.

The second thing that changed the steel workers was the policy of the federal government. In 1933, the new Roosevelt administration passed the National Recovery Act (NRA). It set up the National Recovery Administration, which promulgated codes of conduct for each major industry. While steel companies agreed with much in this program, they did not support Section 7a of the Act that provided for collective bargaining. Essentially the workers were given the right to have employee organizations or unions. The steel companies, however, interpreted the Act to include in its definition of worker organizations the Employee Representation Plans as had been organized at Bethlehem Steel and the small company, Colorado Fuel & Iron. Others claimed that the Act meant the employee organizations to be unions chosen by the workers themselves. A number of court cases then ensued. Before these cases went far, the National Recovery Administration itself was declared unconstitutional in 1935.

Soon, a new law, the Wagner Act, replaced Section 7a as the legal support for unions. The Act also set up the National Labor Relations Board (NLRB). This agency conducted plant-level elections to decide on what organization would represent the workers in collective bargaining. The NLRB also was authorized to settle disputes involving the relationship between companies and unions. Given these favorable political conditions, the workers in the steel industry and members of the labor movement started to unionize the industry. Chronologically, this endeavor can be divided into three parts: (1) the initial organizing effort, (2) the organization of U.S. Steel, and (3) the conflict with the second-level steel companies called "Little Steel."

The initial organizing effort resulting from NRA was centered on the old Amalgamated Association of Iron, Steel and Tin Workers. Before 1933, this union constituted, at most, 10 percent of the steel workforce. It was a skill-based union, which was reluctant to organize workers outside of its original skill set. Many workers in the steel industry belonged in the jurisdiction of other American Federation of Labor unions, and the Amalgamated Association did not want to take in those workers. Nevertheless, the union made efforts to increase its membership, and in May 1934, its newer members attempted to lead a strike against the steel companies. This strike failed due to strong company opposition, but there was also a lack of support from the central office of the Amalgamated.

After this debacle, most workers felt that someone else was needed to organize the steel companies. In 1935, a movement developed within the American Federation of Labor (AFL) to organize workers along industrial lines. It centered around the United Mineworkers (UMW). Its president, John L. Lewis, along with some other union heads formed the Committee of Industrial Organization within AFL to foment an industry-wide union. Due to differences with the traditional AFL leaders, this group split off from the old organization. becoming the Congress of Industrial Organizations (CIO) in 1938.

As for steel, John L. Lewis claimed a special interest because many members of his union worked for the steel firms mining metallurgical coal. Consequently, Lewis and others provided financial backing for the organization of labor in the steel industry. In 1936, they set up the Steel Workers Organizing Committee (SWOC). Headed up by Philip Murray, a Lewis protégée, the SWOC set out to organize the steel workers. Also, the UMW and other unions lent the SWOC field organizers to go among the rank-and-file workers at the plant level. The Steel Workers Organizing Committee took over the Amalgamated, and used it as a skeleton organization, officially making the new local unions part of it.

Initially, SWOC's main target was U.S. Steel. Using the Amalgamated as the official base organization, they started working with rank-and-file workers at U.S. Steel plants. The committee organizers often used the U.S. Steel's Employee Representation Plan as a core from which would come the plant local unions. Within U.S. Steel, discussion on many job issues began between the management and workers who were clearly members of unions. This led to plans for a strike on the question of union recognition.

In early 1937, however, U.S. Steel capitulated without a fight and recognized the SWOC as its union and bargaining agent. Essentially, this agreement came from the top. Chief Executive Officer Myron Taylor approached John L. Lewis and

Philip Murray to initiate a preliminary understanding from which an official contract could be negotiated. There has been much controversy on why the company gave in so easily. Some argue that the U.S. Steel officials were more liberal than other steel firm heads. Some asserted that with what seemed like a booming economy in early 1937, the company did not want to risk a strike.

A stronger reason was the company's relationship with the government. Many scholars have seen this capitulation as a change from the anti-union attitudes of older U.S. Steel leaders like Elbert Gary. Ironically, the change was quite consistent with the main thrust of Gary's policies. He thought that the survival of U.S. Steel depended on the goodwill of the government. At any given time, there were apt to be antitrust and other investigations of the company, the outcome of which could affect the position of the company. Under Roosevelt and the New Deal, the government had become pro-labor, and U.S. Steel management, especially Myron Taylor, felt that an accommodation with organized labor could help the company. Furthermore, events such as the sit-down strikes in the auto industry badly hurt company images. Even local and state governments became more pro-labor; in strikes at other companies, these bodies often actually intervened on the side of the workers. Consequently, most scholars (Rees, 2004) now believe that the change in government attitudes on labor was instrumental in the U.S. Steel recognition of the SWOC.

After U.S. Steel capitulated, several other companies followed, the largest being Jones & Laughlin and Crucible Steel. Shortly after U.S. Steel, they succumbed.

After gaining recognition from U.S. Steel, SWOC focused on the second-tier companies known as "Little Steel." In 1937, SWOC led strikes at Youngstown, Republic, Inland, and Bethlehem. Lasting about a month, these strikes were defeats for the union in that the companies were able to keep their plants going.

Several factors account for this failure. First, the 1937 recession slowed down the demand for steel. Second, the legal standing of SWOC as opposed to the Employee Representation Plans was not yet clear. The company lawyers still continued to fight the SWOC and the NLRB itself in court. Third, the leaders of these firms, especially Tom Girdler of Republic, were militantly anti-union (Girdler and Sparkes, 1943). Fourth, there were some divisions among the workers. Many supported the companies and the Employee Representation Plans. With some firms, the representation plan groups won the NLRB-supervised elections. Consequently, SWOC could not rely on a united front within the rank and file at the mills. A sixth and maybe key factor is that these smaller companies were less dependent on the goodwill of the government than U.S. Steel. It is unlikely that they would be broken up by antitrust action, and often other action against the steel industry would be focused on U.S. Steel and not them. In fact, the small steel companies often had local government support that U.S. Steel did not have. For example, in a strike at Monroe, Michigan, Republic had the support of the local government.

In the prosperous years, 1940 and 1941, the resistance of "Little Steel" to the SWOC lessened. Again, the federal government played a role in that much of the steel demand depended directly and indirectly on defense contracts. Consequently, in 1941 SWOC was able to organize unions in Bethlehem, Inland, Youngstown, Republic and the Great Lakes plant of National Steel.

Thus, in the 1930s, a union independent of the companies became the collective bargaining agent for the bulk of the workers in the steel industry. In 1942, the Steel Workers Organizing Committee acknowledged this triumph by changing its name to the United Steelworkers (USW). Philip Murray resigned from the UMW to become President of the new organization.

The influence of government

In the 1930s, four government initiatives impacted the steel industry: the formation of the National Recovery Administration, the Wagner Act that helped labor to organize independent unions, the Reciprocal Trade policy started by the Roosevelt administration, and a set of antitrust cases. The latter two policies had little immediate impact, but later they would change much in the industry.

The National Recovery Administration (NRA) was set up in 1933 to help business to get the nation out of the Depression. The idea of the NRA was that the government could organize business to deal with the Depression in a way similar to the way it contributed to the war effort in 1917 and 1918. No one, however, had any idea of how to go about this task. There were persistent differences in opinion on just what the appropriate policies were (Hawley, 1956, chapter 2). As a partial consequence of this disagreement, a large number of NRA codes laid out the behavior of the firms in each industry. Since the companies wrote the codes, not surprisingly, these codes effectively organized many industries into cartels. In that way, prices were often raised or at least stabilized.

The general idea was that high prices meant prosperity. The problem was that the causation ran the other way: prosperity causes high prices not the reverse. In fact, other things equal, higher prices would lower output, thereby exacerbating the Depression.

The steel firms cooperated in the NRA code effort; in fact they used their influence to try to get the government to repeal past decisions on basing point pricing (Hawley, 1956, pp. 94–5 and Cheape, 1996). Like many other industries, steel saw the NRA as a way to set high prices. "In 1933 code regulations erected a price umbrella to supplant competition, restore order, and revive profits" (Cheape, 1996, p. 85). Within the National Recovery Administration, there were experts who did not agree with this policy, and conflict abounded. It all became moot in 1935, when the NRA Act was declared unconstitutional, and the agency disbanded.

As much as the steel firms favored parts of the NRA, they did not support the NRA Section 7a which gave labor the right to collective bargaining. Soon after the fall of the NRA, the Wagner Act of 1935 led to the above-described development of the USW.

The third government initiative affecting the steel industry was the Trade Agreements Act of 1934. Arising from the traditions of the Democratic Party, this Act authorized the negotiation of treaties for the bilateral lowering of tariffs between the United States and other countries. As a result of these treaties, the tariffs on certain steel goods were lowered. For instance, the entry tax on steel bars from Sweden was dropped by 37.5 percent , and those on billet bars from Belgium and Brazil were lowered 50 percent (Hogan, 1971, p. 1429). While these changes did not materially affect the American steel companies, they did indicate what would happen when the world economy became more open and the foreign steel firms became more efficient.

The fourth area where government actions could affect the steel industry was antitrust. Three actions indicated the future influence of antitrust, but they did not exert an immediate influence. First, in 1935, the justice department challenged the merger of the Republic Steel Corporation and the Corrigan, McKinney Steel Company. While the government did not succeed, this case was a portent of the merger policy that emerged later (*Iron Age*, May 9, 1935, p. 41).

Second, the multiple base pricing system was challenged; under this system most or all firms would set their transportation charges equal to that from the basing point nearest to the customer. When the government bought steel, cement, and other products, it encountered these practices; Harold Ickes, the Secretary of Interior found the bids quoted by all the companies to be equal. (See *Iron Age*, February 11, 1937, p. 92.) The Federal Trade Commission started an investigation of basing point pricing in steel, cement, and other industries. World War II came before the FTC investigation could be fully developed. The case, however, would have an impact after the war (Rogers, 1983).

Third, in reaction to the above complaints, Congress authorized the study of the Temporary National Economic Committee. Covering many American industries, especially steel, these studies provided data and analyses on which much of the later government steel policy was based.

Conclusion

In the 1930s, the steel industry weathered a very bad time. By the early 1940s, the companies faced a powerful union. Some commentators assert that the strength of the USW was responsible for the troubles encountered by the industry in later decades. Others blame the liberalization of American trade policy and the antitrust enforcement.

The activities of the companies in the 1930s, however, suggest that other factors could explain their later troubles. In the 1930s, the companies not only survived the Depression but also altered their product lines and technology. They moved their production from the old static product lines such as plate and rails to growing products like sheets. In sum, the steel firms adjusted to their situation by varying their product line and increasing efficiency.

As Chapter 7 reveals, these changes in product line and the demands of World War II led to an attenuation of the adjustments made in the 1930s. The developments in World War II may well have contributed much more to the later troubles of the steel industry than did the union, trade policy, or antitrust.

7   Steel and World War II

Introduction

This chapter describes the experience of the American steel industry in World War II. This period encompasses the years 1940 to 1945. Before going into detail, however, it is useful to discuss certain general conditions prevailing in steel at this time. Far more airplanes, ships, and, of course, armaments were produced during the war than at any other time in history. To meet the demands of the war, the industry increased its output. Furthermore, a much different composition of steel products than during the peacetime economy was required, but the change was temporary.

The major firms in the industry remained the same, but the government did finance some new capacity. Most of this capacity was operated under contracts by established steel companies. Much capacity was built in the western United States, which did not have that many plants before the war.

A major development that occurred in steel substitutes was the great increase in aluminum capacity. This increase would have long-run effects on steel because the peacetime economy would not use anywhere near as much aluminum as the war effort did. Incentive developed for aluminum firms to invade the product space once controlled by steel.

In addition, the federal government played an intrusive role in steel. First, indirectly, it became the major customer with all its defense uses. Second, the government attempted to dictate the product mix of the industry. The major initiative impacting the industry was the inclusive and intricate system of price controls administered by the Office of Price Administration (OPA). For many businesses, these controls did not have an appreciable effect on profits. Kennedy (1999, p. 641) states that during the war "Corporate profits . . . nearly doubled." In contrast, steel company profits, which rose between 1939 and 1941, dropped after 1942, when the controls came into effect (Campbell, 1948, p. 229).

This chapter now uses our taxonomy to examine the wartime experience of the steel industry. The next section focuses changes in the nature of the product and its technology. The third section describes the uses of steel during the war. The fourth section discusses the major steel firms. The fifth section examines the substitutes for steel, and the sixth section looks at raw materials and labor. The seventh section discusses the role of government. A final section concludes by presenting some hypotheses on the long-run effect of the war on steel.

Production and the production process

Table 7.1 shows a 69.8 percent increase in steel production between 1939 and 1944. Of this 36,843,000 ton increase, over two-thirds (67.9 percent) were accounted for by increased capacity utilization while the rest, 32.1 percent, came from increased production capacity. This means that 11,823,000 tons of new capacity was added.

To understand this expansion, we look at how the particular parts of the steel-making process changed – starting with the blast furnace. The total number of existing furnaces rose from 231 in 1939 to 243 at the end of 1944, the year when production was at its peak. The number of active furnaces rose from 201 in November 1939 to 232 in December 1944. During the war years, 1941 to 1945, the country built 22 new furnaces. Of these, 11 were financed by the federal government through the Defense Finance Corporation. The new furnaces tended to be large and state-of-the-art. The production per active furnace rose from 177,500 tons in 1939 to 287,900 tons in 1944. Improvements in auxiliary equipment and increases in capacity utilization also increased productivity.

Table 7.2 show the production breakdown by type of steel furnace. Steel capacity rose from 81,829,000 tons to 95,505,000 tons in 1945; most of this increase was in open hearth furnaces. The United Sates built 43 new open hearth furnaces. Of these, private firms financed 14, and the government financed 29. The latter were operated by established steel firms such as U.S. Steel, Republic, Armco, and Granite City. Both the privately financed and government-financed furnaces were larger than the average, leading to an increase in the average furnace size from 111.7 to 126.8 tons per heat. The Bessemer steel furnace "which revived slightly during the war was again on the decline" (Hogan, 1971, pp. 1143–4).

Electric furnaces, however, grew precipitously, increasing over four-fold between 1939 and 1944. The United States installed 33 new electric furnaces during the war period, all of which were privately financed. Most of these furnaces were used to produce alloy steel for special uses. Some important innovations occurred during the war; among them were improved electrical regulators and circuit-breakers.

Table 7.1 Yearly steel production, capacity, and utilization rates, 1939–1945

Year	Steel production	Steel production capacity	Utilization rate
1939	52,798,714	81,829,000	64.5
1940	66,982,686	81,619,000	82.1
1941	82,839,259	84,152,000	98.4
1942	86,032,931	88,570,000	97.1
1943	88,836,512	90,293,000	98.4
1944	89,641,600	93,652,000	95.7
1945	79,701,648	95,505,000	83.5

Source: Moody's *Industrial Manual* and Kanawaty, 1963.

Table 7.2 Yearly steel production broken down by steel furnace type, 1939–1945

| Year | Total production (in tons) | Production for types of furnace | | |
		Open hearth	Bessemer	Electric
1939	52,798,714	48,409,800 (91.7)	3,358,916 (6.4)	1,029,067 (1.9)
1940	66,982,686	61,573,083 (91.9)	3,708,573 (5.5)	1,700,006 (2.5)
1941	82,839,259	74,389,619 (89.8)	5,578,071 (6.7)	2,869,256 (3.5)
1942	86,031,931	76,501,957 (88.9)	5,553,424 (6.5)	3,974,540 (4.6)
1943	88,836,512	78,621,804 (88.5)	5,625,492 (6.3)	4,589,070 (5.2)
1944	89,641,600	80,363,953 (89.7)	5,039,923 (5.6)	4,237,699 (4.7)
1945	79,701,648	71,939,602 (90.3)	4,305,318 (5.4)	3,456,704 (4.3)

Source: Moody's *Industrial Manual* and Kanawaty, 1963.

In rolling mills, there was only one major technological advance, but the change in demand for products led to some interesting improvisations. Almost all types of steel products grew in demand during the war, but some rose much faster than others. World War II required two products in much greater numbers than ever before or since: airplanes and ships. The former required a large number of steel products, not only for the plane itself, but also for manufacturing capital, deployment, and maintenance. For instance, in the South Pacific war theater, the Army and Navy used a steel matting for runways in swampy areas.

Shipbuilding had a major impact on steel plant operations – especially the rolling mills. In order to meet this demand, rolling strip mills, intended to be used for light sheet products, were diverted to making other shapes; about a third of the plates were made in such mills. Other products used in ships, such as pipes, also increased in production as shown in Table 7.3.

The increase in ships, however, did not account for all the growth in steel demand. All major steel products except tin-plate increased in production between 1939 and 1940 as shown in Table 7.3. Ironically, rails, a use not normally associated with the war, increased by almost 100 percent. The wartime demand connected to ships and the oil industry increased the demand for pipes and tubes by 44.7 percent, and the use of wire increased by almost 23 percent. The latter could be attributed to airplane and ship use. Even the use of sheets usually associated with automobiles increased by 3.4 percent, a change not foreseen, since automobile production was virtually abolished in 1942. The need for trucks, trains, and other vehicles apparently made up for this change.

Ironically, the major technological change that occurred during the war years was in a product where production dropped, tin-plate. This fall (5.9 percent) was due to the Japanese conquest of Malaysia, the major source of tin. The situation

Table 7.3 Comparisons of war and peacetime productions of various steel products

Year	Plates	Sheets	Shapes	Bars	Pipes	Wire	Tin-plate	Rails	Others
1939	3,101,981	11,858,772	3,358,985	6,138,350	4,348,630	3,680,297	3,468,358	1,994,796	1,117,384
1940	4,323,408	13,783,700	4,232,346	7,885,261	5,029,966	4,351,848	3,625,551	2,399,494	3,028,795
1943	12,900,000	10,899,000	3,758,000	12,005,000	5,861,000	4,385,000	2,324,000	3,184,000	8,086,000
1944	12,457,356	12,258,903	3,977,790	11,108,920	6,293,709	4,521,991	3,262,044	3,985,464	5,979,947
Percentage change 1939 to 1944	301.6	3.4	18.4	81.0	44.7	22.9	-5.9	99.7	435.4

Source: *Iron Age*, January 3, 1946, p. 80.

encouraged the adoption of the new electrolytic process of tin-plating. It cut the per unit use of tin by 75 percent. Hogan (1971, pp. 1164–5) states, "Virtually all the producers of tin-plate including Bethlehem Steel, National Steel, Youngstown Sheet & Tube, Republic Steel, Jones & Laughlin, Inland Steel, Wheeling Steel, and Crown Cork and Seal Company of Baltimore, installed electrolytic lines."

Thus, the major change in the rolling mill sector resulted from the Japanese conquest of Malaysia. The major technological event, however, was the great increase in total production which impacted all three major sectors: blast furnaces, steel converters, and rolling mills.

The customer industries

Table 7.4 shows steel use by sector. During the war, the steel use of the automobile and the aircraft industries was combined by most data collectors. In 1940, the latter industry used only 51,400 tons of steel or 0.2 percent of total consumption, while this consumption increased to 580,918 tons in 1941. After that, separate aircraft use data was not available. It can be inferred that airplane use increased, but by how much is not certain.

The war temporarily eliminated the major product of the auto industry, the passenger car. The resources of the auto industry were urgently needed by the war effort. Between 1940 and 1944, passenger car production dropped from 3.7 million units to 610 units. Truck production only declined from 754,901 units in 1940 to 737,524 units in 1944. They were needed by the war effort. With the manufacture of its main commodity abolished, the auto industry turned its resources to war materials.

It would seem logical that the industry made war vehicles similar to its peacetime products, and it did – manufacturing scout cars, armored vehicles, and tanks. The

Table 7.4 The breakdown of economic sectors using steel, by percentage, 1939 and 1944

Sector	1939 Tonnage	Percentage	1944 Tonnage	Percentage
Automotive and aircraft (Including trucks and other vehicles)	5,906,358	15.1	4,761,536	7.6
Shipbuilding	517,771	1.3	12,011,301	19.0
Building and construction (including highways)	6,100,386	15.6	6,240,197	9.9
Containers (tin-plate and drums)	2,978,463	7.6	3,878,161	6.1
Agriculture	1,420,697	3.6	1,950,162	3.1
Railroads	3,250,022	8.3	6,134,249	9.7
Oil, gas, water, and mining	1,841,599	4.7	2,464,068	3.9
Machinery	1,460,000	3.7	3,270,156	5.2
Exports	2,817,482	7.2	5,107,690	8.1
Others	12,774,775	32.7	17,276,535	27.4
Total consumption	39,067,553		63,094,055	

Source: *Iron Age*, January 3, 1946, p. 81.

Jeep light truck was one of its best-known wartime products. However, the auto industry's knowledge of manufacturing techniques and its ability to deploy huge amounts of capital enabled it to make other items such as helmets, rifles, and machine guns. Most publicized were the industry's forays into airplanes, such as Ford Motor Company's B24 bomber plant at Willow Run, Michigan and the manufacture of the TBM Navy bomber by General Motors.

Some of the industry's major contributions were less obvious. General Motors developed an efficient way to manufacture the Pratt & Whitney rotor aircraft engine. By 1944, General Motors' engine plant "had completed 50,000 bomber engines and three million cylinder heads" (Hogan, 1971, p. 1320). The latter could equip 200,000 aircraft engines. Another less obvious contribution of the auto industry was the development of a steel bullet shell. The lack of copper, which was used for the brass cartridge, motivated this innovation. Finally, the automobile companies found a manganese steel alloy that could be used for bullet cartridges.

During World War II, shipbuilding became the largest user of steel with industry consumption rising from 999,858 tons in 1940 to 12,011,301 tons in 1944, peaking at 13,318,107 tons in 1943. The United States fought almost all of the war in areas very far from its shores, and it needed ships to transport its troops and their supplies to these areas. Accentuating the problem was, first, the need to supply material to the allies and, second, the opposition of the enemy. Much of the war-making material used by the British and Russians came from the United States almost exclusively by ship. German submarines destroyed a significant portion of the ships going to Europe early in the war, and the large Japanese Navy necessitated the building of a huge American war fleet.

The American World War II Navy became the largest in history with 1,167 combat vessels, including 23 battleships and 50 large and medium aircraft carriers. Building this fleet required steel, most notably the plate for armor but also sheet, pipes, and many other types of metal. To give some examples, a battleship required 100,000 tons of steel; a large destroyer needed over 15,000 tons of steel. In contrast, a standard 10,000 ton displacement freighter used only 3,500 tons.

In total demand, however, the merchant marine accounted for a much larger portion of the shipbuilding industry and its steel than did the Navy. Once oceans were cleared of the enemy, the United States still had to get its troops to the battlefields and supply them. Thus, a huge effort went into building merchant ships. By 1945, a total of 5,452 ships had been built by America. Consequently, between 1939 and 1944, shipbuilding rose from 1.3 to 19.0 percent of total U.S. steel consumption.

This great effort was, however, a short-term endeavor; once the war was over, the demand for these ships declined. In fact, the 1945 consumption of steel from this sector fell to 3,744,403 tons, less than one-third of the 1944 total.

The building and construction sector went through a drastic change during the war. The historically important construction uses of steel, such as bridges and large office buildings, could be delayed, but the war effort required many other projects, such as army camps and shipyards and airplane and munitions factories. A large amount of steel went into new steel mills and, ironically, new aluminum smelters. Military operations themselves often called for construction steels, a good example being the Bailey Bridge, a portable girder bridge developed by the British to help armies cross rivers.

During the war, construction consumption of steel followed an unusual pattern, rising between 1940 and 1941 from 6,935,889 to 10,221,167 tons. In 1942 construction steel use rose further to 10,714,977 tons, and then in 1943 the use fell back to 6,639,509 tons, then 6,240,197 tons in 1944, but it rose to 8,535,027 tons in 1945. Likely the construction needed to deploy the American armed force was done early in the war, and the 1945 increase was due to the initial redeployment of the economy to peacetime use.

The container industries consisted of the tin-plate can makers and steel drum manufacturers. In the former sector, the war not only impacted the demand side of industry, but also the supply of tin, one of its key inputs. The Japanese conquest of Malaysia severed most of the tin supply. Several measures were taken to counter this problem. Tin from Bolivia that had previously gone to Great Britain was diverted to a new American tin smelter in Texas. The recycling of tin was encouraged. A process called bonderizing used in the auto industry to counter rust was adopted to some can uses, but it did not work in most uses.

Efforts were made to cut the demand for civilian tin cans, but the wartime uses counteracted those efforts. Aside from munitions, the Army and Navy required canned food that could be shipped over long distances to the troops. Consequently, even with the restrictions on demand for tin-plate goods, the total use of steel in the container sector increased from 2,978,463 tons in 1939 to 3,878,161 tons in 1944. While much of this increase was accounted for by steel drums, there still was a desperate need for tin-plated containers.

Electrolytic coating, an innovation developed in the 1930s, did much to alleviate this problem. This process not only improved the quality of the tin-plate product but also lowered the per unit use of tin. The amount of tin used in each unit of tin-plate dropped by 38 percent (Hogan, 1971, p. 1394). In total, 28 electrolytic tin-plating lines were under construction in 1942.

The other important part of the container sector also increased. The military needed steel drums to transport fuel. In 1944, 34,000,000 steel drums were manufactured. While no drastic changes in production techniques occurred, improved welding techniques facilitated the production of these drums.

Even though steel was diverted to wartime uses, its use in agriculture increased 37 percent from 1,420,697 tons in 1939 to 1,950,162 tons in 1944. The wartime needs of allies and refugees increased the demand for American food crops. Hampering this increase was a shortfall in labor as farm workers were drafted into military service and were attracted to more lucrative employment in other sectors. To counteract this tendency, the ongoing trends toward mechanization accelerated. This resulted in the use of more steel as mechanized farm implements such as tractors and combines became more prevalent.

During World War II, the railroads prospered. Revenue-tons in freight almost doubled, rising 97.5 percent from 375.4 to 740.6 million. Passenger traffic increased even more, rising 302 percent from 23.8 million passenger miles to 95.7 million. Not only did the war greatly increase travel, but also the termination of car manufacturing and the rationing of gasoline drove the public back to the railroads.

Steel use by the railroads nearly doubled between 1939 and 1944, rising from 3.25 to 6.13 million tons. While rail production rose somewhat, the major change was in the increase in equipment; between 1940 and 1944, the number of locomotives sold rose from 501 to 1,249. This number rose even further in 1945 to 2,845. The number of freight cars also increased with almost half of them being exported.

The war accentuated many of the technological trends already present in the late 1930s. The move to streamlined passenger trains continued when engines and cars could be obtained. The major change, however, was the diffusion of the over-the-road diesel electric locomotive. It was more efficient. The newest diesel could pull a train of 3,500 tons, while the steam engine could only haul 2,000 tons. Thus, the railroad, while not generally thought of as being directly involved in the war effort, increased its share of steel consumption from 8.3 percent in 1939 to 9.6 percent in 1944.

The war significantly increased the demand for steel in the oil and gas industry as well. Not only did the American military and merchant marine run on petroleum fuels, but also the industrial effort to supply the war requirements used a disproportionate amount of petroleum. Combined with water and mining, this sector increased its use of steel by 34 percent, rising from 1,841,599 tons in 1939 to 2,464,068 tons in 1944. Much of this increase came from the wartime expansion in exploration and rising industrial production.

One special wartime circumstance that did much to expand the oil business use of steel was the German submarine activity in the Atlantic Ocean. Much of the oil refined in the eastern United States and Canada came from the Gulf Coast by ship, and in 1942, the German U-boats began sinking these tankers. To avoid this problem and to reallocate tankers to the overseas shipments, two inland oil pipelines were built from Texas to the East Coast. These two projects and some additional pipelines used a large amount of steel – especially seamless tube.

Two parts of the machinery industry were notably impacted by World War II, machine tools and electrical machinery. In total, the sector's consumption of steel increased by over 100 percent from 1,460,000 tons in 1939 to 3,270,156 tons in 1944. For machine tools, the contrast with the previous decade could not have been greater. In the 1930s, machine tool firms suffered from overcapacity; during World War II, their problem was meeting grossly increasing demand with limited resources. The shift from peacetime products to wartime needs led to an increase in the call for machine tools.

The electrical machinery industry shifted its emphasis from building electrical utility equipment to supplying the electrical machinery needed on airplanes and ships. For the former, many of the controls and weapons used depended on electrical motors. In fact, the B29 bomber had 170 electric motors (Hogan, 1971, p. 1345). Modern ships essentially operate miniature electric power systems. Consequently, for both machine tools and electrical machinery, the war caused a gross change in product mix, which greatly challenged the industry and its steel suppliers.

The amount of steel used by the many other consumers of steel greatly increased from 12,774,775 tons in 1939 to 17,276,535 tons in 1944. Supporting the war took a wide variety of products, and steel was a component to many of them. Even with the constraints mandated by the war, the prosperity increased the sales of many consumer goods using steel.

Exports of steel increased by 81 percent (from 2,817,482 tons in 1939 to 5,107,690 tons in 1944). The United States became a major source of steel for many of its allies. First, their wartime demand was much greater than their peacetime use, and second, many of these countries had relied on Germany for steel, and subsequently they could not get it.

In general, the war caused a great increase in the use of steel, not only for the expected uses, such as planes and munitions, but also for the activities that supported the war, such as agriculture, railroads, and oil production. The major shift brought about by the war was the great increase in shipbuilding. This and many other wartime activities would be greatly curtailed on the termination of hostilities. Thus, the steel industry would find itself with excess capacity in many products, such as plate, and a major redeployment of resources would be necessary.

The major competitors

During World War II, there were five particular developments that impinged strongly on the companies themselves. First was a great increase in demand, which first led to a full utilization of capacity and to capacity expansion. However, different companies had different growth experiences. Second, this expansion entailed a change in product composition with the expansion of shipbuilding, the cessation of auto manufacturing, and the buildup of many other products. Third, the government stepped in and financed the construction of several new facilities. Most of these facilities were run and eventually owned by the old companies, but this financing did lead to some new entry. Fourth, there was some merger activity among the large steel firms. With one exception, however, these acquisitions focused on backward and forward integration.

The fifth situation facing the steel firms was the variation in profits. After an initial rise in 1940 and 1941, the wartime profits of most steel companies thinned out. On one hand, the firms were faced with fairly rigid price controls for their products, and on the other hand, these price controls did not contain industry costs.

Here, the experiences of the eight largest companies are described to illustrate the impact of these changes. Then, two new firms that came out of the general expansion are described. With the exception of mergers, United States Steel Corporation experienced all of the above-mentioned phenomena. The company grew in capacity from 28 to 32 million tons a year. It expanded many of its product lines, notably plate steel and its electrolytic tin-plate lines. Like other firms, it used its sheet mills to make plate. In two places, it obtained government financing for expansion: one was in Homestead, Pennsylvania for plates, and the other was for an entire new plant in Geneva, Utah. This mill was designed to supply the West Coast with a wide range of products, including plates and other marine products. Last, like the other firms, U.S. Steel experienced thinning profits as the war progressed. After rising from $102.2 million to $116.2 million between 1940 and 1941, its after tax profits fell to $71.2 million in 1942, $62.6 million in 1943, $60.8 million in 1944, and $58.0 million in 1945.

Like U.S. Steel, Bethlehem Steel expanded and changed its product line during the war. The company expanded by 15 percent during the war, adding plate production to its plants. Its shipbuilding operations grossly expanded; it built 1,085 ships during the war. Unlike the other companies, its profits stagnated rather than fell during the later years of the war with net income remaining between $33 and $36 million between 1941 and 1945, as contrasted with a profit of $34.5 million in 1941. This shipbuilding position may well have bolstered Bethlehem's results.

Republic Steel experienced many of the same phenomena during the war. Its capacity increased 35 percent from 7,280,000 tons in 1939 to 9,791,000 tons in 1945. It changed its production line, moving to electrolytic tin-plate in many plants. It used financing from the Defense Plant Corporation to build a mill to manufacture "high quality electric steel alloy" for ordnance and airplane parts (Hogan, 1971, p. 1242). The expansion of production, capacity, and product line did not particularly help Republic's bottom line. While the company returns improved in the late 1930s, its net income fell from $21.1 million in 1940 to $9.5 million in 1945. Republic was another firm caught between price controls and rising labor costs.

National Steel, the fourth largest firm in the industry, did not experience the same rate of growth as the other firms, but it did expand its product lines developing the steel material used in Quonset huts. It also added electrolytic tin-plate lines. Like the others, its profits dropped during the war from $17.1 million in 1941 to $11.1 millions in 1945.

Jones & Laughlin expanded during the war, and it widened its product line, building more plate and the bonderized sheet for cans and containers. It was the one company that made a significant horizontal merger. In 1942, Jones & Laughlin bought the Otis Steel Company of Cleveland, Ohio. The Otis merger added roughly 1,000,000 tons of capacity to the company. Profits were not affected that much by the merger. As with the other companies, price controls and rising labor cost squeezed the bottom lines with the net income dropping from $15.3 million in 1941 to $8.5 million in 1945.

The steel capacity of Armco rose only from 2,963,000 tons in 1939 to 3,268,000 tons in 1945. The major development with this company during the war was the building of its plant in Houston, Texas. The plant had a capacity of 400,000 tons a year, and it catered to the construction and general steel markets in the Southwest rather than the expected pipe demand. It was partially financed by the Defense Plant Corporation.

Due to some special depreciation expenses, Armco's profit stream did not totally fall. After rising from $7.6 million to $11.2 million between 1940 and 1941, the Armco profits dropped to $7.8 million in 1942 and to just over six and five million in 1943 and 1944 respectively. In 1945, however, the profit rose to $13.4 million. Thus, its pattern differed from the others.

Youngstown Sheet & Tube expanded during the war with production increasing from 2,408,000 tons in 1939 to 3,684,000 tons in 1945. Capacity rose 15 percent.

With the exception of some electrolytic tin-plate lines, Youngstown's product mix did not change that much during the war. Like the other companies, however, its profit stream, after rising in 1940 and 1941, fell back from $16.1 million in 1941 to $7.5 million in 1945.

Inland Steel's experience was typical of the large companies. The company capacity grew by 10 percent between 1939 and 1945. In that it had previously moved its product line to light sheet, the company had to reverse its moves in order to service the war effort. It built capacity to make plate, and it added electrolytic tin-plate lines. Additionally, it became one of the companies using sheet mills to make plate. Like the other companies, its profits during the war were "at fairly modest levels" (Hogan, 1971, p. 1280).

The war effort and the financing of the Defense Plant Corporation added two new companies to the industry. The first and largest was the Kaiser Steel Company of Fontana, California. This new plant catered to shipbuilding and construction with structural products. Its inland location, originally chosen because of fear of Japanese bombing, would create problems later on. A new independent company, Lone Star Steel Company, operated a blast furnace built by the Defense Plant Corporation at Daingerfield, Texas. After the war, it would buy the furnace and integrate forward into steel.

Substitutes

The major substitute for steel, aluminum, experienced two important changes during the war: increases in production and capacity and the de-concentration in the industry resulting directly and indirectly from the Alcoa antitrust case. Aluminum production increased from 148,400 tons in 1939 to 834,800 tons in 1943. Even with the drop to 695,300 tons in 1944, this growth necessitated a great increase in capacity. While most of the increased demand came from the airplane industry, there was an expansion in other aluminum uses. The greater use of the metal familiarized many companies with its advantages. Furthermore, the post-war drop in airplane demand left excess aluminum that could cut into steel use.

The Alcoa antitrust case also increased the use of aluminum. Started in 1937, the prosecution asserted that Alcoa constituted a monopoly and recommended that the firm be broken up into smaller pieces. The case took roughly eight years to adjudicate. While the initial 1942 ruling of the District Federal Court found for the company, the final decree found Alcoa to be a monopoly. This decision was rendered by a special tribunal set up by Congress to substitute for the Supreme Court. Four of its members had to recuse themselves because they had previously worked on the case.

The decision was a landmark because it reinforced the notion that monopoly itself was a violation of the antitrust law, but it was its remedy that was most relevant to steel. While the court decided not to split up the original Alcoa organization, it did two things that attenuated the company's control of the aluminum market. First, the court forced the company to sever its relationship to Alcan, Alcoa's Canadian subsidiary. Much of the aluminum used in the United States was imported from Alcan in Canada. The severance of this relationship made Alcoa and Alcan competing firms instead of cooperating parts of one organization.

The second major change came not directly from the decree but from other parts of the federal government which wanted to act in conformance with it. As in steel, much of the new aluminum capacity built in the early 1940s was financed by the Defense Plant Corporation. The Defense Plant Corporation also owned the new aluminum plants, but the mills were operated by private firms under leasing arrangements. Except for a small plant run by the Olin Corporation, all these aluminum smelters were operated by Alcoa.

At the end of the war, a government body called the War Surplus Property Board was charged with disposing of the Defense Plant Corporation facilities. It was mandated not to enhance Alcoa's monopoly position. While some plants were sold to Alcoa, others were sold to Reynolds Aluminum, which had entered the market in the late 1930s, and had a market share of just over 7 percent by 1944. A second firm, Kaiser Aluminum, which was part of the agglomeration of companies owned by Henry Kaiser, also bought some of these plants.

Consequently, the industry went from being close to monopoly in 1944 with Alcoa having 90 percent of the market to an oligopoly with Alcoa having 50 percent in 1948. This share statistic may even understate the de-concentration of the industry because of the severance of the connection between Alcoa and Alcan. Thus, after World War II, the aluminum industry became much more of a competitor to steel firms than it was before.

Input supplies: ore, coal and labor

In the iron ore industry, the war lowered the amount of ore that could be imported due to the shortfall in ships. This led to a great demand for domestic ore. First, the largest source of ore, the Lake Superior area, increased its production from 61.5 million tons of ore in 1940 to 79.1 million tons in 1944. Additionally, iron mines were developed in the West especially to feed the new mills in Texas, Utah, and California. Furthermore, old iron mines in Pennsylvania, New Jersey, and New York (in the Adirondacks) were reopened.

In coal and coke, the major change was the revival of the beehive coke oven. Most of these ovens had been taken off line but not destroyed. The number of operating beehive ovens increased from 10,934 making 2.6 percent of the coke in 1939 to 18,669 making 10.3 percent of total coke production in 1941. After that, the role of the beehive oven attenuated with the building of modern by-product ovens – the number falling back to 12,179 with 7.7 percent of production in 1945. With these major inputs, the steel industry kept up with demand by using the available resources to their fullest extent whether they were modern or obsolete or, in the case of iron ore, depleted.

The companies faced a similar situation with labor in that the number of workers in the industry rose from 408,000 in 1939 to 511,400 in 1942, but then fell back to 456,700 in 1944. Labor markets were much tighter than in the 1930s, with unemployment dropping from 17.2 percent in 1939 to 1.2 percent in 1944.

Possibly complicating the situation for the companies was the strength of the steel union, the United Steelworkers (USW). By 1942, the USW had organized almost all the major steel companies, and this gave it almost total control of the steel industry's production labor. The USW did cooperate with government in trying to keep wages within the price control guidelines, but wages were less controlled than the product prices (Hogan, 1971, p. 1211 and Campbell, 1948, p. 223). One special problem was the amount of overtime paid, which would raise company hourly totals even if the workers' contract did not change.

Even when the wage increases occurred, labor often did not feel that they were paid as much as they deserved. They had a point in that the cost of living sometimes rose faster than their earnings. This would lead to trouble later.

The influence of government

Three government actions affected the steel industry during World War II. The first was the great increase in defense spending; the second was an increase in the supply of money used to finance the war deficit, and the third was the comprehensive set of wage and price controls from early 1942 until the end of the war.

As stated above, even though automobile manufacture was terminated during the war, the goods necessary for the war more than made up for this loss. In addition to the upturn in the production of munitions, shipbuilding expanded greatly. The prosperity resulting from the war increased many other uses of steel such as railroads and construction. These developments all enlarged the demand for steel. This resulted in upwards pressure on prices.

In addition to the increase in steel demand from the defense build-up, the government method of financing its spending put pressure on steel prices. Not wanting to increase taxes to the full extent of the spending increase, the government ran deficits. While the deficit alone would not lead to inflation, the government authorized the Federal Reserve System to buy government bonds directly from the Treasury (Higgs, 1987, p. 206). This action increased the money supply. The same end could have been effected by the Fed buying bonds through open market operations, which also occurred during the war. Both these practices enlarged the supply of money but tended to lower its value and raise other prices. This action accentuated the pressure on steel prices resulting from the real increase in demand.

There were a number of government agencies that attempted to control prices and the allocation of resources. One initiative, however, affected steel much more than the others, the wage and price control program administered by the Office of Price Administration (OPA). It was instituted in 1942 to counter the inflationary effects of deficit financing and the defense build-up. The price of steel and most other products was mandated to remain at the price charged in March 1942. This regulation created serious allocation problems for the industry.

In normal times, prices fulfill two functions, rationing and incentives. Price rations goods and services; people who are willing to pay the price get the goods. If the availability of a good changes, changes in prices provide incentives for sellers and buyers to alter the production and use of the good. Rising prices lead buyers to forgo the goods or find substitutes, while falling prices lead them to use the goods more. Rising prices lead sellers to increase production, and falling prices lead them to curtail it. Economic theory predicts that in competitive markets, keeping price at a given level during times of changing supply and demand would lead to shortages or surpluses. The war situation with its inflationary government financing and increasing demand put upward pressure on prices, while the OPA capped most prices. Shortages were the likely result. To solve this problem, the OPA and other agencies set up systems of fiat rationing for many goods.

Two factors, however, may have attenuated steel shortages during the war. First, as posited by John Kenneth Galbraith (1946), informal long-term relationships existed between steel company personnel and the customer representatives. This may have led to a seller-imposed non-price rationing process. The customers willingly acquiesced to the system given their trust for and friendship with company personnel. The second reason that allocation could occur without shortages was the oligopolistic structure of the industry. Again this hypothesis was put forth by Galbraith (1946). In markets such as steel, the uncontrolled equilibrium would give the firm above-competitive profits, at least, in prosperous times. In the presence of price controls, companies would not necessarily cease production, but merely sell all the output that customers would buy at the controlled price. This would occur because profits still exist at the controlled prices below those of the unregulated equilibrium.

Consequently, the steel companies earned profits lower than those in the uncontrolled market. As long as their profits were at or above the opportunity cost profit, the firms would meet demand. Thus, they would increase their production in the face of the rising demand, even though price did not increase. This seems to have been the case. As evidenced by steel production, demand increased, and there was little evidence of chronic shortages in the contemporary literature (*Iron Age*, 1942–1946). Additionally, steel company profits dropped (Campbell, 1948, p. 228).

The fall in steel company profits after 1942 is consistent with the hypothesis of the controls limiting company prices and profits, but there is considerable evidence that price controls did not contain steel company costs. It has been asserted that the government was more tolerant of wage increases than of product price increases (Hogan, 1971, p. 1211 and Campbell, 1948, pp. 222–3). Even where the controls were totally effective and wages did not escalate, labor costs could still rise. First, the mobility in the labor market led to a decline in skill levels for given wage categories. This would lower productivity and increase company costs.

Second, the immense immediate demand for product led to the use of more overtime, creating higher wages. Third, many of the inputs used by the steel mills were supplied by competitive markets where shortages could occur with its positive effect on steel costs. Additionally, OPA allowed the price of inputs such as coke and iron ore to rise (Campbell, 1948, p. 217). Interestingly, in one of the two cases where large steel companies were charged with violating the price control laws, the charge was overpayment for an input rather than overcharging for steel (Rockoff, 1981b, p. 125). The profit record of the companies was also consistent with rising costs. Early in the war before the price controls, profits rose, but then they declined after 1942 when the controls went into effect.

What is not pointed out by historians of and participants in the economic administration of the war is the effect of the government financing on who actually paid for the war and its implications for the future (Koistinen, 2004 and Galbraith, 1946). By keeping prices at a low level, the government was essentially taxing the steel company owners to finance the war. Thus, the inflationary policy combined with price controls imposed hidden taxes on these owners.

Making this imposition politically palatable was their hidden nature, which diminished political opposition. A fear arose that price controls combined with inflationary government policy would again lead to partial confiscation of steel company profits. This fear may have had a negative impact on postwar investment. (For more detailed analysis of this circumstance, see Higgs, 1987, pp. 196–236.)

Conclusion

Three World War II events may have had long-run consequences for the steel industry. The first was the change in product composition brought about by the war. The second was the government-mandated price control system, and the third was the great expansion in production.

Much of the increase in steel demand was for products connected to the war. Most of them would not be used again in peacetime in the same numbers. Certain actions, however, weakened this impact. First, the companies and other businesses persuaded the government to change the tax code to allow them to write off the spending on war-related projects. This increased their cash flow, which, in effect, enlarged the real profits on these projects. Second, many of these projects were financed by the Defense Plant Corporation but were operated by the companies. After the war, the facilities were sold at bargain prices to the operating companies.

While the write-offs and government financing could be considered subsidies, they were made for products that the steel companies sold to the government or government contractors. Thus, since the government was the immediate or ultimate customer, the tax breaks and favorable financing could also be considered implicit price increases for the government-bought munitions and other items. Consequently, the product composition changes may not have affected the long-term position of the industry. Supporting this assertion was the ease with which the companies could switch their rolling mills from one product to another as illustrated by the use of sheet mills to make plates.

The price control system may have made it difficult for the steel companies to obtain capital. The possibility that controls would return after the war may have prevented the companies from getting or using capital to expand and modernize. It made the return on the investment uncertain. Indeed, price controls were imposed twice in the decades after the war, in 1952 during the Korean War and in 1971 during the Vietnam War. In the late 1940s and early 1950s, there was a reluctance on the part of the industry to expand capacity. These controls may have had a long-term effect by setting a precedent.

The third situation, the great expansion in production and capacity, probably had the most effect on the industry in the long run. Between 1939 and 1945, the 50.9 percent increase in production led to a 16.7 percent increase in capacity. On the one hand, this increase, especially since much of it was financed by the Defense Plant Corporation, could have helped the industry by giving it new modern plants. On the other hand, the very immediacy of the increasing demand forced the companies to build inefficient capacity. For instance, the Kaiser Steel California and the U.S. Steel Utah plants were located at inefficient inland locations due to fear of enemy bombing. Probably more important was the capacity added onto the older mills. Many of these were not located in areas that would best serve the post-war demand. Furthermore, the existence of this inefficient capacity prevented the building of new mills. With this old capacity in place, the profits on new plants would be constrained. Consequently, the American industry was saddled with World War II vintage capacity that could not compete with the new efficient capacity that was built in Europe and Japan (Rogers, 2001).

Both of the above hypotheses are plausible, though not proven. Thus, while in the short run, the steel industry definitely helped pay for the war effort in the form of attenuated prices, in the long run it may also have paid for it in the form of a weakened competitive position.

David Thomas (Courtesy of
Pennsylvania Canal Society
Collection, Canal Museum).

Sir Henry Bessemer
(Courtesy of Lucidcafe).

Andrew Carnegie (Courtesy of Wikipedia).

Elbert Gary (Courtesy of University Archives, Northwestern University).

Charles M. Schwab (Courtesy of Wikipedia).

John B. Tytus (Courtesy of Ohio Historical Society).

Philip Murray (Courtesy of University Archives, Rutgers University Libraries).

Roger Blough (Courtesy of the Pennsylvania Society).

8   The postwar period

1946 to 1970

Introduction

This chapter covers the postwar years, 1946 to 1970. Other chronological breaks could have been made. Historical, economic, and even statistical analysis points to 1959 as a watershed in the industry (Duke *et al.*, 1977, Mancke, 1968, and Rippe, 1970), but the domestic market structure of the industry changed little. This institutional stability of the industry led this author to use the period 1946 to 1970.

Three major changes in the American steel industry occurred in this period. The first was the growth of an international steel industry which could compete with American companies on their home ground. The second was the appearance of a new segment of the industry, the minimills, which recycled scrap into new steel. The third was the further development of substitute products, such as aluminum and plastics, that cut into the steel market. While these changes later led to major dislocations, as of 1970 they had not materially transformed the basic milieu of the American industry.

To examine the experience of the steel industry in the period, we first examine changes in the production process and then look at the uses of steel. Subsequently, the chapter analyzes various competitors in the industry and, additionally, the international steel industry. Next, the chapter describes the developments in steel substitutes especially aluminum. Then, we examine the conditions in iron ore, coal, and labor. After that, the role of the government is scrutinized. Finally, conclusions are drawn, and some questions are raised.

Production and the production process

In this section, steel production levels and the three major production sectors are described. The three sectors were blast furnaces, steel converters, and the rolling mills. The gross production numbers for the industry exhibit the growth mentioned above, and events in the blast furnaces and rolling mills support this image of stability and prosperity. In contrast, the steel converter sector changed drastically. The basic oxygen process, a new way of converting pig iron to steel, was developed, and an old method, the electric furnace (EH), greatly increased its scope and efficiency.

Table 8.1 Yearly steel production, capacity, and utilization rates, 1946–1970

Year	Steel production	Steel production capacity	Utilization rate
1945	79,702,000	95,505,000	83.45
1946	66,603,000	91,891,000	72.48
1947	84,894,000	91,241,000	93.04
1948	88,640,000	94,233,000	94.06
1949	77,978,000	96,121,000	81.12
1950	96,836,000	99,363,000	97.46
1951	105,200,000	104,230,000	100.93
1952	93,168,000	108,588,000	85.80
1953	111,610,000	117,547,000	94.95
1954	88,312,000	124,330,000	71.03
1955	117,036,000	125,828,000	93.01
1956	115,216,000	128,363,000	89.76
1957	112,715,000	133,459,000	84.46
1958	85,255,000	140,743,000	60.57
1959	93,446,000	147,634,000	63.30
1960	99,282,000	148,571,000	66.82
1961	98,014,000	149,869,000	65.40
1962	98,328,000	150,579,000	65.30
1963	109,261,000	150,913,000	72.40
1964	127,076,000	151,823,000	83.70
1965	131,462,000	152,685,000	86.10
1966	134,101,000	153,434,000	87.40
1967	127,213,000	154,198,000	82.50
1968	131,462,000	155,026,000	84.80
1969	141,262,000	155,575,000	90.80
1970	131,514,000	155,454,000	84.60

Source: Moody's *Industrial Manual,* and Kanawaty, 1963.

As stated above, from examining the production data one would conclude that the period was one of great prosperity. As displayed in Table 8.1, the end of World War II led to a drop in production from 79.7 million in 1945 to 66.6 million tons in 1946. Even though the federal government felt that the steel firms were not adding capacity fast enough, production picked up, rising to 96 million tons in 1950 and to 117 million tons in 1955. With some fall-off in the 1958 and 1961 recessions, the trend continued until 1970 when a total of 131 million tons was reached.

As shown in Table 8.1, the Korean War then strained the industry with the 1951 capacity utilization at 100 percent. This resulted in a great increase in capacity. It rose from 99,363,000 tons in 1950 to 125,828,000 tons in 1955. The expansion in capacity continued until the 1960s, rising to over 150 million tons in 1962.

The one national statistic that portended the future problems was imports – displayed in Table 8.2. In the 1940s and early 1950s, imports stayed between two and three million tons a year. In 1959, however, steel customers increased their purchases of foreign steel in response to a long strike. The buyers continued to import foreign steel in the 1960s increasing to 11.9 million tons in 1965 and 14.6 million

Table 8.2 Production, exports and imports, 1946–1970

Year	Steel production	Steel exports	Steel imports
1945	79,702,000	5,109,229	146,363
1946	66,603,000	5,030,656	70,310
1950	96,836,000	3,093,474	2,029,516
1955	117,036,000	4,553,275	1,466,613
1958	85,255,000	3,463,345	2,136,195
1959	93,446,000	2,128,103	5,523,556
1960	99,282,000	3,470,466	4,087,583
1965	131,462,000	3,089,326	11,963,742
1970	131,514,000	8,139,579	14,609,369

Source: Hogan, 1971, p. 2035, Seely, 1994, p. il, and U.S. Bureau of the Census, 1955.

tons in 1970. Consequently, the American steel firms were no longer isolated from the world steel market.

Examining changes in the production process lends context to the above events. As in the past, almost all iron ore was transformed into purer iron in the blast furnace (BF). There were slightly fewer BFs in 1970 than in 1946 (228 as opposed to 241), but by 1970 pig iron production had doubled. Between 1946 and 1970, 53 new American BFs were built, and at least 66 furnaces were abandoned. The average production of the BF rose from 188,996 tons in 1946 to 398,237 tons in 1970. These numbers imply the same type of incremental progress in BF technology that had occurred for the first forty years of the century.

Consequently, while the BF part of the industry changed slowly, it moved in the direction of larger mills. That might have led to the shutdown of many plants, but that did not occur in the quarter century after World War II. Many old, smaller furnaces remained in production because of, first, geographic markets and transportation costs; second, the low cost of still operating old but fairly good facilities; and third, the political cost of abandoning the old plant communities.

Table 8.3. Total steel production by type of process, open hearth (OH), Bessemer process, basic oxygen (BOF), and electric furnace (EF) in 1946–1970 (1,000s of tons)

Year	Total steel production	Open hearth	Bessemer process[a]	Basic oxygen process[b]	Electric furnace
1946	66,603	60,712 (91.2)	3,328 (5.0)		2,563 (3.8)
1950	96,836	86,263 (89.1)	4,534 (4.7)		6,039 (6.2)
1955	117,036	105,359 (90.0)	3,320 (2.8)	307 (0.3)	8,050 (6.9)
1960	99,282	86,368 (87.0)	1,189 (1.2)	3,346 (3.4)	8,379 (8.4)
1965	131,462	94,193 (71.7)	586 (0.4)	22,879 (17.4)	13,804 (10.5)
1970	131,514	48,022 (36.5)	231 (0.2)	63,330 (48.2)	19,931 (15.2)

Source: Hogan, 1971, pp. 1520, 1527, and 1544.

a The Bessemer data is computed from subtracting the sum of the other processes from the total production.
b The first year of production for the basic oxygen furnace was 1955.

In contrast to the BF, the technology of the steel convertor sector underwent great changes during the period between 1946 and 1970. In the 1950s, a new steel-making system developed, the basic oxygen furnace (BOF). Table 8.3 shows the production levels of these steel-making processes for selected years. Of the older processes, open hearth (OH), the dominant technology up until the 1960s, dropped from 91.2 percent of the total production to 36.5 percent, and the Bessemer process dropped from 5.0 percent to a negligible proportion. In contrast, the electric furnace rose from a small proportion to over 15.2 percent (almost 20 million tons). Starting production only in 1954, the basic oxygen process gained a share of almost 50 percent by 1970.

While the OH process declined later in this period, it expanded greatly in the 1950s. U.S. Steel built an entire new plant with OH furnaces at Fairless, Pennsylvania. U.S. Steel, Inland, Bethlehem, and others added new OH furnaces to their old plants. Furthermore, many furnaces were rebuilt. There were improvements in the OH process, one of which was the use of pure oxygen instead of air in the blow-over part of the process. All this led to lower costs. By the late 1950s, however, the information available indicated that the BOF furnaces could produce at a lower cost than the older process. Thus, in the 1960s, many OH furnaces were replaced by BOF converters (Lynn, 1982).

The Bessemer process basically went out of business during this period, dropping from 3.3 million to 231,000 tons between 1946 and 1970. As of the latter date, only one converter remained in operation.

The electric furnace (EF) greatly increased its market share. Better electric transformers, improved electrodes, and more efficient in-plant procedures led to lower costs and wider product lines. Especially important was the introduction of the AOD (argon-oxygen decarburization) vessels in the late 1960s. These vessels lowered the cost of making stainless steel. Economic growth made for greater availability of scrap steel, the major input into EFs. As the country grew, more new cars and new construction led to the abandonment of old vehicles and buildings.

The advent of the BOF process facilitated the development of the EF. The BOF furnace usually took a much smaller dose of scrap steel than the OH shop, and the BOF dose of scrap was much less variable than the OH dose. Thus, the replacement of OH by BOF provided an opening for the EF. The small dose of the BOF furnace increased the availability of scrap to the EFs. The lower variability of the BOF dose gave them a more stable market environment.

These developments led to a change in the EF's role. For the first half of the twentieth century, the EF was the major producer of specialty items such as alloys, but by the 1960s many EFs were making standard steels such as rebar and wire rod (*Iron Age*, December 3, 1964, p. 83). A whole new sector of the industry materialized, the minimill. These firms either specialized in a narrow product range, an example being Northwestern Steel & Wire, or they sold a range of products in a narrow geographic area, examples being North Star Steel in Minnesota and Cascade Steel in Oregon (*Iron Age*, May 21, 1970, p. 71). As a result, the EF process rose to 15.2 percent of the market.

The fourth type of steel converter used in the middle of the twentieth century was the basic oxygen furnace (BOF). The BOF furnace could be characterized as a Bessemer converter that uses oxygen. It differed from the Bessemer converter in that the gas went into the vessel from the top — not the bottom of the furnace vessel.

From the advent of the Bessemer process, it was recognized that oxygen was the agent that changed pig iron to steel. (In addition to oxygen, air is composed mainly of nitrogen, and it introduces impurities into the Bessemer process that spoiled the steel for many uses; see Chapter 3.) Until the 1930s, however, pure oxygen was too expensive to use in a steel process. The development of the Linde-Frankl process for the separation of oxygen from air made the gas cheap enough to use in steel furnaces. It took until the late 1940s for the Linde-Frankl process to become efficient enough for mass production. With oxygen available, researchers began to work on ways to use it to make steel.

Based on Swiss research, such a process became operational in Austria between 1945 and 1950. The first commercial BOF mill was built in Linz, Austria by Voerst, a government-owned firm. The first American companies to adopt BOF were two smaller firms, McLouth Steel in 1954 and Kaiser Steel in 1955. The latter was part of the large Kaiser organization. Jones & Laughlin added a BOF converter to its Aliquippa, Pennsylvania plant in 1957. A number of the large firms followed suit and built BOF furnaces in the 1960s, often replacing recently installed OH furnaces.

Two characteristics of the BOF converter gave it a lower average cost than the OH. First, the BOF furnaces took only three-quarters of an hour to convert pig iron into steel, while the OH took from eight to eleven hours. Thus, a given amount of equipment would produce more steel with the BOF. Capital costs were, then, lower. Second, the BOF had lower operating costs taking less labor, fuel and material input (*Iron Age*, February 6, 1958, p. 55). These advantages led American firms to invest heavily in the BOF in the middle and late 1960s, raising the process percentage of total production to almost 50 percent (*Iron Age*, October 21, 1965, p. 28).

Although the American firms adopted the BOF fairly fast once they had realized its advantages, they lagged behind the Japanese, who adopted the technology en masse during the years between 1955 and 1970. The Japanese were building a large industry almost de novo, and by 1970, 80 percent of their production was BOF. Observers at the time and also later were critical of the slow pace of innovation in the US (Adams and Dirlam, 1964 and 1966 and Lynn, 1982).

There were two reasons for the Americans' late adoption of BOF. First, the American industry built a large number of OH furnaces in the early 1950s after the Austrian mills had become operational. Second, the efficiency of the BOF had not been reliably established in the early 1950s, when much of the American capacity was built. In fact, once they had decided to build the new furnaces, the Americans came on quite fast, perhaps faster than all the other major steel industries in the Western world (see Slesinger, 1966, Hone and Schoenbrod, 1966, Dilley and McBride, 1967, and McAdams, 1967).

The third major component of the steelmaking process is the rolling mill where steel metal is transformed into a shape that can be used by the customer. Historically, the rolling mill was divided into two parts, the primary mill and secondary mill. The major development in the rolling mill sector during this chapter's period was the replacement of the ingot caster and the primary mill by the continuous caster (*Iron Age*, September 12, 1963, p. 30). This replacement process started in the 1960s, but was only partly underway as of 1970. The continuous caster essentially takes the molten steel out of the converter and casts it into the billet, bloom, or slab. The major advantages of this caster were, first, the lower operating cost resulting from the fewer process steps and, second, the smaller loss of material.

While the initial research had started in the 1930s and 1940s, the successful operation of the machines had only begun in the 1950s. The United States installed 50 continuous casters. Some large companies adopted continuous casters, with U.S. Steel installing six and Armco, four. Nevertheless, a disproportionate number of these machines were put in small company or minimill plants, 25 out of the 50.

The other parts of the rolling mill sector experienced a continuous but slow improvement in productivity often resulting from new practices. Other areas of improvement were sheet rolling mills, especially the areas where the steel was coated with protective covering such as tin and galvanizing.

To summarize, the major technological events in the steel industry in this period were the adoption of the basic oxygen process, the development of the continuous caster, and the great improvement in the EF. Some have asserted the United States was slow to adopt the first two methods, but others argue that the rate of progress was reasonable, given the amount of fairly new and efficient old-technology capacity.

The customer industries

Table 8.4 displays the consumption of steel by various industries: the upper section (A) showing the tons of steel used by various economic sectors and the lower section (B) showing the percentage of the total used by each consumer sector. Even though the data for 1945, 1946, and 1950 are not strictly comparable to the data for 1955–1957 and 1965, the table gives some indication of the trends in consumption. Some sectors significantly increased their steel consumption, and some sectors declined.

In spite of the generally positive statistics, there was a feeling among experts that steel was becoming more susceptible to competition from other materials (*Iron Age*, May 30, 1963, March 3, 1966, and February 11, 1971). Especially vulnerable was the container sector where the aluminum companies were developing methods of making cans for beer and soda (*Iron Age*, November 24, 1960, October 12, 1961, and October 14, 1965). Even with the potential exposure to competition, one could hardly fault the steel companies for being sanguine, especially given the rising national income and such flourishing industries as autos and construction (see *Iron Age*, December 30, 1965, p. 26 for a contemporary view). To understand the situation, we examine the major customer industries starting with the railroads.

The railroad industry is often cited as a declining sector, but this view is deceptive. While passenger service dropped off precipitously, falling 61 percent between 1950 and 1969, the freight business of the railroads rose, with revenue miles increasing over 30 percent between 1950 and 1969.

Table 8.4 The breakdown of economic sectors using steel by percentage, 1945, 1946, 1950, 1955–1957, 1958–1962 and 1965

A. By tonnage (by the 1,000s)						
	1945	*1946*	*1950*	*1955–57*	*1958–62*	*1965*
Railroads	5,300	4,800	4,800	4,200	2,500	3,900
Automotive	neglible	7,400	15,700	17,700	15,800	24,700
Construction	8,400	8,100	12,400	23,500	22,700	26,900
Pressing, forming, & stamping	3,800	3,100	4,600	a	a	a
Machine, tools	4,700	4,400	5,800	a	a	a
Machinery	a	a	a	10,600	10,100	14,700
Oil and gas	2,700	2,500	6,600	3,300	2,600	2,600
Shipbuilding	3,400	300	400	1,100	900	1,000
Agriculture	2,400	2,100	3,100	2,800	2,800	3,300
Containers	4,300	4,700	6,400	7,000	6,800	6,800
Appliances	a	a	a	5,200	5,200	6,100
Defense	a	a	a	1,200	500	700
Aircraft[b]	5,500	Neglible	100	a	a	a
Others	12,600	7,900	9,600	a	a	a
Exports	3,800	3,400	2,800	4,600	2,300	2,500
Total tonnage	57,000	48,800	72,200	81,200	72,200	93,200

B. By percentage						
	1945	*1946*	*1950*	*1955–57*	*1958–62*	*1965*
Railroads	9.3	9.8	6.7	5.2	3.5	4.2
Automotive	0.0	15.2	21.7	21.8	21.9	26.5
Construction	14.7	16.6	17.1	28.9	31.4	28.9
Pressing, forming, & stamping	6.7	6.4	6.4	a	a	a
Machine, tools	8.2	9.0	8.0	a	a	a
Machinery	a	a	a	13.0	14.0	15.8
Oil and gas	4.7	5.1	9.1	4.1	3.6	2.8
Shipbuilding	5.9	0.6	0.5	1.4	1.2	1.1
Agriculture	4.2	4.3	4.3	3.4	3.9	3.5
Containers	7.5	9.6	8.9	8.6	9.4	7.3
Appliances	a	a	a	6.4	7.2	6.5
Defense	a	a	a	1.5	0.7	0.7
Aircraft[b]	9.7	0.1	0.1	a	a	a
Others	22.2	16.2	13.3	a	a	a
Exports	6.7	7.0	3.9	5.7	3.2	2.7

Source: *Iron Age*, January 3, 1952, p. 390 and January 6, 1966, p. 27.

Notes
a Not available in these years. Over the years, the categories which were used to collect data and made estimates changed.
b This includes automotive in 1945.

Steel use then fell off only a small amount from 4,200,000 tons in 1950 to 3,900,000 in 1969. The major reason for this stagnation was greater efficiency. The new rails lasted longer, leading steel rail production to drop from 1,600,000 tons in 1950 to 100,000 tons in 1965. The other railroad uses of steel such as cars and loco-motives actually rose by 300,000 tons. Thus, the steel people had little reason for pessimism in this sector.

In contrast, the automotive sector was unquestionably dynamic. In fact, much of the former passenger and freight business of the railroad was absorbed by this sector. Total United States vehicle production rose from 9,169,276 in 1955 to 11,057,400 in 1965, with automotive steel use rising from 17,700,000 tons to 24,700,000 tons, an increase of almost 40 percent in that decade.

There were signs of future difficulties, however. First, there was a growing demand for smaller cars. According to Hogan (1971, p. 1874), the smaller vehicles used "some 900 pounds less than the standard size motor car." Still, in the late 1960s, automotive steel use seemed destined to stay the same, if not to grow.

During the postwar period the construction industry was the largest user of steel, rising from 23,500,000 tons in 1955 to 26,900,000 tons in 1965. In the large cities, many new skyscrapers were built. New York and Chicago, the traditional centers for these buildings, contributed much to this growth. New York added such edifices as the Seagram's Tower and the Lever, Pan American, and Esso Buildings. Skyscrapers became commonplace in other large cities such as Los Angeles, San Francisco, Houston, Boston, Cleveland, and Pittsburgh. Among these buildings in the latter city were those constructed by two of the actors in this story, the U.S. Steel and Alcoa Towers.

In home construction, steel became more prevalent; much of this increase came from the introduction of home appliances and the increase in indoor plumbing. Hogan (1971, p. 1885) states "The averages use of steel in a six-room house in 1949 totaled 3½ tons versus half a ton in 1938."

Highway construction was greatly enhanced by the building of the Interstate Highway system. Furthermore, many new large bridges were fabricated. Examples were the Chesapeake Bay Bridge in Maryland, the Tappan Zee Bridge in New York, and the Delaware Memorial Bridge between Delaware and New Jersey.

The major technological change, the increase in reinforced concrete, had an ambiguous effect on steel use in construction. While reinforced concrete replaced steel beams in some uses, it meant an increase in rebar, the steel bars used in rein-forced concrete. This product rose from 1,190,000 tons in 1946 to 3,659,000 tons in 1969.

The machinery sector buying steel was composed of many types of equipment. Among them were lathes, saws, road graders, bulldozers, and jack-hammers. Many technological changes affected the demand for steel from this sector. For instance, the development of grain steel lowered the need for steel in transformer cores. In contrast, the increase in automation led to greater use of steel tools, thereby increas-ing the demand for steel. Furthermore, the electrical system grew extensively with population and intensively with greater per capita use. In all, these developments led to a rise in the use of steel in the machinery sector from 10,600,000 tons in 1955 to 14,700,000 tons in 1965.

In the oil and gas industry, the use of steel rose quickly after World War II, and then, in the late 1950s and early 1960s, it slowly dropped. While the data are not complete, Table 8.4 shows that the steel use in this sector rose from 2,500,000 tons in 1946 to 3,300,000 tons in 1955. In the next ten years, however, it fell back to 2,600,000 tons. The early increase was brought about by the great expansion in automobiles and the switch in heating fuel from coal and wood to oil and gas. Counteracting these trends was the leveling off and eventual decline in the exploration and production of oil in the United States. Since demand continued to grow, the United States was transformed from a large exporter to a major importer of oil. The negative effect on steel demand from this sector was somewhat attenuated because the American oil companies were major producers of and explorers for oil in other countries.

Starting with a respite in 1946, the shipbuilding industry in the United States was generally stagnant. This state was reflected in the industry's use of steel, which remained at about 1,000,000 tons a year through most of this period. In merchant ship building, the United States was not competitive with countries like Japan and Germany. Three things counteracted this trend: the demand for Navy ships, the presence of government subsidies, and the need for ships on the Great Lakes.

The major product in the container sector was tin-plated cans for food, beverage, and motor oil. Research on the preservation of food increased demand. In addition, more people were buying beer and soda pop in cans. In the 1960s, however, aluminum made inroads into the tin-plate market (*Iron Age*, November 24, 1960, p. 196). In 1960, the Standard Oil Company of New Jersey (Esso) started to put lubrication oil in aluminum cans (Reutter, 2004, p. 415–16). Aluminum also started to invade the beer can market (*Iron Age*, October 24, 1963, p. 42).

Even with these intrusions into its market, steel for containers still almost maintained its sales, only falling from 7,000,000 tons in 1955 to 6,800,000 in 1965. Drums for oil and chemical products maintained their level of production during this period.

The agricultural sector used about 3.5 percent of the steel made in this country during the 1950s and 1960s. While the number of farms dropped (from 5.8 million in 1945 to 3.2 million in 1964), the production of most crops increased. Generally, steel use was stable during the postwar years, varying from 2.8 million tons in 1955 to 3.3 million in 1965. The increased use of large machinery compensated for the fall of the number of farms.

The appliance sector became a large user of steel, more than 5,000,000 tons a year from 1955 onward. Rising family income increased the demand for appliances. These were considered luxury items before World War II, but they became customary for middle-class families. Thus, for most of this period, the demand for steel from this sector increased.

A major development in the immediate postwar periods was an increase in the amount of steel sold through Steel Service Centers. These firms were essentially wholesalers who do some processing for some customers. Most of the buyers serviced by these centers were small users such as contractors, local governments, and manufacturers who do not use much steel. On one hand, the service centers would do processes which require large outlays on the part of customers. On the other hand, these particular processes would not then generate enough revenue for the steel companies to do it themselves. Roughly 18 percent of the steel consumed in the United States was sold through these centers.

The steel service center industry consisted of many independent firms such as Earle M. Jorgensen Company and Central Steel & Wire Company. However, some steel companies had integrated forward. Notable among them were Inland and U.S. Steel who respectively owned the largest and second largest service centers, Joseph T. Ryerson & Son, Inc. and United States Steel Supply Division.

In contrast to many other sectors, exports had dropped off by 1965. This can be attributed to the growth of new large steel industries in Europe, Japan, mainland Asia, and South America.

In examining the steel customers, one is struck by the growth and stability of steel use in many sectors. While much has been made of the possible substitutes for steel, tin-plated steel was the only sector for which an alternative material, aluminum, had made much of an inroad. Consequently, optimism was a reasonable attitude for steel firms in the late 1960s (*Iron Age*, April 24, 1969, p. 84).

The major competitors

In this section, the competitors in the industry are discussed. At the time, the problem considered most important by policymakers was pricing. Until 1948, the steel industry used the basing point pricing system to quote prices to individual customers. Since 1924, there were multiple basing points; among them were Chicago, Pittsburgh, Baltimore, Middletown, Ohio, and Birmingham, Alabama, places where large companies had important mills. The steel companies could very well have used this pricing technique to charge supra competitive prices (Chapter 5 and Carlton, 1983). Cases against this practice in the steel and cement industries were brought by the Federal Trade Commission (e.g. *Federal Trade Commission* v. *Cement Institute*, 1948). The *Cement Institute* Decision against the cement companies led the steel companies to abandon the practice.

The companies began to charge FOB (Free on Board) price or price at factory plus transportation to customer. Thus, the customer would pay the price at the mill plus the cost of transporting the product to his premises. Often, however, the firms discounted off of these formulas. Research has found, however, that the other-things-equal steel prices dropped after this decision (Rogers, 1983 and 1987).

From 1948 until the 1960s, changes in price were usually announced by U.S. Steel and then followed by industry. Other firms, however, often shaved prices to certain customers. U.S. Steel itself could very well have shaved price from its book level. Many scholars still maintained that this price leadership by U.S. Steel was a device sufficient to keep prices above the competitive level (Adams and Dirlam, 1964, Broude, 1963, Comanor and Scherer, 1995, Duke *et al.*, 1977, Mancke, 1968, Rippe, 1970, and Rogers, 1987). The 1959 strike changed the situation. Buyers looking for product that could not be obtained from the companies on strike found that they could get foreign steel at viable prices and terms.

In 1962, a confrontation between President John F. Kennedy and Roger Blough, the chief executive officer of U.S. Steel, showed the weaknesses of the price leadership system. In 1962, the steel firms had obtained a favorable labor settlement with the help of the federal government. According to the administration principals including President Kennedy, U.S. Steel had promised not to raise prices. In April 1962, U.S. Steel raised them, anyway, and Bethlehem and several other firms followed. In order to persuade U.S. Steel and other firms not to raise prices, Kennedy threatened to bring antitrust suits and to renege on government contracts. Inland, Armco, and some other firms did not raise prices. Whether this was due to Kennedy's action is not clear; one investigator asserts that competitive forces were instrumental in these actions (McConnell, 1963). The other firms that had followed U.S. Steel now took back their price hikes, and finally U.S. Steel followed.

After that episode, U.S. Steel was usually not the first company to raise prices. Often it was Bethlehem, but sometimes others. It has been asserted that this change was due to the Kennedy–Blough confrontation. (See the Kennedy quotation in Davis in Seely, 1994, pp. 398–400.) While U.S. Steel behavior may have been modified, statistical evidence points to no change in price level, other things equal, after 1963. Rather, the evidence points to an other-things-equal price change occurring in 1959 after the strike. (See Duke *et al.*, 1977, Mancke, 1968, Rippe, 1970, and Rogers, 1987.)

For this change, one can plausibly point to two causes. First, U.S. Steel had a lower market share in the 1960s, lessening its influence. Second, foreign firms had moved into the U.S. market; imports rose from 2.1 million tons in 1958 to 11.9 million tons in 1965 and 14.6 million in 1970.

A second issue concerning the individual companies was the great expansion in the 1950s. Many thought that the firms had inefficiently stayed with the OH technology instead of using the better BOF. The choice, however, was not the major problem with the steel expansion.

The problem rather was that the firms retrofitted new furnaces (including BOF) onto old plants rather than building new ones. New plants could have been efficiently laid out as they were in Japan. Many scholars have made that point (Crandall, 1981, Barnett and Crandall, 1986, and Lynn, 1982). The steel industry, however, consisted of large plants in relatively small towns, and moving these plants out of these places may have been politically impossible.

Now that the general issues have been analyzed, the experiences of some firms will be perused. Additionally, the development of the major world steel industries will be examined to ascertain their competitive impact on the United States. The analysis starts with U.S. Steel. Company market share figures are shown in Table 8.5. In the 25 years after World War II, U.S. Steel expanded and then contracted its production, and over time its market share fell. While the firm built many new furnaces and two entirely new mills, its market share dropped from 32.5 in 1950 to 23.9 in 1970, its production staying about the same.

Table 8.5 Total steel production and market share for the leading firms and concentration in the United States (1946–1970).

Year	Total production (1000s of tons)	Market share of US Steel	Bethlehem	Republic	National	Jones & Laughlin	Armco	Youngstown	Inland	Total Big eight	Rest of industry
1946	66,603	32.0	15.0	9.4	4.9	5.7	4.1	4.9	4.2	80.2	19.8
1950	96,836	32.5	15.6	8.8	4.8	5.1	4.1	4.3	3.8	79.0	21.0
1955	117,036	30.2	16.1	8.3	4.8	5.3	4.4	4.8	4.4	78.1	21.9
1959	93,446	26.2	15.3	8.0	5.7	5.2	5.3	4.4	4.5	74.6	25.4
1960	99,282	27.5	16.1	7.8	5.8	5.8	5.0	4.2	5.2	77.3	22.7
1965	131,462	24.8	16.0	7.5	6.5	5.5	5.9	4.6	4.9	75.7	24.3
1970	131,514	23.9	15.7	7.5	7.5	5.3	6.0	3.9	5.4	75.1	24.9

Source: Moody's Industrial Manual and Kanawaty, 1963.

Even so, expansion seemed to have been the company policy in the 1950s. First, U.S. Steel bought the large integrated plant at Geneva, Utah from the Defense Plant Corporation. Second, it built a new "greenfield" plant, called the Fairless Works, in eastern Pennsylvania, near Trenton, New Jersey. Third, it built a new plant to make slabs in Texas using EFs.

The company also centralized its operations, eliminating many of the divisions that were left over from the original organization of the firm in 1901. The firm diversified into other industries such as chemicals, engineering, and real estate. While the strategy was fashionable at the time, it may not have benefited the stockholders.

Bethlehem Steel was the second largest firm in the industry during the postwar period. Its production went from 15,116,000 tons in 1950 to 20,586,000 tons in 1970. Bethlehem grew by several methods. It undertook large investment programs, and it widened its product line and geographic scope. In the 1950s, Bethlehem enlarged its older mills. It built new OH furnaces at the Lackawanna, New York and Sparrows Point, Maryland plants. Stewart P. Cort, the company's chief engineer, was a believer in the older OH process, and his influence may have held up Bethlehem's move to the basic oxygen process. Nevertheless, in the 1960s, Bethlehem did start to install BOF furnaces, ironically when Cort's son, Stewart S. Cort, had become Company President.

To increase its geographic and product scope, Bethlehem tried to merge with Youngstown Sheet and Tube in 1955. The justice department, however, opposed the merger because the merger increased concentration. The Supreme Court agreed in 1958, and Bethlehem did not merge with Youngstown. Bethlehem then built a plant in the Midwest at Burns Harbor, Indiana in 1963. Burns Harbor was the last fully integrated steel mill built in the United States.

In 1957, Eugene Grace retired; he had been president or chairman of the board since 1913. Some authorities have argued that there was an inbredness to the Bethlehem management that discouraged innovation (see Reutter, 2004, and Leary and Sholes, in Seely, 1994, pp. 41–6).

As of 1950, Bethlehem operations were concentrated on the East Coast with large plants in Bethlehem, Johnstown, and Steelton, Pennsylvania, and at Sparrows Point near Baltimore. It had a large plant on Lake Erie that sold into the Midwest at Lackawanna, New York. By 1970, its new Burns Harbor plant gave it a presence in the growing Midwest markets, especially with the auto industry.

The third largest American steel firm during this period, the Republic Steel Corporation, consisted of a group of mills put together by Cyrus Eaton in the early 1930s. Most of these mills produced specialty products. Republic's production did not grow much during the postwar period. Its market share actually declined from 8.83 percent in 1950 to 7.48 percent in 1970.

This seemingly stagnant performance was not the result of inactivity. Republic bought the facilities in Chicago and Cleveland financed by the Defense Plant Corporation. It modernized and expanded its older plants, especially the one in Cleveland, and in the 1960s, it adopted the BOF process. It participated in the development of taconite ore and the acquisition of foreign iron ores.

Nevertheless, its strategy was still relatively conservative. It stayed with its scattered plant configuration with facilities making specialty products. When it added capacity, Republic retrofitted it to the old facilities. Arguably, it was relatively slow at adopting the new steel furnace technologies, the EF and the BOF. Republic continued to use relatively old technology to produce specialty products. This was especially problematic because many of these products could be produced by minimills.

In 1956, Thomas Girdler, who had been with Republic from the time Cyrus Eaton had taken control, retired. He was succeeded by his protégés, Charles M. White and Thomas F. Patton. Some argue that these people had difficulty responding to a new environment, but at the time many saw the firm as quite strong, "one of the most competitive firms in the steel industry" (Miller in Seely, 1994, p. 369).

Geographically, the firm changed little. It had major plants in Cleveland, Chicago, Buffalo, and Gadsden, Alabama. It also had a number of specialty and fabricating operations around Canton and Massillon, Ohio. It was still a very scattered operation at a time when the BOF required larger capacity plants, but it did not readily adopt the minimill formula, which subsequently was used by firms such as Nucor and Florida Steel.

The fourth largest American steel firm in the postwar period was National Steel. Its production was concentrated at only two plants at Ecorse, Michigan and Weirton, West Virginia. Unlike Republic, National focused on only two high-volume items, sheet steel for automobiles and tin-plate for canning. The former product was concentrated at Ecorse, while the latter was concentrated at Weirton. Weirton, however, did produce automobile sheet and other coated sheet products.

To strengthen its position, National Steel bought into coal and iron ore mines. It also bought land in California, Delaware, and Indiana with the idea of someday building plants. Only in the latter area did the plans come to fruition with the building of rolling mills in Portage, Indiana near Chicago. More important, National Steel modernized its old facilities. It built modern BFs at Ecorse and Weirton. Even though it had new OH furnaces, National installed BOFs in both locations. In fact, by 1970, its total production was in BOF. Additionally, the company built a continuous caster at Weirton.

To lessen its dependence on the auto and can producers, National Steel integrated forward, setting up a steel service center named the National Steel Products Company. Additionally, National Steel made some efforts to diversify. Among the moves was the buying of some aluminum fabricators. In a joint venture with the Southwire Company that it partly owned, National built an aluminum reduction plant at Hawesville, Kentucky.

Like the other firms, National Steel's management was stable; the company founders, George Fink and E. T. Weir, retired in the mid-1950s. They were replaced by George Humphrey, the former U.S. Secretary of the Treasury, who had come up through the ranks at the M. A. Hanna mining and lake shipping part of the firm, and by Thomas Millsop, a Weir protégé. As of 1970, National Steel was among the strongest firms in the industry.

The fifth largest company, Jones & Laughlin, continued to hold between 5 and 6 percent of the market throughout the period. Its main strategy for most of the period was internal expansion and the broadening of its product line. To fulfill this goal, Jones & Laughlin modernized and expanded its three mills at Cleveland, Ohio, Pittsburgh, and Aliquippa, Pennsylvania. Notably, Jones & Laughlin was the first large American firm to adopt the BOF in 1957 (at Aliquippa). In the 1960s, it also installed BOF furnaces in the other two plants. With plans to move into the Midwest market, it built a new rolling mill in Hennepin, Illinois. Later, it planned to add BFs and BOF or electric steel converters, but this plan did not materialize.

In 1968, the conglomerate Ling-Temco-Vought (LTV) bought Jones & Laughlin. LTV was originally an electronics and airplane manufacturer. Its leaders believed in the efficacy of generalized management. They thought any properly trained manager could run any company. They did not believe that given industries needed specialized management.

Some have claimed that another motive led LTV to Jones & Laughlin. Being capital-intensive, steel companies generate very large cash flows due to major depreciation expenses. Often a lag existed between when the firms got money and when they had to spend it. In that time period, the management of LTV may have seen an opportunity to use the money to make other investments.

These plans never worked out. First, LTV's take-over of the steel firm created a vacuum in the management, and the company operations deteriorated, lowering the firm's cash flow. "One former director remarked that in 1969, J&L was run like 'a company that isn't owned by anyone,' . . ." (Heitmann in Seely, 1994, pp. 250–3). Second, the cash needs of Jones & Laughlin were greater and more urgent than had been anticipated.

Armco Incorporated was the sixth largest American steel firm in this period. Between 1950 and 1970 its total production grew, leading to a market share increase from 4.09 to 6.01. The company engaged in a roughly even expansion in all of its plants. It integrated backward and forward, buying interests in coal mines, iron mines, and steel products companies, including pipes, container drums, and oil field rigs. Consistent with this policy, it expanded its stainless steel operation at Baltimore. Armco sold a large number of products in the international market, operating fabricating plants in Mexico, South Africa, and England. It maintained a research division that emphasized developing new products. In the late sixties, Armco undertook a major expansion called PROJECT 600, which included the installation of BOF converters at Middletown and Ashland and of EFs at the other plants (Hogan, 1971, pp. 1808–1810).

In 1967, C. William Verity, a member of the founding family became president. While he was another member of the Verrity family, they did not totally control the company. Many other executives such as Charles Hook, W. W. Sebald, and Logan Johnston had great influence and obtained high position.

The seventh largest company, Youngstown Sheet & Tube, started to lose its position during this period. While its production rose from 3,242,000 tons in 1946 to 5,142,000 tons in 1970, its market share dropped from 4.87 to 3.91. Its expansion plans emphasized the plant in Indiana Harbor, Indiana. Brier Hill and Campbell, the two mills in the company's namesake city, Youngstown, Ohio, were neglected.

A major factor in this firm's history was the possibility of mergers. In 1955, Bethlehem Steel tried to merge with Youngstown. The justice department, however, prevented it. The problem for Youngstown was that, while the merger permission was being sought, its plans were on hold, and it could do little to expand or improve its facilities. One account states that "The worst damage to Youngstown was the disruption of planning during the five years of waiting" (Sypolt and Seely in Seely, 1994, p. 502).

In 1969, Youngstown Sheet & Tube was bought by a conglomerate, Lykes Industries. As with many conglomerates, Lykes operated under the assumption that any good manager could run any company. Furthermore, Youngstown proved attractive because it had "a high cash flow and a sizeable gap between per-share market price and book value" (Sypolt and Seely in Seely, 1994, p. 502). Steel companies, however, needed a large cash flow for capital spending. As with the Bethlehem episode in the 1950s, this merger diverted management attention away from technical and marketing problems on which the company's prosperity depended.

Often the Inland Steel Company has been cited as the most successful of the Big Eight. Between 1950 and 1970, its production rose from 3,676,000 tons to 7,051,000 tons, and its market share rose from 3.80 to 5.36. The company's main emphasis was on its single plant at Indiana Harbor, Indiana. After the war, it reconverted much of its product line back to automobile sheet. The company undertook some diversification mainly into housing, but generally it stuck to steel. Installing BOF converters in the late 1960s helped make the Indiana Harbor plant one of the largest in the Western Hemisphere. Like other firms, Inland Steel bought coal mines and iron ore sources.

The company encountered greater competition in the late 1960s. Youngstown and U.S. Steel expanded their plants, while Bethlehem, National, and Jones & Laughlin built rolling mills in the Chicago area. While these infringements lowered Inland profits, they did not affect the basic health of the company.

As with Armco, Inland Steel's founding family continued its influence. J. L. Brock was chairman of the board during much of this period. He was succeeded by P. D. Brock in 1967. Other people were important in Inland's management, such as the company presidents Wilfred Sykes, who organized the firm's move to sheet in 1930s, and Clarence B. Randell, a lawyer who acted as a spokesman for the whole industry in its many disputes with the government.

The market share of the small Non-Big Eight firms rose during this period from 19.81 in 1950 to 24.91 in 1970; it is important to see what led to this change. The increase did not mean all was well with the smaller steel firms. In fact, some had great difficulties in the postwar years. For instance, Wheeling Steel's poor performance led to a merger with Pittsburgh Steel in 1967. A general pattern, however, can be discerned among the smaller steel companies. The companies using the conventional fully integrated blast furnace-steel converter set-up usually did poorly, while the firms using scrap steel to feed EFs prospered.

Several factors contributed to the problems of the smaller integrated firms. Some firms had difficulty in applying new technology. Wheeling Steel and Colorado Fuel & Iron were slow to build the BOF converters. Sharon Steel adopted the Kaldo converter, a new steel furnace that did not work out.

Many of these firms were also confronted with greater competition in both their geographic areas and product lines. For instance, Kaiser Steel's West Coast location made it vulnerable to Japanese competition. Furthermore, all these firms faced new competition from the minimills.

Last, many of these firms became targets for take-over from conglomerate firms in the 1960s. Examples were Crucible Steel which was taken over by Colt Industries, CF&I which was purchased by Crane, and Sharon Steel which was bought by the corporate raider, Victor Posner. These companies often had large cash flows, which made them attractive buys. While the attention of the target firm management was diverted from the company's economic and technical problems during the merger process, the new conglomerate managements did little to improve performance.

With all these problems, the smaller firms as a whole still gained market share. Some integrated firms such as Lukens and Interlake did well in the 1960s, but the bulk of the market share increase came from the EF firms. During the postwar period, these companies expanded the use of the EF technology from specialty products to standard items such as rebar and wire. Many were steel users who integrated backward to the EF and then started to sell their excess steel on the market, examples being Timken and Nucor. Between the late 1950s and 1970, the market share of the minimills rose from 2 to 6 percent (Crandall in Seely, 1994, p. 310).

Another group cutting into the position of the integrated firms was the foreign steel industry. Between 1945 and 1970, world steel production rose from 123,000,000 tons to 628,800,000 tons. The United States share dropped from 54.5 to 22.5 percent, even while its production actually rose from 66,600,000 to 131,514,000 tons. The great expansion in world production made it likely that some foreign firms could compete in the U.S. market.

At first, however, foreign penetration of the United States market was minimal with imports being just over 2,000,000 tons, but then the 1959 steel strike led many buyers to buy foreign steel. They discovered that they could get the product they needed from overseas. At first, Europeans provided most of the imports, but later Japan became the major steel exporter to the United States. Japan not only had lower wages, but also more efficient mills, making the American firms very vulnerable.

The domestic firms often complained that foreign firms sold product in the United States at prices below costs, a practice that was against the American antidumping laws. While complaints were made in the late 1960s, the government did not vigorously pursue them. In 1968, several foreign countries, including Japan and those in the European Community were pressured into setting a quota for exports to the United States. This action actually accentuated the problems facing some specialty steel product firms such as stainless, tool, and tubular steel (Hogan, 1971, pp. 2049–73). Foreign firms could increase their sales of these high-priced products and still stay within the quota.

Table 8.6 Market share for the leading firms in the aluminum industry, selected years, 1956–1971

Year	Market share of Alcoa	Reynolds	Kaiser	Others
1950	51.0	31.0	18.0	0.0
1955	43.9	27.4	26.6	2.1
1960	34.6	28.4	24.7	12.3
1971*	31.6	20.9	15.2	32.3

Source: Smith, 1988, pp. 271, 285, and 366.

* The 1971 data are in terms of capacity.

Substitutes

The closest substitute for steel in the postwar years was aluminum. The major event affecting the aluminum industry in this period was the 1945 antitrust decision against Alcoa, the leading aluminum firm. The results of this decision are described in Chapter 7. Alcoa now had three strong competitors, Reynolds, Kaiser, and Alcan. The new, more competitive, industry was more likely to invade steel's product domain. Table 8.6, which shows the market shares of the major aluminum firms, indicates a downward movement in industry concentration. Since these figures represent domestic production and capacity, they understate the possible increase in competition because they do not take into account the imports from Canada made by Alcan.

While the contest between the two metals for automobile components continued, the major changes were in construction and containers. Encouraged by its experience in building its new headquarters building in Pittsburgh, Alcoa, followed by its competitors, offered new ways to use aluminum in construction, which cut into steel use.

The third major area where steel and aluminum competed was the beverage part of the container industry. At first, the aluminum companies only provided the tops of the beer and soft drink cans. Later, however, Reynolds and Alcoa developed an aluminum sheet that could be used for the whole can. As of 1970, steel still had over 50 percent of the beverage can market, but aluminum cans rose from no share in 1963 to 14.6 percent by 1972. That had grave implications for steel.

Cement could be considered both a substitute and complement to steel. They were used together mainly in construction. The major development in the postwar period was the replacement in many buildings of steel girders and beams by reinforced concrete. With reinforced concrete, however, the loss in structural steel was compensated somewhat by the gain in the rebar rods.

In many situations, plastics were becoming a substitute for steel. As of 1963, 4,500,000 tons of plastics were being manufactured (*Iron Age*, February 6, 1964, p. 41). The major uses for which this material competed with steel were in construction and containers, especially storage tanks. By 1970, plastics had not cut into steel that much, but the potential was there.

Input supplies: ore, coal, and labor

At the end of World War II, the United States seemed to be running out of iron ore. The high wartime production rates led to a depletion of the rich ore deposits in Minnesota and Michigan. The industry responded to this problem in two ways: exploring for new deposits and making greater use of the low grade ores. Many American firms formed joint ventures with other steel firms and mining companies to exploit foreign deposits. They developed new mines in Canada, Venezuela, Brazil, West Africa, and Australia.

The second response was to use the lower grade iron ores found in the Lake Superior region. This involved beneficiation, the removal of non-iron parts of the ore before it was sent to mills. Two processes were primarily used separately but sometimes in conjunction: sintering and pelleting. Sintering was the process of making the fine-grained pieces of the purified low grade ore into large clinker-like shapes, called sinters. Developed for mining other metals, this process was used in iron in the 1920s. In the postwar years, however, sintering declined, being replaced by the pelletization of taconite, the most common low grade ore in Minnesota and Michigan. The pelletization process enriched the low grade ore, raising the iron content from around 20 percent to 60 percent. This process worked well in the new, large BFs.

The second major input into steel in the postwar period was coal (usually refined into coke). Unlike iron ore, coal was not in short supply, but there were changes in the supply of coal and coke to the steel industry. First, strip mining became more important in the coal industry, although most metallurgical coal still came from underground mines (about 80 percent). Second, foreign steel companies began to buy American coal. By 1969, 42,200,000 tons of metallurgical coal was exported, roughly 7.5 percent of total American coal production.

Significant changes in coke ovens counteracted the pressure from coal exports. First, the beehive ovens were almost eliminated. Second, the by-product ovens became more efficient. Additionally, coke usage per ton of steel lessened. In 1945, 1,800 pounds of coke were used to make 2,000 pounds of pig iron. By 1969, only 1,200 pounds of coke were needed to make 2,000 pounds, or a ton, of pig iron.

The major input into steel was labor. At the end of World War II, the United Steel Workers (USW) represented the bulk of production workers in the steel industry. Given that the union had held down its wage demands during the war and steel profits actually declined toward the end of the war, a conflict between the union and the companies was inevitable. Besides wages, other issues such as health care, pensions, and job rules became problems.

That the government still maintained its World War II price and wage controls into the peace (until November 1946) exacerbated the conflict. The USW wanted a $0.25 per hour raise, but the companies were willing to give only $0.15. The government proposed a $0.18 raise. The result was a strike in January 1946. After a 28-day shut down, the companies granted a $0.185 per hour raise and a yearly contract with the union. In return, the government allowed them to raise prices.

Between 1947 and 1956, the companies and the USW continued to negotiate yearly contracts. After no-strike settlements in 1947 and 1948, a strike occurred in

1949. This strike was followed by settlements in 1950 and 1951, but the companies and union again reached an impasse in 1952. Accentuating the problem were the Korean War institution of price controls and the urgency of the war demands for steel. To prevent a strike, President Harry S. Truman seized the steel mills and had the government operate them. This occurred in April 1952. In June, however, the Supreme Court declared the seizure unconstitutional. Seven weeks later, a settlement was reached that gave the union a wage increase and allowed the companies to raise prices. This episode was followed by three years of relatively peaceful relations between steel labor and its management. In 1956, however, there was a short strike, which resulted in a three-year contract.

In 1959, public concern with inflation and a relatively slow economy put pressure on the steel industry to keep prices down. The union, however, responding to inflation, wanted higher wages. The result was a 116-day strike, which ended with the federal government intervention and a three-year contract.

In the 1960s, quiet relations existed between labor and management. With the help of the John F. Kennedy administration, a strike was averted in 1962. (This led to the above-described confrontation between President Kennedy and U.S. Steel Chairman Roger Blough.) In 1963, a five-year contract was negotiated. It allowed for some wage and benefit increases.

The 1959 contract set up the Human Relations Committee, which the union and the companies used to settle disputes arising from work rules. While it helped smooth union–company relations, the committee illustrates the problems facing the union and industry. From the onset of United Steel Workers, both the companies and the union had assumed an adversarial stance. This attitude discouraged cooperation and internal governance issues. It may have prevented the two from addressing the many problems affecting the competitive position of the union companies.

Some have argued that the structure and internal politics of the USW prevented it from addressing these problems (Hoerr, 1988 and Serrin, 1992). In fact, many union officials who understood the issue were driven out of the organization in the 1940s (Serrin, 1992, pp. 249–52). The union hierarchy was averse to new ways of dealing with management. Likewise, the steel management did not want to change its dominant position within the plants.

The Human Relations Committee may have been a casualty of this syndrome. Neither labor nor management saw the value of the group, and consequently, it fell victim to union politics. It had been proposed and developed by USW President David McDonald, who had trouble dealing with the local plant-level leaders. When the new union President, Iorwith W. Abel, came into power in 1965, he got rid of this vestige of McDonald. That internal union politics could destroy it indicates that neither management nor the union wanted to work together.

Some critics blame the high wages demanded by the union leadership for the subsequent troubles of the industry, but accusing the USW of lack of foresight does not seem justified. The evidence at the time was that the steel industry was here to stay. Not only was there a large growing production, but also employment was stable if not growing. While steel employment dropped from 674,000 in 1950 to

657,000 in 1965 and 627,000 in 1970, it had not fallen that much. Furthermore, the industry had recovered from similar falls in the past. Therefore, optimism on the part of the union seemed justified.

The influence of government

In this period, three issues pervaded the relationship between government and the steel industry: the capacity controversy, steel pricing, and imports. In the late 1940s, the government put a great deal of pressure on the steel industry to increase capacity. Many government experts, most notably Louis Bean of the Department of Agriculture, thought that more steel capacity was needed to keep the economy growing, but the steel companies were reluctant to build new capacity. They had lived through the 1930s, when the industry operated at very low rates of capacity utilization. The Korean War ended the debate. Defense needs – let alone growth – called for much more steel. Consequently, there was a big unambiguous push to add capacity.

As stated above, the urgency of this drive may have led firms to increase steel capacity by add-ons to old plants rather than by new efficient greenfield mills. Additionally, much of the capacity added in the early 1950s was with the soon-to-be obsolete OH technology.

The second government–steel industry conflict was on pricing. This concern was motivated by a belief that steel pricing was not competitive. Much evidence supports this assertion (Adams and Dirlam, 1964, Comanor and Scherer, 1995, Duke, *et al.*, 1977, Mancke, 1968, Rippe, 1970, Rogers, 1984 and 1987, and Stigler, 1965). Government officials often complained about steel pricing. The Federal Trade Commission did prohibit basing point pricing in 1948, and this act seems to have lowered prices (Rogers, 1987). Other than that, the federal government seemed at a loss as to what to do. Some scholars proposed breaking up the large companies, but no action commenced, partly due to political considerations and partly due to the uncertainty as to its effect. The steel companies were not particularly profitable.

Others wanted the steel price to be regulated. Actually, steel prices were regulated after World War II up to November 1946 and during the Korean War between 1950 and 1953. Often, however, the government yielded to the companies and allowed them to raise prices. Nevertheless, often when the companies raised prices, the politicians would threaten to investigate and bring antitrust cases, only to back off when their attention was diverted to other issues.

As a result, the government intervened in pricing on a haphazard basis, when it seemed politically expedient. Sometimes, steel firms could raise price and sometimes they could not. This could very well have explained why they went to add-ons instead of greenfield plants. Given the off-and-on attitude of the government in this area, firms were often in an uncertain position where they could not make rational long-run plans. In the long run, what assurances did the companies have of getting their return if sometimes they could raise price in response to market conditions and sometimes they could not? To sum up, the government failed to address the pricing problem.

The last area where the government and steel industry were in conflict was imports. Until the late 1960s, the government, even the pro-business Eisenhower administration, resisted industry appeals for tariffs or other kind of trade protection (*Iron Age*, October 2, 1954, p. 136). In the latter part of the 1960s, influential legislators such as Senator Vance Hartke of Indiana and Hugh Scott of Pennsylvania prevailed upon the government to obtain import quotas from Japan and the European Community nations (*Iron Age*, October 19, 1967, p. 73, October 2, 1969, p. 19, and January 16, 1969, p. 36). Given subsequent events, it is not clear that this action did much to improve the long-run performance of the industry.

The above statement could be made about almost all the government steel initiatives in the postwar period except perhaps the proscription of basing point pricing. The government did little to help the steel industry, and it may have done certain things that exacerbated its later difficulties.

Conclusion

It is hard to draw any definite conclusion about the performance of the steel industry during the 1950s and 1960s. While there was considerable growth in both size and productivity, many authorities see the firm policies in this period as the cause of the great decline in the late 1970s and early 1980s (Seely, 1994, pp. xxxv–xliv, Hoerr, 1988, and Serrin, 1992). Numerous causes of the later decline could be traced to the postwar period, including unhealthy labor relations, technological conservatism, and disorderly add-on expansion.

Still, the industry was much larger in 1970 than in 1946, and the above problems had been present in the past. Thus, one could very well be optimistic in 1970. In fact, one noted contemporary expert stated the following:

> The steel industry in the United States faces a number of problems ... [that] can and will be solved and as these solutions are developed and the new equipment performs up to expectations, the industry can function efficiently and profitably.
>
> (Hogan, 1971, p. 2095)

With an endorsement like that the difficulties of the next decade and a half were not all that obvious.

9   Troubled times
1970 to 1989

Introduction

This chapter covers the years 1970 to 1989. For the steel industry, this was a time of falling production, plant closings, and layoffs. These events occurred in the face of a growing economy – especially in the late 1980s.

As often happens, a great deal of blame was passed around. (For a list and discussion of the villains involved, see Bolling and Bowles, 1982.) Many commentators attribute the problem to imports and the lack of technological progress. There is some support for these theories in that other countries, especially Japan and Germany, became the major sources of new technology. Thus, there is considerable controversy, and it is important to put it in perspective.

Before applying our taxonomy, however, an examination of some of the statistics in Table 9.1 can give a useful overview of the industry. These data lend support to the decline story. Steel production dropped over 25 percent from 131,514,000 tons in 1970 to 97,943,000 tons in 1989. Imports rose by 50 percent between 1970 and 1989 – going from 14,609,000 tons to 22,056,000 tons.

American steel production increased greatly in 1972 and 1973. The 1973 steel production (150,800,000 tons) was the highest in U.S. history. After that, there were some revivals, but production never again reached its 1973 peak. In 1989, steel production was more than 24 percent below the 1981 level and 35 percent below the record 1973 production.

Table 9.6 (on page 153) shows the fall in employment; it is much greater proportionately than that of production. Between 1970 and 1990, employment in the steel industry dropped over 59 percent. Ironically, this statistic has a positive aspect. There was a great increase in labor productivity; steel output per employee rose 148 percent from 144 to 358 tons.

To better understand the situation behind these facts, we first examine the steel production process. Subsequently, we analyze customers and competitors. Then, we discuss the international steel situation. Next, we describe substitutes. Then, the major input markets, iron ore, coal, electricity, and labor, are examined. After that, we focus on the impact of the government, and finally, we end with some tentative conclusions.

Table 9.1 Steel production, exports, and imports, 1970–1988

Year	Total production	Imports	Exports
1970	131,514,000[a]	14,609,000	8,139,000
1971	120,400,000[a]	19,630,000[b]	3,547,000[a]
1972	133,200,000	19,558,000	3,606,000
1973	150,800,000	17,008,000[b]	5,060,000
1974	145,700,000[a]	17,962,000[b]	7,132,000
1975	116,600,000[a]	13,919,000	4,146,000[a]
1976	128,000,000	16,294,000[b]	3,865,000[a]
1977	125,300,000[a]	21,658,000[b]	3,218,000[a]
1978	137,000,000	24,068,000[b]	3,499,000
1979	136,300,000[a]	20,327,000	3,762,000
1980	111,835,000[a]	17,878,000	5,107,000
1981	120,828,000	22,639,000[b]	3,775,000[a]
1982	74,577,000[a]	18,770,000	2,588,000[a]
1983	84,615,000	19,301,000[b]	1,765,000[a]
1984	92,528,000	29,548,000[b]	1,727,000[a]
1985	88,359,000[a]	27,633,000	1,569,000[a]
1986	81,606,000[a]	24,238,000	1,452,000[a]
1987	89,151,000	23,836,000	1,708,000
1988	99,924,000	25,659,000	2,757,000
1989	97,943,000[a]	22,056,000	5,374,000

Source: American Iron and Steel Institute, *Annual Statistical Report*, various years.

Notes
a indicates a drop in the statistic from the previous year.
b indicates an increase in the statistic from the previous year.

Production and the production process

To analyze the situation, we start by looking at the changes in steelmaking technology. As discussed previously, this process can be divided into three parts: the smelting of iron ore, the refining of iron into steel, and the rolling of the steel into the pieces used by customers.

The blast furnace (BF) sector experienced a slow and steady increase in productivity. The average output of a single furnace rose from 398,237 tons in 1970 to 1,114,000 tons in 1988 (Casey in Seely, 1994, p. 47). The reasons for this progress can be divided into three categories, size, equipment, and practice. With greater physical size, BFs can produce more output per unit of physical input. There were some very large American units. Among the largest were Inland Steel's Furnace 7 with 2,920,000 tons and Bethlehem Steel's furnace L at Sparrows Point, Maryland with 3,398,000 tons of production. As the 1988 average size indicates, however, most of the BFs were much smaller.

Improved equipment and practice led to greater efficiency, even in small BFs. One authority observed: "Meanwhile, there are all kinds of opportunities for upgrading existing furnaces. Most of the improvements will have to come on existing furnaces because no one is rushing out to build new blast furnaces these days" (McManus in *Iron Age*, March 7, 1983, p. MP-5).

These improvements came from better equipment which often led to better procedures. *Iron Age* noted: "The incremental changes being made in blast furnace technology include better refractories, better controls, and longer campaigns". (McManus in *Iron Age*, September 1987, p. 39).

The term "campaigns" refers to the periods between the re-linings of the furnaces when the bricks on the inside are replaced. Better controls lowered the amount of coke used in the furnaces.

The downside of this progress was that fewer people were employed in this sector. A suggestive statistic is the decline in the number of operating "active" BFs. They dropped from 169 in 1970 to 50 in 1988 (Casey in Seely, 1994, p. 47).

Throughout the 1970s and 1980s there was talk about the direct reduction process replacing the BF. Direct reduction uses natural gas or a gas derived from coal or crude oil to provide heat to purge the impurities from iron ore. This process is very old, dating back to ancient times, but there are several modern variants on it. The rising price of oil and gas, however, did much to prevent the spread of this process. While it was installed in two gas-producing countries, Saudi Arabia and Venezuela, it found only a small place in the United States. Still, periodic shortfalls of scrap steel and coke led to interests in this process.

In the steel converter sector, the basic technology did not change significantly. Instead, the proportions of production used by the old technologies changed. As shown in Table 9.2, the basic oxygen process (BOF) continued to replace the open hearth furnace (OH). By 1989, the BOF process accounted for 59.6 percent of U.S. production, while the open hearth took up only 4.5 percent of the total. The basic oxygen process, however, did not continue to grow absolutely; it reached its height in production in 1978 with a total of 83,433,000 tons. After that, its production fluctuated, but in total declined: falling to 45,309,000 tons in 1982 and recovering to 58,348,000 tons in 1989.

By the late 1970s, BOF had become the dominant mode for the integrated steel sector, and its production fluctuated with the demand of product from this sector. Consequently, the BOF production fell somewhat in the 1980s. This resulted in some plant closings in the BOF sector. Sadly, America's first three BOF plants, McLouth at Trenton, Michigan and Kaiser at Fontana, California, and Jones & Laughlin at Aliquippa, Pennsylvania, were among those shut down. In all, 10 of the 32 BOF steel plants operating in 1974 had either shut down or switched to the EF process by 1985 (Barnett and Crandall, 1986, p. 38).

Thus, the use of the basic oxygen process was beginning to decline by the 1980s. A major problem was that the BOF converters were placed in old plants where the other parts of the mill did not fit well with the new converter. This problem also arose with other new processes such as continuous casters and rolling mills.

The primary change in the steel converter sector during this period was the growth of the electric furnace (EF). In spite of a drop in total steel production, the EF total actually rose during this period, increasing from 19,931,000 tons in 1970 to 35,154,000 tons in 1989. The EF market share went from 15.2 percent to 35.9 percent.

The EF had almost always used scrap steel as an input. Historically, the EF converter was used to make high grade steels such as alloys and stainless steel. A few

Table 9.2 Total steel production by type of process: basic oxygen (BOF), electric furnace (EF), and open hearth (OH) selected years, 1970–1989 (1,000s of tons)

Year	Total production	Basic oxygen process (BOF)	BOF percentage*	Electric furnace process (EF)	EF percentage*	Open hearth process (OH)	OH percentage*
1970	131,514	63,330	48.2	19,931	15.2	48,202	36.7
1973	150,800	83,242	55.2	27,747	18.4	39,112	25.9
1975	116,600	71,826	61.6	22,620	19.4	22,154	19.0
1980	111,835	67,615	60.5	31,166	27.9	13,054	11.7
1982	74,577	45,309	60.8	23,158	31.1	6,110	8.2
1983	84,615	52,050	61.5	26,615	31.5	5,951	7.0
1984	92,528	52,822	57.1	31,369	33.9	8,336	9.0
1985	88,359	51,885	58.7	29,946	33.9	6,428	7.3
1989	97,943	58,348	59.6	35,154	35.9	4,442	4.5

Source: American Iron and Steel Institute, *Annual Statistical Report*, various years.

* For some years, there was a small amount of Bessmer production; thus the percentages do not add up to 100.

firms such as Northwestern Steel & Wire focused on narrow but conventional product lines. In the 1960s, the furnace was improved to the point that it could efficiently make a wide line of the generic products such as rods, rails, and rebar (*Iron Age*, May 5, 1980, p. MP-5 for a contemporary analysis).

Three kinds of firms adopted the EF in a major way. The old large traditional firms found that, at least for some plants, EFs made more sense. Bethlehem Steel converted its plants in Johnstown and Steelton to fully EF mills, as did Jones & Laughlin with its Pittsburgh plant.

Many smaller integrated basic and specialty steel companies also switched their entire production to EF. Examples were Lukens, an eastern Pennsylvania maker of ship plate and CF&I, the former Colorado Fuel & Iron Corporation which specialized in rails.

The third set of firms building EFs was a more recent phenomenon, minimills. These firms, starting in the 1960s, built small furnace plants that either serviced a narrow geographic market or focused on a narrow product line. Several reasons can be given for the rise of the minimills. First, the EF became much more efficient compared to the other technologies. Barnett and Crandall (1986, pp. 56–8) document the rise in EF total factor productivity. Among the most important changes used by the minimills was the continuous casters, which these mills had adopted much faster than the others.

Second, the price of scrap steel was so low that the metal resource cost of the scrap-fed EF was lower than that of the integrated mill. As of 1985, it was only 38 percent of the hot metal cost of the integrated mill (Barnett and Crandall, 1986, p. 31).

Third, minimills generally had lower labor costs. These firms often operated in low wage areas without unions. Another advantage of being non-union was the greater ability to manage as a result of fewer work rules.

Certain non-technological products, such as rebar, rods, and wire, were especially amenable to minimill production. Consequently, many minimills became specialists in certain products. These firms would often sell to a wide region.

Some, such as Raritan River, produce only wire rods while others, such as Quanex and Newport, specialize in tubular products (Barnett and Crandall, 1986, p. 31). Other minimills developed a somewhat larger product line but sold in a geographically confined area. Many of the firms were located in the south and southwest.

Until the late 1980s, there seemed to be limits on the product lines that could be produced by EFs. They expanded into rod, wire, pipe production, and in the early 1980s, they moved into shapes for construction. Sheets, however, had remained the province of the old integrated mills with BFs. In 1986, however, Nucor Corporation began to build an EF mill that made sheets. As of 1988, the mill was still under construction.

In general, the 1970s and 1980s were characterized by competition between different processes for refining steel. At first, the BOF continued to replace the open hearth furnaces. Later, however, the BOF was often replaced by the EF.

In the rolling mill sector of the steel industry, improvement continued in the secondary mills where the products for the customers are shaped, but the major change was the widespread adoption of the continuous caster. The chief advantage of the continuous caster was the lower operating cost. This came as a result of the fewer steps in the process and the decreased loss of material. The continuous caster takes molten steel from a ladle that comes from the converter furnace, and shapes it into the billets, blooms, and slabs from which final products are rolled. The continuous caster replaced two steps in the steel process: the casting of ingots from the molten steel and the use of primary rolling mills. Generally, the caster used less labor and capital.

With all its advantages, the implementation of this innovation took some time. While the initial research began in the 1930s and 1940s, the successful operation of the machines only began in the 1950s. By 1975, only 9 percent of American steel was made with continuous casters, but by 1980, the percentage had increased to 20 percent.

By 1983, the percentage of continuous caster steel was 31 percent (Hogan, 1984, p. 126). The traditional integrated companies had made a commitment to this technology in the early 1980s. In contrast, the great bulk of the EF mills operated with continuous casters, including almost 100 percent of the minimills. By 1986, most of the industry was committed to continuous casters. The advantages were clear. By one estimate, the continuous caster saved companies between $40 and $50 a ton. "That means the new batch of casters could reduce the industry costs as much as $800 million a year" (McManus in *Iron Age*, February 7, 1983, p. MP-4). By 1988, continuous casters made 77 percent of the steel in the United States.

Concomitant with the introduction of the continuous caster were developments in refining the composition and even molecular structure of the steel product. This refining was often done in the ladle, hence the term "ladle technology." The ladle was the large vessel into which molten steel was poured after it is processed in the converter furnace. In the ladle, these compositional and molecular changes can be made by stirring and injecting material (McManus in *Iron Age*, October 3, 1986, p. 37).

The secondary rolling mill sector improved incrementally during the 1970s and the early 1980s, but by 1984 there was a growing interest in replacing old rolling mills and developing new ones. Three developments seemed to motivate this interest. First, the adoption of continuous casters led firms to examine how to coordinate the rolling mills with the new technology (McManus in *Iron Age*, February 7, 1984, p. 19). Second, customers began to demand better-quality product, often asking for special steel treatments for their particular needs. In the forefront of these customers were the automobile companies and the canning firms. Several steel companies, including National Steel, Armco, Wheeling-Pittsburgh, and Bethlehem responded to their demands (See Berry in *Iron Age*, September 1987, p. 32 and September 1989, p. 55).

The third event accentuating progress in this sector was the entry of the small firms into rolling products. With relatively new mills, they often opted for the latest rolling equipment. Continental Steel Company of Kokomo, Indiana and Heidtmann Steel Products Inc. of Toledo, Ohio were examples of this type of mill. The former company was a minimill that built an advanced rolling mill for rods, while the latter was a distributor that integrated into rolling mills for sheets.

Responding to technological imperatives and customer desires, both the old, integrated companies and the smaller EF firms developed new rolling mills to improve product quality.

The major question about this period concerned not the particular innovations, but their implementation. The minimills and integrated firms followed different strategies. The former built new mills to respond to new opportunities. In contrast, the integrated firms followed a policy of "rounding out." Instead of building new plants, they merely installed new technology in their old plants.

Often such plans created major problems. It was sometimes difficult to coordinate the new BOFs and the continuous casters with the complementary parts of the works like the BFs and the rolling mills. With old plants, it was often difficult to place the continuous caster near the secondary mills that made the final product. Often, the companies came up with creative solutions to the problem (McManus in *Iron Age*, March 1987, p. 43).

The other integrated firms abandoned plans to fully integrate some separate rolling mills and modernized the old plants. Jones & Laughlin and its successor firm, LTV Steel, merely kept operating its rolling mills in Hennepin, Illinois, and National Steel did the same thing with its partly integrated plant in Portage, Indiana. A major impediment to these plans was the 1982 recession that dried up capital. Consequently, many of the mills were left only partly modernized. Often, they had higher costs than even the old-fashioned plants (Barnett and Crandall, 1986, pp. 39–40).

The customer industries

This section focuses on the change in the demand composition for steel from 1970 to 1988. Tables 9.3A and 9.3B show the changing uses of steel over that period. The former shows the amount of steel shipped in tonnage to the major groups of customers, and the latter displays each group's percentage of total domestic steel shipments. These tables confirm other data in the chapter, in that steel production, consumption and shipments dropped.

An examination of the various steel customer sectors helps one to understand the nature of this decline. Tables 9.3A and 9.3B show the domestic shipments to ten different sectors along with exports and the shipments to the sectors so small that they are aggregated into one category, "Other."

The tables show the ten sectors that accounted for between 73 and 83 percent of the steel shipments. The "Other" category represents the shipments to smaller consumer sectors. There are, however, some problems with these definitions, which are further discussed below.

To clarify the nature of the change in consumption, some general trends are examined. Except for steel service centers and distributors and the "Other" category, all sectors experienced a decline in sales between 1970 and 1988. The total drop between 1970 and 1988 was only 6,958,000 tons, but the steel sold in the steel service centers and the "Other" categories increased by 5,012,000 and 8,152,000 tons respectively. Thus, the other nine sectors and exports decreased by just over

Table 9.3A The breakdown of economic sectors using steel by tonnage (by the 1000s), 1970, 1973, 1975, 1980, 1985, and 1988

Year	1970	1973	1975	1980	1985	1988
Total shipments	90,798	111,430	79,957	83,853	73,043	83,840
Steel service centers & distributors	16,025	20,383	12,700	16,172	18,439	21,037
Automotive	14,475	23,217	15,214	12,124	12,950	12,555
Construction, including maintenance	13,353	17,190	12,046	11,890	11,230	12,102
Containers, packaging and shipping mat.	7,775	7,811	6,053	5,551	4,089	4,421
Machinery, industrial and electrical	7,863	9,699	7,346	6,984	4,140	5,257
Oil & gas	3,550	3,405	4,171	5,371	2,044	1,477
Railroads (*adj. 1980)	3,098	3,228	3,152	3,155	1,061	1,146
Appliance and home Equipment	3,938	4,737	3,043	3,426	2,681	2,838
Agricultural	1,126	1,772	1,429	1,240	629	568
Shipbuilding	859	1,019	1,413	1,201	337	303
Other	12,751	15,831	11,635	14,144	14,949	20,903
Export	5,985	3,138	1,755	2,595	494	1,233

Source: American Iron and Steel Institute, *Annual Statistical Report*, various years.

Table 9.3B The breakdown of economic sectors using steel by percentage, 1970, 1973, 1975, 1980, 1985, and 1988

Year	1970	1973	1975	1980	1985	1988
Total shipments	90,798	111,430	79,957	83,853	73,043	83,840
Steel service centers & distributors	17.7	18.3	15.9	19.3	25.2	25.1
Automotive	15.9	20.8	19.0	14.5	17.7	15.0
Construction, including maintenance	14.7	15.4	15.1	14.2	15.3	14.4
Containers, packaging and shipping mat.	8.6	7.0	7.6	6.6	5.6	5.3
Machinery, industrial and electrical	8.7	8.7	9.2	8.3	5.7	6.3
Oil & gas	3.9	3.0	5.2	6.4	2.8	1.7
Railroads (*adj. 1980)	3.4	2.9	3.9	3.7	1.5	1.4
Appliance and home Equipment	4.3	4.3	3.8	4.1	3.7	3.4
Agricultural	1.2	1.6	1.8	1.5	0.9	0.7
Shipbuilding	0.9	0.9	1.7	1.4	0.5	0.3
Other	14.0	14.2	14.6	16.9	20.4	24.9
Export	6.6	2.8	2.2	3.1	0.6	1.5

Source: American Iron and Steel Institute, *Annual Statistical Report*, various years.

20,000,000 tons, meaning that large parts of the industry experienced enormous drops in sales. The fall in the nine domestic sectors, excluding service centers and others, adds up to 15,370,000 tons.

Hogan (1984 and 1986) attributes this fall mainly to declines in five sectors: automobiles, containers, oil and gas, railroads, and industrial and electrical machinery. Between 1970 and 1988, these sectors accounted for 77.5 percent of the fall in the declining domestic sectors. Therefore, we emphasize these sectors.

Additionally, the presence of the steel service centers obscures some information on the declines in these sectors. While three sectors, containers, oil and gas, and railroads, consisted of firms that usually dealt directly with the steel companies, the automotive and machinery sectors included significant firms that bought through the steel service centers. Consequently, the figures in Tables 9.3A and B give a reasonable indication of the actual decline in steel sales for three sectors but perhaps not for the other two.

Automobile companies usually dealt directly with the steel companies, but they had suppliers that worked through the steel service centers. In the 1980s, the auto companies increasingly outsourced their production and that increased the portion of the process handled by small firms. Thus, the figures may overstate the fall in consumption from the auto industry. Similarly, machinery makers consisted of many different firms, some large and some small. Many of them dealt through the service centers.

Table 9.4 shows the breakdown by consumption sector of the sales for Joseph T. Ryerson & Son, Inc. which was the United States' largest steel service center. It gives a fair representation of the number of the customers buying through service centers. The machinery industry took up 37.5 percent of this firm's shipments, while transportation, including automobiles, railroads, and airplanes, took up only 9.2 percent of the Ryerson shipments. Accordingly, it is very likely that the above figures in Table 9.4 greatly overstate the decline in the sale of steel to the machinery sector. The bias is probably somewhat less in the automotive sector's figures. With these general caveats, we now examine the developments in the 1970s and 1980s in each of these five sectors. Then, we summarily look at the other customer sectors.

The automotive sector experienced the greatest overall fall in steel consumption. The average steel shipments to the automotive sector fell from 19,025,000 tons in the 1970s to 12,047,000 tons in the 1980s. This change was the result of a large decrease in consumption between the two decades. The recovering economy of the

Table 9.4 Shipments by market percentage by Joseph T. Ryerson & Son, Inc., the country's largest steel service center

	1986	1987
Construction-related	4.1	4.6
Metal mills & foundries	3.0	3.4
Electrical machinery	6.5	6.5
Transportation equipment	9.7	9.2
Wholesale distributors	5.1	4.6
Metal products & fabricators	22.8	22.5
Machinery manufacturers	37.1	37.6
Other	11.7	11.6

Source: *Iron Age*, May 1987, p. 37.

mid and late 1980s did not raise automotive steel consumption to its 1981 level – let alone the 1970s peaks.

The reasons for this drop have been discussed extensively (Hogan, 1983, p. 132, Hogan, 1986, pp. 3–4, Guiles in *Iron Age*, October 26, 1972, p. 21 and Berry in *Iron Age*, July 1987, p. 31). First, motor vehicles sales dropped in those two decades: the largest year in the 1970s was 1978 with 13.1 million vehicles, while in the 1980s the largest year was 1986 with 12.1 million vehicles. Also, the United States imported more motor vehicles. Furthermore, the amount of steel used for each car dropped during this period. With the rising demand for higher gasoline mileage, the cars became smaller and lighter.

The demand for containers also declined during these two decades. The consumption from this sector dropped from 7,775,000 tons in 1970 to 4,421,000 tons in 1988. The main reason for this fall was the virtually total replacement of steel by aluminum in the beer and soft beverage industries. While the movement started in the 1960s, it became much more pronounced in these two decades. In addition, plastics started to penetrate some food container markets.

Just like the container and automotive sectors, oil and gas decreased its use of steel. The demand for steel from oil and gas fell 35 percent. The fall in this sector received much attention because the drop in demand for what were called oil country goods coincided with the general fall-off resulting from the 1982 recession.

Over the period, however, the behavior of consumption in this sector was different from the first two sectors. Oil country shipments in 1974 reached 4,210,000 tons, the decade's highest level, and the lowest yearly level was 2,653,000 tons in 1976. The yearly shipments for 1980 and 1981 were higher than any in the 1970s; in 1980 they were 5,371,000 tons, and in 1981, they were 6,238,000 tons. The year with the lowest was 1986 with 1,023,000 tons.

The demand in this sector boomed in the late 1970s and early 1980s with the run-up in world oil prices in 1979. Between 1978 and 1981, crude oil prices rose $14.95 to $38.00 per barrel. As a result, oil drilling activity in the United States increased enormously. From 1978 to 1981, the number of oil rigs operating in the United States rose from 2,259 to over 3,970. This increased the demand for steel, especially pipe and tube (McManus in *Iron Age*, January 4, 1982, p. MP-8).

After 1981, however, a drop in crude oil prices led to a collapse in drilling activity. From 1981 to 1982, the crude oil price dropped to $31. This drop started a trend. Thus, steel shipments to the oil and gas sector fell from 6,238,000 tons in 1981 to 2,745,000 tons in 1982 and 1,296,000 tons in 1983. While these shipments recovered somewhat in 1984 and 1985, they dropped more in 1986 to 1,023,000 tons – reaching only 1,477,000 in 1988. Thus, oil and gas demand for steel dropped 76 percent between 1981 and 1988. Essentially, instead of continual decline in sales between 1970 and 1988, oil country steel rose precipitously in the early 1980s only to fall back later in the decade.

The railroad industry, once the major customer of steel, became insignificant in this era. Between 1970 and 1988, steel sales to the railroads declined from 3,098,000 to 1,146,000 tons. The decade average of steel shipments to the railroads went from 3,258,000 tons in the 1970s to 1,165,000 tons in the 1980s. The problem of falling railroad demand was accentuated by the over-optimistic predictions by the steel companies in the 1970s. This attitude led to the building or expanding of some rail mills. In the 1980s, the demand from the railroads dropped for not only rails but also other steel products, such as locomotives and cars. "Freight car construction hit an all-time low of 5,772 cars in 1983, down from a range of 52,000 to 95,000 in the late 1970s" (Hogan, 1987, p. 5). Essentially, the amount of trackage dropped off, and railroad spending on other capital also fell.

Between 1970 and 1988 steel shipments to the industrial and electrical machinery sector dropped from 7,863,000 tons to 5,257,000 tons. The decade average dropped from 8,269,000 tons in the 1970s to 5,014,000 tons in the 1980s. Hogan (1987, p. 5) asserts that at least part of the reason for the decline of sales in this sector was import penetration. The fall in capital spending in the early 1980s also lowered steel demand from this sector. Another reason for the falling figures may have been more benign. Part of the increase in the sales of steel through the steel centers may have gone to machinery makers. They accounted for over 37 percent of Ryerson's steel service center shipments in 1986 and 1987. Therefore, the falling numbers for the sector may indicate a change in distribution channels as much as a fall in total demand.

Thus, it is important to examine the steel service centers and distributors. Service centers do more than just distribute the product. Often, it was not economical for a steel mill to prepare the product exactly to the customer's specifications. Thus, the steel service centers arose to prepare the metal for the specific needs of the customer. It is not surprising that more such services were needed given the ever increasing diversity of the economy's products. As one authority put it, "The idea is to find clients, put in special equipment to serve them . . . " (Bennett in *Iron Age*, April 21, 1975, p. 34).

Four other major sectors used significant amounts of steel during the 1970s and 1980s. As shown in Tables 9.3A and 9.3B (the changes in shipments for these sectors), construction, the largest of these sectors, dropped its shipments 9.3 percent from 13,353,000 tons in 1970 to 12,102,000 tons in 1988. This sector also bought from the steel service centers. Construction took 4.6 percent of Ryerson's shipments. Thus, this drop could very well overstate the fall in construction steel usage.

The decline in steel shipments in the other three sectors was proportionately much larger. The fall in steel used in the appliance and home equipment industry was 27 percent. A major portion of it probably came from the substitution of other materials (mainly plastics). The steel consumption drops in agriculture and shipbuilding were much more drastic: 49.6 percent in the former and 64.7 percent in the latter. Given the drop in the number of farms, it is likely that the decline in demand accounted for most of the drop in the former.

Even with the diversion of some product to the service centers, the overall use of steel dropped during these two decades. Three major factors seem common to all consuming sectors. First, steel imports increased greatly, and thus, some business was lost by the domestic firms to foreign companies. Second, there was substitution of other materials – mostly to aluminum and plastics. Third, the composition of the economy seems to have moved to a less steel-intensive set of products. Early in economic development, countries build up their physical infrastructure. Once this foundation is built, countries consume fewer steel-intensive goods and services. (For a more thorough analysis of this sequence, see Barnett and Schorsch, 1983, pp. 39-44 and Hogan, 1994, pp. 92–6.)

The firms in the steel industry

This chapter focuses now on the particular steel companies during the 1970s and 1980s. The steel companies can be divided into three classes: the old integrated firms that mainly made steel from iron ore, old firms that completely switched their production to the EF, and the minimills which also used EFs from the onset.

Table 9.5A shows the available production and market shares for the first class of firms. Two things stand out. First, production dropped for most firms. Second, two of the Big Eight merged with a third firm, the Jones & Laughlin Steel Corporation (now called LTV). Table 9.5B presents the market share of a sample of firms in the two other categories. Those labeled with "OI" are the old integrated firms that switched to the EF process, while those labeled by "M" are the minimill producers.

To understand the particular firms, this section discusses the Big Eight integrated firms and three smaller integrated firms. Then, some firms in the other two classes are analyzed to illustrate certain trends and problems. Finally, we examine the overseas industry selling steel in this country.

U.S. Steel

The first firm in Table 9.5A is the United States Steel Corporation. Even though its production and market share dropped, it was still the largest firm as of 1988. The boom in 1973 and 1974 led the firm to increase its capital spending plans. It upgraded its older plants and made plans to build a large "greenfield" at Conneaut, Ohio.

Its lackluster performance in the late 1970s led the firm to reconsider its position. The replacement of Board Chairman Edgar B. Speer by David M. Roderick signaled this change. Roderick hired, as company president, William R. Roesch, an operations expert from Jones & Laughlin who started a program of retrenchment. The Conneaut plans were discarded. This mill would have had lower operating costs than the other plants, but once it was financed its total costs would have been higher than those of the old ones. As part of this fallback, U.S. Steel also closed down its integrated plant in Youngstown, Ohio.

U.S. Steel could not endure the steel Depression of 1982 and 1983 without further cutbacks. On the death of William R. Roesch, Roderick appointed another outside operations expert, Thomas C. Graham, as U.S. Steel president. His mandate was to supervise further consolidation. In the Chicago area, the company eliminated some of the rolling mills at Gary, Indiana and abandoned its rail mills. In Ohio, U.S. Steel closed its plant in Cleveland.

After shutting down the Fairfield, Alabama plant for two years, the company installed a continuous caster and upgraded its blast and BOF furnaces and its pipe

Table 9.5A Steel production and market share for ten large steel integrated firms, 1970–1988

Year	Total production (1,000 tons)	Company production[a] US Steel	Bethlehem	LTV[b] J & L	Republic[c]	National Steel	Armco	Youngstown[d]	Inland	Wheeling-Pittsburgh	Weirton[e]
1970	131,514	31,400 (23.9)	20,586 (15.7)	6,965 (5.3)	9,838 (7.5)	9,869 (7.5)	7,908 (6.0)	5,142 (3.9)	7,051 (5.4)	N/AVAL	N/A
1973	150,800	34,968 (23.2)	23,702 (15.7)	7,986 (5.3)	11,288 (7.5)	11,321 (7.5)	9,464 (6.3)	5,846 (3.9)	8,155 (5.4)	4,407 (2.9)	N/A
1975	116,600	26,385 (22.6)	17,500 (15.0)	5,734 (4.9)	8,768 (7.5)	8,578 (7.4)	7,183 (6.2)	4,448 (3.8)	7,287 (6.2)	3,277 (2.8)	N/A
1980	111,835	23,300 (20.8)	14,998 (13.4)	9,699 (8.7)	8,530 (7.6)	7,569 (6.8)	7,290 (6.5)	N/A	7,049 (6.3)	3,119 (2.8)	N/A
1985	88,359	16,700 (18.9)	10,440 (11.8)	13,112 (14.8)	N/A	4,785 (5.4)	5,347 (6.1)	N/A	6,069 (6.9)	1,754 (2.0)	2,744 (3.1)
1988	99,924	15,545 (15.6)	12,900 (12.9)	10,461 (10.5)	N/A	5,393 (5.4)	5,771 (5.8)	N/A	6,126 (6.1)	2,490 (2.5)	2,700 (2.7)

Source: *Iron Age*, various issues.

Notes
a Under the company production tonnages are the market shares of total U.S. production.
b This firm was merged with Youngstown in 1979 and Republic in 1984.
c This firm was merged with LTV in 1984.
d This firm was merged with LTV in 1979.
e This firm was spun off by National Steel in 1983.

N/A denotes not applicable. The firm was not in business or had been merged into another firm.
N/AVAL denotes not available.

Table 9.5B Total steel production and market share for samples of the old integrated firms that switched to electric furnace and the minimill firms, 1970–1988

Year	Total production (1,000s)	Company* production CF&I(OI)	Lukens (OI)	Northwestern Steel & Wire (M)	Nucor(M)	Korf Georgetown(M)	Florida Steel(M)
1970	131,514	N/AVAL	N/AVAL	N/AVAL	N/AVAL	N/AVAL	N/AVAL
1973	150,800	1,794 (1.2)	887 (0.6)	1,444 (1.0)	N/AVAL	N/AVAL	N/AVAL
1975	116,600	1,571 (1.3)	775 (0.7)	1,391 (1.2)	N/AVAL	N/AVAL	N/AVAL
1980	111,835	1,574 (1.4)	734 (0.7)	1,447 (1.3)	1,193 (1.1)	1,389 (1.2)	794 (0.7)
1985	88,359	606 (0.7)	476 (0.5)	866 (1.0)	1,893 (2.1)	N/AVAL	N/AVAL
1988	99,924	752 (0.8)	N/AVAL	N/AVAL	2,100 (2.1)	N/AVAL	N/AVAL

Source: *Iron Age*, various issues.

* Under the company production tonnages are the market shares of total U.S. production.

N/A denotes not applicable. The firm was out of business or had been merged into another firm. N/AVAL denotes not available.

and tube mills. As a result of this upgrade, U.S. Steel shut down its Baytown, Texas plant, since the Alabama plant could provide the same product.

U.S. Steel also closed its plant at Geneva, Utah. The company then entered a joint venture with the Korean steel firm, Pohang Iron and Steel, Ltd (POSCO), to renovate the Pittsburg, California rolling mills. Thus, POSCO supplied it with the steel to be rolled. Similarly, U.S. Steel also attempted to use foreign steel for its rolling mills at Fairless, Pennsylvania. This deal with British Steel did not work out.

One of the most publicized U.S. Steel actions was its consolidation of the mills in its Pittsburgh district (Hoerr, 1988 and Serrin, 1992). Essentially, it eliminated the two integrated steel plants at Homestead and Duquesne, Pennsylvania. Keeping its coke-making facility at Clairton, Pennsylvania, it used its BFs at Duquesne and Braddock, Pennsylvania to feed the Braddock BOF converters. These converters supplied steel to rolling mills at Irvin, Homestead, and other places. In effect, U.S. Steel set up a fully integrated works with different parts in different towns in the Monongahela River valley. In the process, many people were laid off. This and the demand for lower wages eventually led to a strike in 1986.

Consistent with the emphasis on increasing profitability was the acquisition policy of the company. U.S. Steel always had been more diversified than most steel companies, owning cement, chemical, and fertilizer companies. It now went much further by buying two large integrated petroleum companies, Marathon Oil Company and Texas Oil & Gas. These acquisitions were designed to make the company's profit more stable. The company, however, financed the acquisitions with debt. Critics asserted that U.S. Steel should have used the debt to build up its steel mills. As Hogan (1984, p. 29) noted, however, the firm could not have borrowed money to build steel mills.

While the charge that U.S. Steel's Marathon acquisition diverted resources from rebuilding its steel plants may be unfair, another criticism has some credibility. It is that the management used the corporation's resources to invest in the oil industry, but there is no evidence that U.S. Steel management had any special knowledge of the energy industry that qualified them to invest other people's money in that area. In fact, it is not clear that the investment worked out that well.

Nevertheless, in the merger and the other activities of Roderick, there is a consistent pattern. He wanted to make the company show a profit, and he went to any length to do it. Buying Marathon and Texas Oil & Gas did put black ink on the U.S. Steel income statements, as did bringing in outside operations experts, like Roesch and Graham.

Other acquisition plans were also consistent with this goal. U.S. Steel tried to buy National Steel, but the justice department enjoined it. U.S. Steel would have obtained two efficient steel mills at a low cost. When it exited the rail business, U.S. Steel attempted to buy the steel rail firm, CF&I. This also could have been a way to obtain cheap capacity. Thus, if enhancing the U.S. Steel profits was Roderick's goal, his policies were rational.

By some standards, Roderick's actions may have been wrong, but the fault may lie with the incentive system, not the individual. His fiduciary goal was making the profit sheet look good, even if some stakeholders, like workers, were badly hurt.

The role of the corporate manager was not always totally clear. Does management have the right to deploy the firm's money and credit in any way it wants? Or should there be restrictions on the uses to which corporate managers can put firms' resources?

On Roderick's policy, however, one comment is in order. As of 2006, U.S. Steel was one of the few large steel companies not to have gone through bankruptcy, and its pensioners were receiving their contracted annuities. Possibly, Roderick's drastic policies were responsible for this result.

Bethlehem

As of 1970, the second largest steel firm in the United States was the Bethlehem Steel Corporation. It had six integrated steel plants. It made money every year up until 1977, which was the first year that the company lost money since the 1930s.

In reaction to this loss, the company cut back production in two mills that year. At Lackawanna, New York, the company cut capacity. A second cutback was at Johnstown, Pennsylvania where Bethlehem replaced the BF and open hearth furnaces with electric converters.

In the 1980s, Bethlehem Steel got into financial trouble. One company history states that: "From late 1982 through 1986 the company experienced its first unbroken string of losses since the Depression" (Leary and Sholes in Seely, 1994, p. 45). Unlike U.S. Steel, this firm did not diversify, following a policy of staying almost totally in steel (McManus in *Iron Age*, April 15, 1981, p. 43).

To reduce costs, Bethlehem cut back on more plants. Except for coke ovens and one rolling mill, it abandoned its Lackawanna works. It converted its Steelton plant to an EF works. On the positive side, it installed new continuous casters in its Burns Harbor, Steelton, and Sparrows Point plants. By 1984, the firm had reduced its labor force to 48,000 employees from 115,000 employees in 1975. Further cuts were made in the late 1980s. By 1988, Bethlehem Steel had three fully integrated BOF steel plants, Sparrow Points, Burns Harbor, and Bethlehem, and it ran two EF plants, Steelton and Johnstown.

LTV, Republic, Jones & Laughlin, and Youngstown Sheet & Tube

In 1970, the fourth largest firm in the American steel industry was the Republic Steel Corporation with a market share of 7.5 percent. In 1984, Republic merged with Jones & Laughlin, owned by LTV Corporation. Earlier in 1979, LTV Steel bought the Youngstown Sheet & Tube Company.

While most of the top management of the new entity came from Jones & Laughlin, the new company centered its activities around the mills owned by Republic and Youngstown. A detailed discussion of the original companies shows why this was the case.

In the 1970s, these firms were not as profitable as U.S. Steel and Bethlehem. In 1977, all three lost money. In the 1970s, Youngstown had essentially focused its investment in its large Indiana Harbor plant, neglecting its two Youngstown plants. In 1977, the company abandoned these two locations.

Jones & Laughlin had very thin profit margins in the 1970s. They started with two serious handicaps. First, when LTV bought the company, the parent company did not clearly take control, and there was a period when management was at loose ends. Second, the firm had spent a great deal of money in the 1960s to build the Hennepin, Illinois mill, and it became clear that it would not be profitable to finish it.

These handicaps were somewhat offset by two strong managers, William R. Roesch and Thomas C. Graham. They instituted programs to update the plant technology. They worked with foremen and the unions to change the work procedures, and they rationalized many of the plants.

Republic, meanwhile, worked, through the 1970s and early 1980s, to update and modernize its plants in a piecemeal fashion. While it built a modern rolling mill and a continuous caster, the company still had low profits. After losing $239 million in 1983, the firm merged with Jones & Laughlin in 1984 to become the LTV Steel Corporation. The justice department saw an anticompetitive effect from this merger, even though Republic was on the verge of bankruptcy. The merger was allowed on the condition that the new company sell its integrated plant at Gadsden, Alabama and a stainless steel rolling mill at Massillon, Ohio.

At the time, the Republic plants in South Chicago and Buffalo, New York were closed. Even these drastic actions were not enough to solve the new company's problems. In 1984, LTV lost $378 million, and in 1985, it lost $724 million. These losses were not sustainable, and the company went bankrupt in 1986.

With the reorganization, the two former Jones & Laughlin plants at Aliquippa and Pittsburgh, Pennsylvania were shut down. In 1988, the company was operating only the integrated mills in Indiana Harbor, Indiana and Cleveland and Warren, Ohio as well as an EF plant in Canton, Ohio.

National Steel

With a production of 9,869,000 tons, National Steel was the third largest steel producer as of 1970. It focused mainly on automotive steel and tin-plate for cans. Throughout the next decade, National Steel had positive profits, and at first, it expanded.

While it made moves to diversify its product line by going into aluminum, real estate, and drug distribution, it still attempted to increase its steel production. In 1971, it bought Granite City Steel Company, with a plant in the St. Louis area. Also, the company started to build a new plant in Portage, Indiana.

In the late 1970s, National Steel responded to the lackluster steel market by canceling its steel expansion and re-emphasizing diversification. Thus, the Portage, Indiana mill was left with only its rolling mills.

The depressed steel market in the early 1980s led the company to a series of actions de-emphasizing the steel business. First, it changed its name to National Intergroup, stating that it was a diversified general products firm, not a steel company. The steel assets were put under a separate organization. It spun off the Weirton plant to the employees by setting up an Employee Stock Option Plan (ESOP, which gave the new company some tax advantages). National Intergroup then cut back on the capacity of its other plants. It also attempted to sell its steel mills to U.S. Steel, but the justice department enjoined the transaction on antitrust grounds.

When this transaction did not work out, the National Intergroup management sold half of the steel division to a Japanese company, the Nippon Kokan Steel Corporation. By 1988, the National Steel Division of National Intergroup was half owned by Nippon Kokan with two plants, Granite City, Illinois and the Ecorse, Michigan plant.

The actions of National Intergroup raise the same questions as the policies of David Roderick at U.S. Steel. Was the management of National Intergroup any better at investing the funds generated by the steel company in other areas than the stockholders?

Armco and AK Steel

In 1970, the fifth largest steel company was Armco, Inc. The company produced 7,908,000 tons of steel in 1970. The four integrated steel plants had a capacity of 8.4 million tons.

The company became diversified very early, owning a major oil drilling supply firm (National Supply), and maintaining interests in titanium. In the 1960s, it modernized its operations. Consequently, it made money in the 1970s, when some firms lost money. The steel mills were well positioned and modern, while the company's diversification effort seemed to work. By 1981, only 37 percent of the company's assets were in steel.

The diversification did not prevent the losses in the period after 1981. In fact, the oil supply company increased the company losses by its exposure to the oil country Depression. As a result of the recession, Armco retrenched. It shut down its Houston plant, sold off the two EF plants, and cut capacity at its Middletown plant.

In 1985, the company highlighted its diversification by moving its headquarters to New Jersey. In 1988, it sold a 40 percent interest in its carbon steel division to Kawasaki Steel of Japan. Later the Middletown, Ohio and Ashland, Kentucky plants were put under a new company called AK Steel.

Inland Steel Company

Inland Steel Company was, in many ways, the most successful large integrated steel firm during this period. Like the others, however, it suffered losses in the 1980s for four straight years (1982 to 1985). Inland operated only one integrated steel plant located at Indiana Harbor, Indiana. Like other companies, it did diversify some, but not much. Steel accounted for 95 percent of the firm's sales.

The recession of the 1980s, however, forced this firm to cut back. In 1986, the open hearth part of its mill was shut down. In 1988, it did follow other companies by entering a joint venture with a Japanese firm, Nippon Steel, to build a rolling mill and cold reduction. As of 1988, Inland Steel was in a strong position for a steel company. It was profitable, and as Hogan says (1987, p. 28) "its pension liabilities are fully funded."

The smaller integrated companies

There were a number of smaller integrated steel firms other than the largest eight (down to six by 1988). While some of the smaller firms, such as CF&I, changed into EF firms, others remained integrated producers. Two of these firms illustrate particular problems faced by "Little Steel."

Wheeling-Pittsburgh Steel Corporation came from a 1968 merger of the Pittsburgh Steel Company and the Wheeling Steel Company. Its two steel plants were rather small, and had old equipment. To rectify the situation, the firm modernized the facilities. At Monessen, the company built a new rail mill, which was financed by the Small Business Administration.

Alas, Wheeling-Pittsburgh was hit by the 1982 recession. After three years of losses, the company went into bankruptcy in 1985. It tried to get its workers to take lower wages, but the union balked, and there was an 83-day strike. As a result of the bankruptcy settlement, the BFs and the steel converters were shut down at Monessen. The new rail mill was taken over by the government, the major company creditor. Later, that mill was bought by Bethlehem Steel. Thus, as of 1988, Wheeling-Pittsburgh Steel Corporation was running one mill.

Another firm that underwent bankruptcy was McLouth Steel Corporation, forced into it by heavy capital expenditures and heavy losses in 1980 and 1981. Cyrus Tang, a scrap steel dealer, took over the company, and he resumed the company's operation under the name McLouth Steel Products Corporation.

Several new steel firms were formed as a result of either spin-offs from larger companies or reorganizations of older companies. The largest of these companies, the Weirton Steel Corporation, was spun off by National Steel. The employees agreed to take an average 20 percent cut in pay, and the company kept its product quality high. Consequently, it was quite profitable during the first years of its existence (1984 to 1988).

Three other firms were founded in the 1980s to take over facilities that other companies had divested. The Dearborn, Michigan steel plant of the Ford Motor Company was spun off and run by a new firm, the Rouge Steel Company; it was a fully integrated firm with BFs and a BOF shop. As a result of the antitrust restrictions on the merger of Jones & Laughlin and Republic, a new steel firm, the Gulf States Steel Corporation, was organized to run the steel plant at Gadsden, Alabama. It also had a BF, a BOF furnace shop, and rolling mills. The Kaiser Steel Corporation in southern California lost a great deal of money in the early 1980s because of low demand and high capital expenditures. As a result, a new group backed by the Kawasaki Steel Company of Japan and CVRD, a Brazilian iron ore company, reopened the mill. It abandoned the front-end iron and steel facilities and proceeded to purchase steel slabs and blooms for its rolling mills from Japan.

In general, this period was one of retrenchment for both large and small integrated steel firms. Almost all of them experienced losses in the 1980s. One very large (LTV) and two small firms (Wheeling-Pittsburgh and McLouth) went into bankruptcy and came out with smaller capacity.

Old EF firms

The second class of steel firm in this era consisted of the old integrated firms that changed their basic technology from the fully integrated process to the scrap-fed EF. Among these firms were CF&I, Lukens, and McLouth after its bankruptcy.

Two examples can give an idea of the situations of these firms: CF&I and Lukens. In 1970, CF&I was owned by the Crane Company. CF&I operated its home plant in Pueblo, Colorado and four steel plants in the East. By the 1980s, it had abandoned the East Coast plants. Its Pueblo plant was fully integrated with BFs, BOF converters, and a new rail mill. CF&I's market focus was on rails for the railroads and tube and pipe for the oil industry. The 1982 recession hit CF&I especially hard due to its focus on rails and oil country goods.

In response to these conditions, the company shut down its BFs and BOF shop and became an EF producer. The parent company, Crane, tried to sell CF&I to other firms, but failed. Then, it offered the plant to the employees who set up an Employee Stock Option Plan (ESOP). Under the leadership of Frank J. Yaklich, the company had returned to profitability by 1988.

In 1970, the Lukens Steel Company was a fully integrated steel firm that specialized in plate steel used on navy ships. The company prospered in the 1970s. Lukens built two new EFs, thereby relying totally on that technology. In 1978, it purchased the plate rolling mills of the bankrupt Alan Wood Steel Company. Because of its dependence on defense work, this company was less affected by the 1980s recession than its larger rivals, but it still lost money in some years. By 1988, it was profitable.

The minimills

The third class of steel firms operating during this period were the EF firms called minimills. Most of these firms started out as EF companies that either serviced a small geographic market, sold a narrow product line, or both. Most firms remained small one-plant operations, but some grew to be quite large, building more than one plant. Here, we examine two of the latter type of firm: Nucor and Florida Steel (Ameristeel).

The Nucor Corporation was the successor company of the REO Motor Company. It originally built automobiles and trucks but then switched product lines to various high-tech defense products and building materials. One division made joists, the steel frameworks that hold up the roofs of a large building. F. Kenneth Iverson, the head of that division, was never satisfied with the prices of the steel. Using his background in metals, Iverson built an EF mill. Not only could he supply Nucor with joist steel, but he could also sell construction items to other customers.

From the plant in South Carolina, Nucor expanded into other parts of the country, selling construction bars and other low-tech materials. Steel plants were built in Nebraska, Utah, and Texas. This success led the firm to broaden its horizons. First, Nucor formed a joint venture with Yamato Steel of Japan to make large structural beams at Blythesville, Arkansas. Nucor's second move out of its niche was a plan to use EF steel to make sheets at Crawfordsville, Indiana.

Nucor was notoriously anti-union, and none of its plant had a union. While the base wages were lower than the union plants, incentive systems often led to higher pay.

A second firm, the Florida Steel Corporation, had a more conservative strategy than Nucor. Its main thrust was selling rebar, rods and small structurals (special steel pieces used in construction). In the 1980s, it had five plants in Florida, North Carolina, and Tennessee. One authority stated, "Unlike some of the larger minimill companies, Florida Steel has maintained a narrow product line and geographic focus" (Crandall in Seely, 1994, p. 137).

Throughout this period, the bulk of the minimills remained one-plant firms. While most focused on simple construction items like rebar, wire rods, and structurals, some moved out into other areas. Looking at the following two firms gives one an idea of the situation faced by most minimills: the Georgetown Steel Corporation and the Roanoke Electric Steel Corporation.

The first firm, the Georgetown Steel Corporation, followed the usual practice of producing rebar and rod for wire. Like many firms, the Georgetown workers were organized by the USW, but the pay was still not as high as integrated mills. The plant was unusual in one way. In the 1980s, it was the only minimill plant in the United States that had a direct reduction furnace for making iron from ore. Therefore, Georgetown Steel did not totally rely on scrap steel.

Built in 1962, the Roanoke Electric Steel Corporation of Roanoke, Virginia was one of the oldest minimills. It produced rebar and other construction items. It was non-union, and it paid lower wages than the traditional steel firms. While conservative on technology, Roanoke Steel did install a continuous caster in the 1960s. In many ways, it typified the minimill firm.

Imports

In the 1970s and 1980s, the American steel firms were not alone in the market. Imports to the United States had become a major influence in the 1960s, and the influence grew in this period. In absolute terms, imports rose from 14,609,000 tons in 1970 to 22,056,000 tons in 1989 (see Table 9.1). Their market share rose from 11.1 percent in 1970 to 22.5 percent in 1989. Steel imports did not increase in a linear fashion. In 1984, both the absolute amount and the percentage reached their peak of 29,548,000 tons and 31.9 percent respectively. Still, the general trend was up.

Many authorities have criticized the inability of American companies to hold onto their home market, citing technological ineptness. Some Japanese and European firms did have lower costs than those in the United States. The former companies not only paid lower wages but also had greater total factor productivity. Japanese and other foreign firms had also used newly discovered sources of iron ore that reduced their costs to below those of the United States. Given the new advantages of foreign firms, and the high cost of many American plants, it is not surprising that imports increased. However, these conditions alone could not explain the rise of imports.

To see why, first one must look at conditions in the world steel industry. From 1950 to 1974, world steel production rose at an almost steady rate from 207,000,000 tons to 767,000,000 tons. After 1974, world production leveled off. In 1988, it was 859,539,000 tons. Many countries, including the United States were caught with excess capacity.

This led to the problem of steel companies operating below capacity. Such firms were faced with an incentive to increase their output, even if it meant selling some steel at prices below total unit cost. Typically, steel firms had relatively high fixed costs, and their variable costs could be quite low compared to the price that would cover total average cost. If the price obtained for a given amount of steel was greater than the average variable cost, they could increase profits (lower losses) by making the sale. The problem was that they could not make a profit or break even if they sell all their output at the price near average variable cost. Therefore, they have to price discriminate, charging some customers a price high enough to cover incremental cost plus the bulk of the fixed cost but charging just above incremental costs to others. This calls for separating the high-price customers from the low-price customers.

National borders can be ideal separators. Therefore, a firm could sell its output in its home country at the high price and at lower prices to customers in other countries. Often the latter prices would be below the fully covered unit cost. Usually, the home government helped the domestic companies by preventing firms from other countries from selling steel within its borders. The practice of taking advantage of this situation and selling below total cost steel in other countries is called dumping.

American companies believed dumping to be very common in this period. While not all, or maybe not even most, steel coming into America was dumped, it is certain that some of it was. The 1974 slowdown in world steel growth put many firms in positions to dump, and other factors increased its likelihood. Political considerations in many countries prevented firms from eliminating obsolete plant capacity. To keep these plants going, many foreign governments gave their companies subsidies, either direct or in the form of low interest loans. While many foreign firms were government owned, private companies often received similar subsidies. Howell *et al.* (p. 24) states:

> A large integrated steel plant employs thousands of people and can account for most of the economic activity (employment, taxes, income, etc.) in a given community or geographic region. This means that any changes in the plant's economic fortunes have a huge impact on the local economy, one of the major reasons that intervention by national governments has been pervasive.

Furthermore, in many countries, firms continued to add plants even when it was obvious that the new demand for product was not there. For instance, Italy continued to build its plant at Tarento in the south.

Even in the United States, political considerations led to some expansion. In spite of surfeit of rail capacity, the federal government lent Pittsburgh-Wheeling Steel the funds to build its rail mill at Monessen. Foreigners often brought up this case when Americans confronted them with the problem of steel subsidies. The consequence of all this expansion was that many foreign plants operated at below capacity, and therefore, they had high incentives to dump steel into the United States.

In the United States, no firms (with the exception of Pittsburgh-Wheeling Steel for its plant at Monessen) were given major subsidies to either expand or maintain production. Consequently, American steel firms felt that they were at a disadvantage because the government did not subsidize their operations. To them, this situation justified the various trade barriers that the Nixon, Carter, and Reagan administrations instituted (*Iron Age*, June 27, 1977, p. 22, *Iron Age*, May 21, 1981, p. 39, and *Iron Age*, May 7, 1984, p. 24). In spite of the trade restrictions, the import of steel into the United States continued to increase.

Among the companies, this period was characterized by much more change than the postwar and even Depression years. First, two of the Big Eight firms, Republic Steel and Youngstown Sheet & Tube, ceased to exist, being merged with Jones & Laughlin into LTV Steel. Some of the smaller steel firms, such as CF&I and Lukens, changed from fully integrated operations to EF firms. One other firm, Alan Wood, went out of business. All of these firms were challenged by a new set of companies, the minimills. Finally, imports continued to increase, further weakening the hold of the old large integrated firms.

Substitutes

One of the reasons given for the troubles in the steel industry was the growth of substitutes. To see the situation in substitutes, we re-examine the customer sectors where substitutes were important: containers, automotive, construction, and appliances. With containers, steel definitely lost market share in this period, mostly to aluminum and some to plastics. Between 1970 and 1988, aluminum's share of the beer and soft drink can market rose from 9 percent to 96 percent. Tin-plated steel was essentially driven out of the beer and soda can segment. In the food sector of the can industry, however, tin-plate held onto its market share because it worked better with most foods. Thus, it was not clear how much more business aluminum would get (Marley in *Iron Age*, November 1988, p. 28). Hogan (1994, p. 134) stated: "Tinplate seems to have a dominant share of the food-can market and to some extent general-line cans."

As discussed on pages 135–136, steel use in the automotive industry declined in this period, but it was not that much due to the substitution of other materials. Between 1977 and 1990, the average amount of steel in a car dropped from 2,202 pounds to 1,564 pounds (Standard and Poors, July 4, 2002, p. 13 and Hogan, 1994, p. 127). This change came partly from the redesign of the car body to a less metal intensive configuration called unibody construction (Guiles, in *Iron Age*, October 26, 1972, p. 21 and Berry in *Iron Age*, July 1987, p. 31). In the 1980s, the total amounts of aluminum and plastic in the average car rose from 130 and 195 pounds respectively to 158 pounds and 220 pounds. Nonetheless, neither plastics nor aluminum were close to replacing steel as the main part of an automobile.

The third area where steel encountered major substitutes was construction. From the 1940s to the 1970s, steel structural products lost market share to reinforced concrete, especially in the commercial and industrial sectors of the construction industry. In the 1980s, steel structurals began to hold onto the commercial and industrial construction sectors. Against reinforced concrete, the steel structural share of the market varied between 42 percent and 52 percent in the years of that decade.

In the 1980s, steel started to make inroads against wood in some construction uses. Prefabricated steel buildings were being built more often, especially for warehouses. Steel started to replace wood as the studs used in room partitions. In the 1970s, almost all studs were wood. After that decade, steel studs became very common.

Thus, in construction, steel seemed to be holding its share. One of the reasons for the contrary impression was the way the steel consumption statistics are compiled. Construction is listed in a separate heading which shows the product that the steel companies shipped directly to the construction firms. As Table 9.3A shows, that figure dropped slightly over the period. In contrast, the consumption listed under the steel service centers increased. Much of the output going to the service centers went to construction firms. This further implies that steel held its own against substitutes in this sector.

The fourth sector where substitutes were important was appliances. In this sector, steel was often replaced by plastics, but some of the loss can be accounted for by the use of lighter steel instead of substitutes. By the mid-1980s, however, the steel firms had started to strike back by working with the manufacturers on how to use steel better in their products.

Therefore, while having some truth, the claim that substitutes cut into steel in this period is somewhat overstated. More important in explaining the losses to the steel industry were three other changes: the decrease in the portion of GDP taken up by steel-intensive products, the use of lighter and stronger steel, and the growth of imports (Hogan, 1994, pp. 92–6).

Input supplies

Five steel inputs evoked significant concern in this period: iron ore, coal, scrap steel, electricity, and labor. The fifth, labor, constituted the largest part of steel costs, and its complex problems call for a separate subsection. Before getting to labor, however, the events concerning the other inputs will be discussed.

Iron ore, coal, scrap steel, electricity

Iron ore, coal, scrap steel, and electricity were resources with which North America was well endowed, but special problems were encountered with each in the 1970s and 1980s. Most North American iron ore deposits were located in northern Minnesota, Michigan, and Canada. There was still ample supply, but over time its average quality had deteriorated. The average iron content of the ore mined in the early twentieth century was about 60 percent, and by the 1970s, the steel companies used ore with a content of between 20 percent and 30 percent. Exacerbating these problems were the large amounts of capital needed for plants to prepare the low grade ore for use in the BFs.

In the meantime, extensive exploration efforts found huge deposits of high grade iron ore in Venezuela, Brazil, Africa, and Australia. Most of these new non-American deposits went to Japan, Europe, and other areas.

In the early 1970s, the worldwide steel boom led American firms to build additional plants to refine the low grade American iron ore into the pellets suitable for the BFs. The companies feared that foreign ores would become overly expensive. When world demand declined in the late 1970s and early 1980s, American firms were caught with too much ore-refining capacity. With the 1980s demand conditions, they could easily obtain iron ore on the world markets. (For a more in-depth discussion of this problem, see Barnett and Schorsch, 1983, p. 297–307.)

The total cost of obtaining ore from the refining plant was often greater than the cost of importing ore. For some firms, however, it still made sense to use the refined ore. The incremental cost of the refined ore was still less than that of the imported ore. In other situations, the cost of buying the foreign iron was lower than the incremental cost of the firm using its refined ore. In those cases, it would have made sense to import iron ore. In many cases, however, the companies felt that there were risks from using foreign ore that justified the continued use of the refined ore. One article put it this way:

> Whether iron ore is owned or purchased, there has to be a fixed obligation, says E. G. Jaicks, chairman of Inland Steel. He doubts that outside purchases can be made in quantity without strings. "I assume these people have some sort of liability," he says.
>
> (*Iron Age*, May 4, 1981, p. MP-25)

Still, while they may have wasted a great deal of money securing a domestic source, American steel companies did not face a major problem obtaining iron ore during this period.

As with iron ore, obtaining coal was not a major problem for American steel firms. By one estimate, the United States had enough metallurgical coal to last almost 200 years (Hogan, 1994, p. 101). There was some concern with differing qualities of the coal, but most experts did not see a major problem (Hogan, 1994, p. 102).

Rather, the major difficulty facing steel firms was the lack of coke ovens to convert coal into coke. Partly because of new environmental requirements, these ovens required a great deal of capital. Consequently, in the late 1980s, some companies were caught short of coke, and thus, they occasionally imported (usually from Canada). Hogan (1983, p. 102) summed up the situation in the 1980s: "At the current rate of operations, the existing coke ovens are adequate. If demand for steel should increase significantly, there could be a problem."

The third major input was scrap steel. To understand the scrap problem, one has to examine the types of scrap. Three classes of scrap existed: mill revert scrap, which was generated within the steel mills; prompt industrial scrap, which came from the process of manufacturing steel products; and obsolete scrap, which came from abandoned steel products such as cars, appliances, and torn-down buildings. The move by integrated firms to the basic oxygen furnace (BOF) initially increased the supply of revert scrap to the minimills. Like its open hearth predecessors, the BOF uses scrap steel, but the maximum proportion of the BOF iron charge from scrap was about 30 percent. The open hearth furnace could and did use much more, and thus its replacement by the BOF temporarily led to an excess supply of scrap.

The problem with obsolete scrap was its quality. Without very careful screening of the scrap input, it could be very difficult to produce a high-quality steel from scrap. Thus, the EF firms needed to be very careful about the quality of scrap they used. While scrap quality seemed to be a concern in the 1980s, moves by Nucor and other firms into high-quality products suggest that it was solvable.

Electricity, the fourth major input into steel, increased in importance with the advent of the minimill. Electricity accounted for about 12 percent of the total cost of a minimill. Some of the electricity went to the rolling mills (as it would in integrated mills), but most was used by the steel furnace. (For a contemporary analysis of the electricity supply situation, see Barnett and Crandall, 1986, pp. 85–94.)

Between 1974 and 1982, industrial electricity prices rose almost 300 percent, but they leveled off in the mid 1980s. Even with this great increase, the ratio between minimill costs and integrated mill cost still dropped. The energy costs of the latter rose by 325 percent, while the basic energy cost of the state-of-the-art minimill rose by only 290 percent (Barnett and Crandall, 1986, pp. 87–8). Consequently, electricity prices did not hinder the growth of the EF.

There was, however, some concern about the availability of electricity to the minimills in certain areas. (For an example of this problem, see Preston, 1992, pp. 179–80.) Thus, the electricity situation did not present a major problem for the steel industry.

Labor

With labor, the major development in the 1970s and 1980s was the decline in steel industry employment. Table 9.6 documents the drop in both total employment in SIC 3312, Blast Furnaces and Steel Mills. SIC 3312 is the statistical data unit used by the Department of Commerce that best represents the steel industry. While production fell, its descent is not anywhere near as great as the drop in employment. Between 1970 and 1988, steel production dropped 24 percent, while total steel employment dropped over 59 percent. Here, we first give an indication of the proportion of the total drop that can be assigned to either falling production, increasing labor productivity, or imports. Then, we look at the reactions to this situation by the steel unions and companies.

The Appendix to this chapter details an analysis of the causes of the employment loss between 1970 and 1988. The analysis shown in Table 9.A first breaks down the

Table 9.6 Average number of employees of SIC 3312, blast furnaces and steel mills and total steel production per employee, 1965–1988

Year	All employees	Total steel production	Production per employee
1950	674,000	96,836,000	144
1955	635,000	117,036,000	184
1960	651,000	99,282,000	153
1965	657,000	131,462,000	200
1970	627,000	131,514,000	210
1973	606,000	150,800,000	249
1975	548,000	116,600,000	213
1980	512,000	111,835,000	218
1982	394,000	74,577,000	189
1984	335,000	92,528,000	276
1985	303,000	88,359,000	292
1990	276,000	98,906,000	358

Source: U.S. Bureau of the Census, 1960–2005.

loss in employment between the declining output and increasing labor productivity. For the year 1990, the Appendix calculations indicate that the loss of 155,460 jobs can be attributed to lower output, and 195,540 lost jobs can be attributed to increased labor productivity. The percentage breakdowns were 44.3 for decreased output and 55.7 for increased productivity. Therefore, increased productivity, on the average, accounted for over half of the drop in employment.

With the method described in the Appendix, we estimate the effect of imports by breaking the output change-induced job loss into two components: that accounted for by rising imports and that accounted for by falling domestic demand. For 1990, our estimate of the losses from 1970 due to imports is 12,930, 3.7 percent of the total. Because imports vary from year to year, we look at the changes for 1988, a year when imports were particularly high. For that year, our estimate of the losses from 1970 due to imports is 62,093, 17.7 percent of the total. As shown in the Appendix, these are upper bound estimates for both years due to a conservative productivity assumption. Given these figures, it is clear that while their impact was not trivial, imports were not responsible for the bulk of the job loss. Rather, the increasing labor productivity was responsible for most of it.

With the rise in productivity, there are several issues. Increasing labor productivity can be attributed to either the substitution away from labor due to rising wages or to labor-saving technological improvements. For integrated mills, however, the installations of the BOF furnaces and continuous casters were labor saving. Larger BFs and new rolling mills were also labor saving. The move of much production from integrated firms to minmills also lowered the labor use because the iron-making step of the process was eliminated. These changes provided the environment for the actions of the unions and companies.

The production worker sector of the steel labor market can be viewed as one with a dominant firm and a fringe. Most steel production workers were members of the

United Steelworkers (USW). Some plants, however, either did not have a union or had their own. Examples of the latter were the Weirton plant of National Steel and the Middletown plant of Armco Steel. A significant portion of the minimills (but not all) were non-union, examples being Nucor and Roanoke. Therefore, it is important to analyze first, the activities of the USW during this period, and second, the issues concerning non-union labor.

The 1970s started well for the USW with a settlement in 1971 that gave them a 30 percent wage increase over three years and a cost-of-living escalator. One problem, however, concerned the union President, Iorwith W. Abel. Stockpiling of steel in anticipation of a strike led customers to build up inventory. This all led to layoffs once the strike was settled.

To deal with this problem, Abel considered the no-strike compulsory arbitration proposal, made by U.S. Steel labor negotiator, Richard C. Cooper, in 1968. By this plan, the union and companies would automatically submit their differences to arbitration rather than strike or lockout. Many union officials in the union hierarchy favored the idea, but there was strong opposition from some in the rank and file. In 1973, Abel won his final election to the presidency of the USW before compulsory retirement. Therefore, he did not fear the repercussions of an unpopular stance.

In 1974, he negotiated a new contract with U.S. Steel Vice Chairman, R. Heath Larry, who represented all the large steel firms, through the Coordinating Committee Steel Companies. As a result of this contract, the union renounced the strike, and the companies promised not to use the lockout. Other differences were to be submitted to outside arbitration. Since the companies and the union agreed to end or renew this provision at the end of each contract period, the plan was called the Experimental Negotiating Agreement (ENA).

In the 1974 contract, the union received a 35 percent raise (Kalwa in Seely, 1994, p. 118). To placate any opposition, Abel inserted in the 1974 ENA an allowance for local strikes on local issues.

In 1976, Abel's hand-picked successor as union president, Lloyd McBride, was challenged by Edward E. Sadlowski, a local official in the Chicago area. While McBride easily won the election, Sadlowski ran a strong campaign. It was obvious that he represented a militant view that the leadership had to consider. Sadlowski and his followers thought that the workers should get more wages and benefits than the union central leadership thought prudent or possible.

The union was able to negotiate a renewal of the ENA in 1977. In return, they got an extensive set of benefits relating to retirement and layoff pay.

In 1980, a new contract was negotiated, which gave the workers some wage increases but did not renew the Experimental Negotiating Agreement. By the next contract date in 1983, the troubles of the industry had caught up with the union, and the resulting contract actually lowered the worker's wages. McBride had difficulty getting the local unions to agree to the contract, and in the middle of the discussions, he had a heart attack. The union vice president, Joseph Odorcich, finished the approval process. McBride died later that year.

After the 1983 contract, the union no longer bargained with the Coordinating Committee Steel Companies, but made separate contracts with each company.

With most companies, it made for further concessions. With U.S. Steel, the result was a strike in 1986, which still led to concessions by the union. The most noted thing about the USW experience in this period was the wage successes in the 1970s and the rollbacks in the 1980s.

In the 1970s, American steel wages rose in comparison with other industries. Between 1973 and 1982, steel wages rose from being 50 percent greater than the average for all manufacturing to about 100 percent greater than the average (Barnett and Crandall, 1986, p. 4). In the 1980s, the union lowered wages in often futile efforts to keep plants open. The actions of the union were relevant to the dramatic increase in labor productivity during this period.

Some would argue that the wage increases led companies to substitute capital for labor, even in situations where the total factor productivity did not rise. Were this the case, the unions were irrational. Earlier concessions on wages and work rules might have allowed more plants to continue operations.

Another theory is that technology was changing in a labor-saving way, and union wages had little to do with the loss of jobs. In that case, there was little the union could do to prevent the catastrophe to its workers. In fact, the rational course would have been to get as much benefit as possible before the fall. Barnett and Crandall (1986, p. 42) explain this view, "One suggestion is that the union may have been playing an endgame, extracting as much of the quasi-rents as possible from the industry . . ." (For other views, see Blonigen and Wilson, 2005 and Tornell, 1997.) Which of these scenarios corresponded most with reality is not clear.

The final labor question concerns the role of the non-union sector. Among the minimills, many firms were totally convinced that their success was due to their ability to run their plants without the restrictive union rules. Nucor was the prime example of this situation (Iverson, 1998). While their wages were lower than those of the union firms, the company incentive systems were such that their workers often had more income than the union members. The success of these companies leads one to wonder what would have happened if the USW and the old integrated companies had been able to reach a better accommodation.

The influence of government

Government policy had a significant impact on the steel industry in three areas: antitrust, environmental protection, and trade policy. Of the three, the last had the most importance, but the others were not insignificant.

The major focus of antitrust policy was on joint ventures and mergers. In the late 1980s, the department became more lenient than in the past. This led to approval of a series of ventures between American and Japanese firms in the late 1980s. Among them were the co-ownership of National Steel by National Intergroup and Nippon Kokan and the joint venture between Kobe Steel and U.S. Steel at Lorain, Ohio.

In contrast, the justice department was reluctant to approve any merger that increased concentration. Almost the only way that firms were allowed to merge was with the "failing firm" argument. This provision allowed the two largest steel mergers in this period, those between Jones & Laughlin and Youngstown Sheet &

Tube (1979) and between LTV and Republic Steel (1984). Both of the acquirees, Youngstown Sheet & Tube and Republic, were on the verge of bankruptcy (McManus in *Iron Age*, March 5, 1984, p. 48 and Benedict in *Iron Age*, March 7, 1983, p. 7).

A good indication of the department's attitude was its proscription of the merger between U.S. Steel and National Steel in 1984. Since National Steel was not a failing firm, the justice department felt its acquisition would increase concentration.

The second area where government policy impacted the steel industry was pollution control. The passage of the Clean Air Act of 1970 and the Federal Water Pollution Control Act of 1972 plus the founding of the Environmental Protection Agency (EPA) led to a major effort to clean up pollution. It was not surprising that attention would be given to the steel industry. The pollution from the mills was well known. According to one historical account, "In the late 1960s the [steel] industry was responsible for 10 percent of the air pollution in the United States and a third of all industrial waste-water discharge"(Reynolds in Seely, 1994, p. 354).

The industry did succeed in reducing the pollution coming from its plants. By 1979, the amount of particulates it removed reached 95 percent of the total. By 1977, it removed 80.7 percent of the acid from its fluent discharges (Reynolds in Seely, 1994, p. 354). Still, many people were not satisfied, and as more and more contaminants were eliminated, the law of diminishing returns set in, raising the cost of eliminating the remainder.

By 1984, the steel companies had spent about $6 billion on pollution control. Many critics have pointed to this expenditure as one of the reasons that American steel had such a difficult time in this period (Mueller, 1984, p. 129). Nonetheless, other countries also had high pollution standards. Japan spent $5.5 billion fulfilling its requirements. Consequently, although not insignificant, the pollution control effort was not the major cause of the industry's troubles.

In the 1970s and 1980s, the United States government made three attempts to protect the domestic industry from imports. First, the Voluntary Restraint Agreements (VRAs) were instituted under the Lyndon Johnson administration in 1969 and carried forward by President Richard Nixon. Under VRA, Japan and the European Community agreed to limit their U.S.-bound exports to 5,400,000 tons in 1969 and somewhat higher amounts in 1970 and 1971. Other countries did not go along with the program. Imports decreased in 1969 and 1970, but due to the fear of a steel strike, they rose in 1971. Consequently, the VRAs were renewed in 1972 with quotas of 6,500,000 tons for Japan and 8,000,000 tons for the European Community. With the world steel boom of 1973 and 1974, quotas seemed no longer necessary, so they were dropped.

After 1974, the steel industry went into a recession, and imports increased as steel mills in other countries became desperate for customers. This led to accusations of dumping and pressure to find ways to protect the industry. As a result, the James Carter administration instituted a rather unique program called the Trigger Price Mechanism (TPM). It set a floor on the prices of steel imports into the United States. This floor was essentially a calculation of the average Japanese per ton cost of production plus an 8 percent unit profit. This action did seem to lower imports in

1979, 1980, and 1981. With the 1982 recession, the companies demanded even more import controls. Furthermore, certain products, such as specialty steels, seemed to come into the country despite the TPM.

In response to a rash of dumping cases in 1982, Ronald Reagan's administration made an agreement with the European Community to limit its share to 5.44 percent of the American market. This was essentially a return to Voluntary Restraint Agreements. Japan did not get a quota, and its exports to the United States increased, but political pressure resulted in them dropping imports in 1983. There was also a large flow of steel from undeveloped countries. This resulted in more dumping cases.

This situation led the government to renegotiate the quotas in 1985 to cover the years through 1988. This time the quotas pertained to the narrowly defined products. Certain countries, however, would not go along with the program. Thus, the steel companies were not satisfied. (For detailed accounts, see Jones, 1986 and Howell, *et al.*, 1988.)

An important thing to question is the reason for these trade programs. Crandall (1981, p. 94) cites two normative arguments, unfair competition and national defense, but he found little that could support either of them. Others asserted that trade protection would give the industry a chance to rebuild itself, but Mueller (1984, pp. 75–82) argued that, during the VRA periods, the industry lessened its efforts to increase its efficiency.

A definite reason for the existence of the trade policy was the political clout of the steel companies and the USW. In the late 1960s, a group of federal legislators, led by Senators Hugh Scott of Pennsylvania and Vance Hartke of Indiana, organized the Steel Caucus to look after the steel industry (Bowers, *Iron Age*, October 23, 1978, p. 45). It did much to foment the U.S. trade policies.

Conclusion

Another look at the events of the 1970s and 1980s will help put the period in perspective. During this time, American steel production dropped 24 percent, and steel industry employment fell 59 percent. Two major firms, Republic Steel and Youngstown Sheet & Tube, went out of existence, and many steel plants owned by other firms shut down.

Accompanying the fall in production was an increase in imports and the rise of a new set of steel companies – the minimills. Previously, it was shown that the import increase could not have destroyed that many jobs. A rough estimate of the jobs lost from 1970 due to imports for 1988 and 1990 are 62,093 and 12,930 respectively out of the total of about 398,000.

Consequently, other things led to the drop in employment. EF production rose from 10.5 percent to 35.9 percent of output. Since they used less labor, they did contribute to the employment drop. Furthermore, the major technological innovations in the integrated sector (larger BFs, the BOF converters, and the continuous casters) were labor-saving. Thus, technological change led to lower employment.

This still leaves the question of whether there was a major substitution of capital for labor, due to the high wage settlements obtained by the USW. It is not clear at this time how much of an impact these settlements had. One theory posits that there was little the union could do to prevent employment from dropping, and therefore, its best policy was to extract as much money as it could. Aside from experts, some union leaders believed this theory; among them was Edward E. Sadlowski, the unsuccessful 1976 candidate for USW president (Serrin, 1992, p. 321).

The fourth element present in these decades, and for the first time in the twentieth century, was the intermittent, but systematic, effort by the federal government to protect the steel industry from imports. Again, it is not clear that the policy was successful; imports rose from 11.1 percent to 22.5 percent of American production. Since imports did not account for much of the employment loss, this protection effort did little to protect jobs. The great loss of jobs in the steel industry points to a general problem that may need attention from society as a whole. With large industries, where jobs are not that secure, how can society protect people from these great changes? Perhaps, a compensation or insurance plan can be established that would protect people from the effects of change.

Appendix

Table 9.A breaks down the loss in employment into parts that can be accounted for by (1) declining output, (2) changing imports, (3) declining output net of import and productivity change, and (4) increasing labor productivity. The table shows the losses in total employment between 1970 and selected years and the drops that can be associated with each of these changes. Table 9.A first splits the total loss into that due to falling output and that due to increased labor productivity. For the change due to falling production, we calculate the number of workers needed to produce the later years' output assuming the 1970 labor/output ratio, and then subtract it from the 1970 employment (column 5 in Table 9.A). The following formula portrays this figure:

Year I job loss due to falling production =
1970 employment – [(1970 labor/output ratio)* year I output]

To find the change in employment due to increasing labor productivity or better technology, we calculate the difference between the number of workers needed to produce the later years' output with the 1970 labor/output ratio and the actual number of workers employed in that year (column 8 in Table 9.A). The formula for this figure is:

Year I job loss due to productivity =
[(1970 labor/output ratio)* year I output] – actual year I employment

These two differences added together amount to the total loss in employment between 1970 and the given years (column 9 in Table 9.A). To illustrate, for the

Table 9.A Analysis of the change in steel industry employment (SIC 3312, blast furnaces and steel mills), 1970–1988

(1)	(2)	(3)	(4)	(5)	(6)	(7)	(8)	(9)
				Loss in total employment*				
		Total production (in tons)	Tons per employee	Due to production change	Due to change in imports	Net of import and technology change	Due to technology change	Total loss
Year	Employment							
1975	548,000	116,600,000	213	71,103 (90.0)	-3,290 (-4.2)	74,393 (94.2)	7,897 (10.0)	79,000
1975	548,000	116,600,000	213	71,103 (90.0)	-3,290 (-4.2)	74,393 (94.2)	7,897 (10.0)	79,000
1980	512,000	111,835,000	218	93,821 (81.6)	15,585 (13.6)	78,236 (68.0)	21,179 (18.4)	115,000
1985	303,000	88,359,000	292	205,744 (63.5)	71,222 (22.0)	134,522 (41.5)	118,256 (36.5)	324,000
1988	277,000	99,924,000	361	150,607 (43.0)	62,093 (17.7)	88,514 (25.3)	199,393 (57.0)	350,000
1990	276,000	98,906,000	358	155,460 (44.3)	12,930 (3.7)	142,530 (40.6)	195,540 (55.7)	351,000

Source: U.S. Bureau of the Census, 1960–2005.

* Percentages of the total loss are in parentheses under the relevant number.

year 1990, these calculations indicate that the loss of 155,460 workers can be attributed to lower output, and 195,540 workers lost jobs can be attributed to increasing productivity.

To account for the influence of imports, we separate loss due to falling output from the drop in output due to rising imports. To do this, we assume that imports stayed at their 1970 level, and then we calculate the difference between the 1970 imports and the current year imports. This gives the change in production that would result from keeping imports at their 1970 level. From this, we calculate the jobs lost by multiplying the difference in imports between the two years by the 1970 labor/output ratio. This gives an estimate of the jobs lost due to the increase in imports (column 6 in Table 9.A). Here is the formula:

Year I job loss due to imports
= (year I imports – 1970 imports)* (1970 labor/output ratio)

In the one year listed, 1975, there were fewer imports than in 1970, and consequently, this loss would be a gain. Thus, it is listed as a negative loss in Table 9.A.

There is an assumption worth mentioning: the use of the 1970 output/labor ratio to compute the employment losses due to changing imports. Since technology is obviously progressing, an increase in output due to lower imports might be better reflected by a change based on the current technology. Thus, our estimates of the import-caused losses are overstated, but some authorities assert that if the industry was protected more from international competition, the technological progress would be lower (Mueller, 1984). Thus, our job loss estimate could reasonably be seen as an upper bound. To give us a lower bound of the jobs lost from imports, we computed the job loss assuming current technology. For 1988, it was 36,104 job compared to the estimate in Table 9.A of 62,093, and for 1990, when imports were much lower, it was 7,568 job compared to the Table 9.A estimate of 12,930. Thus, these calculations convey a reasonable idea of the range in impacts of increasing imports.

10 Uneasy stability
1990 to 2001

Introduction

The last period covered by this book is the eleven years between 1990 and 2001. Here we refer to this period as the 1990s. Until its very end, this was a period of stability with minor fluctuations in production, but there were signs of trouble. The minimills continued to grow and expand into new products. This boded especially ill for integrated companies. In addition, other countries ran into economic difficulties thereby cutting off their demand for steel. This led to increased exports to the United States, often making minimill companies just as vulnerable to import competition as the integrated firms.

Before proceeding, however, an examination of some data from this period provides perspective. As Table 10.1 shows, total production fluctuated, but it did not change drastically during the period, going from 98,906,000 tons in 1990 to 99,321,000 tons in 2001, fluctuating with the American business cycle from the recession in the early 1990s to the boom of the late 1990s.

Table 10.1 Steel production, imports, net sales (in dollars) and profits, 1989–2001

Year	Total production	Production share of electric furnace	Imports	Net sales	Net income
1990	98,906,000	37.3	17,321,000	$30,635,000,000	$54,000,000
1991	87,896,000	38.4	15,845,000	26,871,000,000	−2,042,000,000
1992	92,949,000	38.0	17,075,000	26,855,000,000	−4,068,000,000
1993	97,877,000	39.4	19,501,000	29,416,000,000	1,870,000,000
1994	100,579,000	39.3	30,066,000	33,890,000,000	1,285,000,000
1995	104,930,000	40.4	24,409,000	34,884,000,000	1,534,000,000
1996	105,309,000	42.6	29,164,000	34,702,000,000	442,000,000
1997	108,561,000	43.8	31,157,000	36,367,000,000	1,031,000,000
1998	108,752,000	45.1	41,520,000	37,917,000,000	1,110,000,000
1999	107,395,000	46.3	35,731,000	36,099,000,000	−464,000,000
2000	112,242,000	47.0	37,957,000	36,962,000,000	−1,007,000,000
2001	99,321,000	47.4	30,080,000	28,636,000,000	−3,801,000,000

Source: American Iron and Steel Institute, *Annual Statistical Report*, various years.

Imports grew but they did not reach the previous high level (1984) until 1997. In 1998, however, imports rose almost 25 percent. This was partly due to high American demand and partly due to the crash in the East Asian economies that attenuated their demand for steel.

By then, these problems caught up with some firms, resulting in the bankruptcies of Bethlehem Steel and LTV Steel. In 2001, production dropped in line with the recession, and total steel firm losses rose to $3,801,000,000.

An analysis of steel during the 1990s using our taxonomy is an efficient way to examine these issues. As in other chapters, the changes in the production process are first examined. Then, the uses of steel during this period are scrutinized. Subsequently, we analyze competitors including integrated firms, minimills, and foreign producers. Next, we look at developments in steel substitutes. Then, the conditions in the major input markets, coal, iron ore, electricity, and labor, are analyzed. After that, we study the role of the government. Finally, some tentative conclusions are made.

Production and the production process

During this period, electric furnace (EF) production rose from 37.3 percent of output to 47.4 percent. Interestingly, the shift was not so much due to the changes in steel converters as to changes in the shaping and rolling technology. A new type of continuous caster, the thin slab machine, made it economical to produce usable steel sheet with an EF.

To fully understand the importance of this change, it is necessary to examine events in each part of the steel process: the smelting of iron, the conversion of iron into steel, and the shaping (or rolling) of the steel into useable pieces. As of the late 1990s, the major way to smelt iron ore into iron remained the blast furnace (BF), but the growth of the scrap using EF steel lessened its importance.

Aside from EFs, there was one serious problem with the BF system, coke. Because of the increasingly strict environmental standards, there was a constant worry about shortfalls of coke. Due to the incursion of EF minimills, and the coke problem, the number of American BFs dropped from 50 in 1988 to 42 in 2001.

Scrap became the iron input of more and more mills, but this trend led to an interest in alternative ways of smelting iron from ore. There was a constant fear that scrap prices would rise to the point where minimills would not be competitive.

In response to this fear, research continued on alternatives to the BF (BF) – especially ones that could be coupled with EFs. Two major technologies came forth. One, direct reduction iron (DRI) furnaces, had been used earlier. Research continued on how to lower its cost. Several more DRI furnaces were built or planned for the United States.

Another technology was the iron carbide process where ore was converted into iron carbide, which could be fed into the EFs in conjunction with scrap. Nucor built an iron carbide plant in Trinidad. In 1999, however, the project was abandoned because it could not be commercialized and scrap prices dropped (Table 10.2). Anyhow, this price drop lowered the urgency of finding a new way of smelting iron.

Table 10.2 Steel scrap prices (per ton of No. 1 heavy melt scrap), 1987–2001

Year	Price
1990	$107.15
1991	93.26
1992	84.33
1993	128.67
1994	132.14
1995	141.98
1996	132.70
1997	132.54
1998	109.92
1999	95.61
2000	97.42
2001	76.18

Source: Standard & Poor's, September 2, 1993, p. S26 for 1987–1992, Standard & Poor's 1994–1996 and Standard & Poor's, 1997–2003 for the other dates.

"At present, the need to find solutions to the technological obstacles is not very pressing, given that scrap prices are too low to permit either of substitute projects – iron carbide and DRI – to be very profitable" (Standard and Poor's, January 17, 2002, p. 10).

As of 1988, there were three steel converter technologies operating in the United States, the basic oxygen (BOF), the Electric Furnace (EF), and the old open hearth (OH) processes. Due to an unusual rise in demand for certain products, the OH furnaces experienced a temporary resurgence in the late 1980s. With the 1990 recession, however, that died down, and the last OH furnace was closed in 1991.

Thus, the field was left to the BOFs and EFs. As of 1988, the type of product determined the type of furnace used. Sheets were the main product of the BOF integrated mills; specialty products, stainless steel, and simple construction items such as rebar and angles were the major products of the EF mills. Structurals, pipes, rails, and plates were made by both.

In the 1990s, the minimills moved into steel sheets. This was the result of the development of the new thin slab caster. This caster produced a slab that was only $1\frac{3}{4}$ inch thick as opposed the conventional slab that was 7 inches thick. The thinness of the slab cut down on the amount of rolling needed to make the final pieces. Since less rolling meant less machinery and labor, costs went down. Also, with lower capital costs, it became easier to enter the market. Thus, the integrated mills now faced competition from the minimills in sheets.

This new caster was first put into operation by Nucor at Crawfordsville, Indiana. At the beginning, the quality was not that high, but plans were made to develop better sheets. In 2001, Nucor had built two more sheet plants, and four other minimill firms used the thin slab caster to make sheets. Nucor and others also built plants to make structural products. By 1999, the minimills had completely taken over the structural beam market when Bethlehem dropped out.

Furthermore, since economies of scale were less important with the thin-strip casting, smaller mills were able to enter the market. There was interest in a newer caster that made even thinner slabs that could be rolled directly into sheets. However, the technology had not yet been commercialized (*Wall Street Journal*, September 25, 1995, p. B10C).

With the rest of the rolling mill process, there was a general trend toward greater sophistication in catering to the product preferences of individual customers. Notable in this endeavor was the joint venture between Inland Steel and Nippon Steel for a rolling mill in Carlisle, Indiana. It fit the needs of a varied set of customers.

To sum up, the major development in the rolling part of the steelmaking process, the thin slab caster, accentuated the trend toward the minimill plants.

The customer industries

Given the popular impression of decline, it is surprising that this was a period of increasing steel usage for many customers. Table 10.3 displays the shipments of the steel industry by customer sector. Of the nine domestic steel use sectors, only two, machinery and containers, dropped their consumption during the eleven years of this period. To understand these trends, we examine the major consumption sectors and see how use changed in order to eventually answer this question.

In this period, the largest consumption sector in steel was the steel service centers and distributors. During the 1990s, the consumption by this sector rose from 21,111,000 tons to 30,108,000 tons, and its percentage of total consumption went from 24.8 to 27.6. This sector served the firms that were too small to deal directly with the steel companies. It also further processed the product to fit the particular needs of customers. This sector's growth in the 1990s demonstrated an increasing demand for steel from many parts of the economy.

Table 10.3 The breakdown of economic sectors using steel by tonnage (by the 1,000s), 1990, 1995, and 2000

Years	1990	1995	2000
Total shipments (1,000s of tons)	84,979	97,494	109,051
Steel service centers & distributors	21,111 (24.8)	23,751 (24.4)	30,108 (27.6)
Construction, including maintenance	12,115 (14.3)	14,892 (15.3)	20,290 (18.6)
Automotive	11,100 (13.1)	14,622 (15.0)	16,063 (14.7)
Oil & gas	1,892 (2.2)	2,643 (2.7)	2,885 (2.7)
Agricultural	712 (0.8)	746 (0.8)	907 (0.8)
Machinery, industrial and electrical	4,841 (5.7)	4,707 (4.8)	3,839 (3.5)
Household and communications equipment	2,617 (3.1)	2,493 (2.6)	3,043 (2.8)
Containers, packaging and shipping material	4,474 (5.3)	4,139 (4.2)	3,708 (3.4)
Other	23,630 (27.8)	25,059 (25.7)	25,359 (23.3)
Exports	2,487 (2.9)	4,442 (4.5)	2,849 (2.6)

Source: American Iron and Steel Institute, *Annual Statistical Report*, various years.

Additionally, the increase reflects a change in the organization of the economy. Many large manufacturers, including auto companies, had become less integrated – outsourcing the manufacture of components to smaller companies who often found it more efficient to deal with service centers.

The major change in this period was that the service centers became completely independent of the steel firms. This trend had started in the 1980s, when cash-strapped integrated companies sold off their assets not directly involved in the manufacture of steel. This included their affiliated service centers. Ironically, when the last service center became disaffiliated with its steel company, it was the service center, Ryerson-Tull, that sold the steel firm (Inland Steel) in 1998.

The second largest steel using sector in the 1990s was the construction industry. For steel in construction, the period was one of growth. The amount of steel that went to construction grew from 12,115,000 tons in 1990 to 20,290,000 tons in 2000. The 1990s were generally a time of prosperity for the construction industry. Steel use increased in home building. Steel started to make inroads into wood in the 1980s, and the metal became much more prevalent in the 1990s in home construction. According to Hogan (1994, p. 132), the number of homes with steel frames rose from 500 to 10,000 between 1992 and 1993. In the other construction sectors, steel held its own in most areas, but made gains in some. One use where steel gained was partition studs. Hogan (1994, p. 131) states that steel studs "have become a preferred material for use in such buildings as hospitals, office buildings, and shopping malls." Thus, the boom in construction and steel's ability to hold its own against substitutes led to increased sales to this industry.

The next large steel user was the automotive sector. Between 1989 and 2001, the use of steel in this industry rose from 11,500,000 to 14,059,000 tons. This compares to an auto industry consumption of 21,490,000 tons in 1977. During the 1990s, auto consumption fluctuated with the business cycle. From 1989 to 1991, automotive steel consumption dropped from 11,761,000 to 10,015,000 tons. Then, it rose almost steadily (except in 1995, when it fell 0.88 percent), reaching 16,711,000 tons in 1999. After 1999, steel consumption in motor vehicles declined to 14,059,000 tons in 2001.

Three developments in the automotive industry led to greater steel use. First, the auto industry did well in the 1990s with motor vehicle production rising from 11,212,000 in 1989 to 12,771,000 units in 2000. Second, the fall in real fuel prices in the 1990s helped make the sport utility vehicle (SUV) popular, and then, the average motor vehicle became larger and heavier, increasing the use of steel. Third, the slow substitution away from steel characteristic of the auto industry in the 1970s and 1980s abated.

Thus, steel more than held its own in the automobile industry. Additionally, due to the outsourcing of many parts to small firms, much steel going into the auto industry was sold through the service centers, and therefore, the increase in automotive steel usage shown in the tables may even be understated.

The fourth largest user of steel was the container industry, made up mainly the makers and users of metal cans. In the late 1980s and early 1990s, steel in this sector seemed to be holding its own. While consumption dropped in 1994, it surpassed that of 1989. After that, steel consumption in containers dropped. Overall, the amount of steel used in containers dropped 18.5 percent from 4,474,000 tons in 1990 to 3,708,000 tons in 2000.

The literature does not have a good explanation for this fall. Since aluminum totally dominated the canned beverage sector, the loss did not come there. Aluminum had not been able to repeat in food canning the take-over that had occurred in beverages. A possible explanation for the fall in steel usage in containers was the incursion of plastics into food canning. The amount of goods in the grocery stores using plastics definitely increased in the 1990s, especially toward the end of the decade.

Of the smaller steel-using sectors, four, oil and gas, agricultural, household and communications, and "other," increased consumption, while one, machinery (industrial and electrical), lowered its consumption. Oil and gas, agricultural, and household and communications rose by considerable amounts, respectively, 37.6, 26.1, and 17.1 percent. These changes likely reflected the increased prosperity of the nation. Special circumstances probably did explain some increases. Oil prices started to rise toward the end of the decade, which pushed up steel usage.

In household equipment, the steel firms began an effort to replace plastics with steel (Hogan, 1994, p. 136). The increase in the "other" category indicates that comparatively small users of steel increased their demand during this period. The 21.3 percent drop in consumption in the machinery, industrial and electrical sectors could have come from several things. Aluminum substitution may have hit this sector especially hard. The development of lighter steel could have lowered the total usage. Also, the firms in this sector had started to buy more through the steel service centers. This would lower the apparent usage.

An analysis by Hogan (1994, pp. 92–6) does much to explain the rather strong performance of steel consumption in the 1990s. According to Hogan, seven factors lowered the demand for steel in the 1970s and 1980s. They were (1) the movement of GDP away from physical goods to services, (2) the change in capital spending from heavy equipment and construction to lighter items such as computers, (3) the completion of the building of the nation's physical infrastructure, (4) substitution in the motor vehicle industry of aluminum and plastics for steel, (5) the movement of other materials such as aluminum, plastics, ceramics, and concrete into steel uses, (6) the development of lightweight steels that lessened the needed consumption, and (7) the use of computer-aided design to fabricate the steels that can do the job efficiently.

Hogan, then, states that by the 1990s, these trends played themselves out. American manufacturing had revived, with a concomitant demand for steel; a need for new infrastructure had arisen as the old roads and public buildings had worn out. Additionally, limits had been reached on how much other material could be substituted for steel in products such as automobiles, other consumer durables, and capital equipment.

All these counter-trends contributed to the increased use of steel in the 1990s. This still raised the issue of why certain steel firms were not more prosperous than in the 1980s.

The firms in the steel industry

An examination of the individual steel firms in the 1990s will increase our understanding of the paradox between growing steel demand and the weaknesses of many firms. By the 1990s, the firms in this industry could be divided into two classes, the integrated and the EF firms. The latter were often called minimills, but the term electric furnace companies was more descriptive because many of the companies such as Lukens and CF&I did not start off as minimills, and many other firms, like Nucor and Ameristeel, had grown out of the minimill term. Table 10.4 shows the production and market share of some companies.

It is instructive to describe the fortunes of the six largest old line-integrated firms during the 1990s. Then, we analyze a sample of the other firms, and last, we look at the situation in imports.

U.S. Steel/USX

As of 1989, the largest firm in the industry in production was still U.S. Steel. It started the period with five fully integrated steel plants. By 2001, only three of these plants remained with the company, Mon Valley, Pennsylvania, Fairfield, Alabama, and Gary, Indiana.

In this period, U.S. Steel production went from 11,000,000 tons in 1990 to 11,400,000 tons in 1995 and 11,791,000 tons in 2000, but its market share dropped from 12.9 to 10.5 percent. Therefore, while U.S. Steel's production did not keep up with the industry, it did not decline as it had in the 1970s and 1980s. In 1990s, it made money in some years and lost money in others. Losing a small amount of money in 2000 ($21 million), its losses widened to $218 million in 2001. In spite of these losses, it was still solvent at the end of our period.

The policy of the company was generally to increase its efficiency and narrow its product line. These efforts did not shelter it from controversy, however. In the late 1980s and early 1990s, the largest stockholder, Carl C. Icahn, continually urged the firm to divest itself of its steel division and go mainly with the oil property, but the majority voted with management to keep the steel operations.

In 1991, however, Thomas Usher, the new president of USX, the parent company, did separate the oil and steel divisions into independent subsidiaries with their own stocks. Some thought that this division was done in order to prevent the oil business from absorbing the losses of the steel division. A better explanation is that having two stocks, one for steel and one for oil, would give investors a wider choice of what to hold in their portfolios.

The 2001 losses did not prevent the company from making and planning some acquisitions. In 2001, U.S. Steel bought Vychodoslovenske Zeleziarne AS (VSZ), a large steel company in Slovakia with a capacity of 4,000,000 tons a year. This was the first acquisition by an American company of a major foreign steel firm. The Slovakian company could give U.S. Steel an offset to its cyclical American business.

As 2001 ended, U.S. Steel was contemplating buying National Steel, but the details had not yet been worked out. Thus, U.S. Steel was not only solvent, but also making plans to expand and move into foreign markets.

Table 10.4 Total steel production (1,000 of tons) and market share for selected steel firms in the United States for 1990, 1995, 1999, and 2000

Year	Total production	Production for selected integrated companies						Production for selected electric furnace companies			
		USX/US Steel	Bethlehem	LTV	National Steel	Inland Steel	AK Steel	Nucor	Birmingham	North Star	steel dynamics
1990	85,000	11,000 (12.9)	8,900 (10.5)	7,300 (8.6)	4,900 (5.8)	4,700 (5.5)	4,800 (5.6)	3,400 (4.0)			
1995	97,500	11,400 (11.7)	9,000 (9.2)	8,000 (8.2)	5,600 (5.7)	5,100 (5.2)	4,100 (4.2)	7,900 (8.1)			
1999	107,395	10,629 (10.0)	8,416 (7.8)	7,469 (7.0)	6,110 (5.7)	N/AVAL	6,541 (6.1)	8,734 (8.1)			
2000	112,242	11,791 (10.5)	10,028 (8.9)	8,155 (7.3)	6,171 (5.5)	N/AVAL	6,392 (5.7)	11,020 (9.8)	3,100 (2.8)	2,900 (2.6)	2,000 (1.8)

Sources: For 1990 and 1995, Bernstein, 1997, for 1999, Standard & Poor's, 2001, and for 2000, Cooney, 2003, p. 10.

Bethlehem Steel

In 1989, the second largest steel company in the United States was Bethlehem Steel. Like U.S. Steel, Bethlehem increased its production from 8,900,000 tons in 1990 to 10,028,000 tons in 2000, but its market share still dropped from 10.5 to 8.9 percent.

Like U.S. Steel, it had lost money during the recessions and made money during the boom times. Alas, the losses during the late 1990s recession were so great that it could not cover its day-to-day financial obligations, and it declared bankruptcy in 2001.

Most of the activity of Bethlehem during this period seemed rational. It concentrated on its strong mills, especially Burns Harbor and Sparrows Point. It abandoned inefficient plants and unprofitable products. Sadly, this led to the closing of its home city plant at Bethlehem, Pennsylvania. This meant that the firm abandoned the structural market to the EF firms. This change left Bethlehem with only administrative and research employees in its home city.

In plates, the firm decided to increase its presence by a merger. Bethlehem bought Lukens Steel. Buying this old company strengthened Bethlehem's position in plates, but the increased debt and the costs incurred by the shutdown of some Lukens facilities raised the break-even point of the company, and contributed to its final failure.

Three money-losing years, 1999, 2000, and 2001, exhausted Bethlehem's ability to cover its debt payments. Thus, at the end of this chapter's period, the company was in bankruptcy.

LTV Steel

The third largest American steel firm in 1989 was LTV Steel. Its Massillon and Warren (Ohio) plants had been spun off into independent companies, Republic Engineered Steels and WCI Steel. The former had bar products, while WCI made flat rolled products.

The production at LTV rose during this period from 7,300,000 tons to 8,155,000 tons in 2000. Profits, however, fluctuated in the early and mid 1990s. However, it lost money, $38 million, $212 million, $868 million, in 1998, 1999, and 2000 respectively.

In the prosperous years, it participated in a number of joint ventures and bought two large companies. With British Steel and Sumitomo Metal Industries of Japan, LTV set up a company, Trico Steel, to make steel sheets with an EF in Decatur, Alabama. It encountered opposition from the United Steelworkers because the plant was not automatically union (*New York Times*, December 20, 1994, p. D5 and December 13, 1995, p. D1, and *Wall Street Journal*, December 20, 1994, p. A2).

LTV also entered into a joint venture with the iron ore firm, Cleveland Cliffs, called Cliffs and Associates Limited (CAL) to smelt iron by the direct reduction (DRI) process (Standard & Poor's, July 15, 1999, p. 8). LTV divested its interests in this company in 2001. In February 1998, LTV bought Copperweld, a specialty steel firm that made, among other things, tubes and pipes. It also bought VP Buildings, a fabricator of metal buildings in July 1999.

All these schemes did not compensate for the recession and high imports in the late 1990s and early 2000s. LTV experienced a series of losses, which it did not have the resources to bear. Consequently, it declared bankruptcy in December 2000, and it was forced to shut down its plants in December 2001.

As with Bethlehem, with its merger with Lukens, the question arises as to whether LTV should have bought Copperweld and VP Building and participated in the joint ventures. While those projects may have had profit potential, they could also increase expenses, and whether successful or not, they added to LTV's debt and its interest payments. Thus, these mergers and ventures could very well have contributed to the company's bankruptcy.

National Steel, AK Steel, and Inland Steel

The next three companies in production as of 1989, National Steel, AK Steel, and Inland Steel, had two things in common. First, they were or became partially owned by foreign steel companies, and second, they survived this period (1989–2001) without bankruptcy.

National Steel was controlled by the Japanese firm, Nippon Kokan (NKK) and the parent, National Intergroup. The latter sold out most of its interest and turned itself into a drug distribution company. NKK improved the state of National's mills. Its production rose from 4,900,000 tons in 1990 to 6,171,000 tons in 2000. Its profits fluctuated with the business cycle, but the company remained solvent.

During this period, the company had a checkered management history. Due to dissatisfaction with the people who ran the steel division under National Intergroup, NKK hired from U.S. Steel V. John Goodwin as president. Goodwin had been head of the U.S. Steel Gary works. In spite of a considerable improvement in efficiency and profitability, National Steel set Goodwin aside in 1996. Finally, in 2001, NKK decided to abandon the National Steel Company and made an offer to sell it to U.S. Steel.

AK Steel was also controlled by a Japanese Company, Kawasaki Steel. In 1989, the company was split into two subsidiary organizations: AK Steel which operated two integrated steel mills, and Armco which ran the specialty steel business. In 1992, Armco bought Cyclops which had a specialty plant in Baltimore, Maryland and an EF plant at Mansfield, Ohio. During this period, AK Steel increased its production from 4,800,000 tons in 1990 to 6,392,000 tons in 2000. It lost money in 1990, 1991, and 1992, but after that it was quite profitable until 2001. The AK Steel profits held up when those of the other firms became negative in the late 1990s.

Going into the 1990s, the company's efficiency was not up to that of most of the other firms; this contributed to its losses in the early part of the period. In 1992, Thomas C. Graham was hired from U.S. Steel where he had retired as company president. AK Steel was the third company which Graham had headed. As with the other two, he succeeded in substantially improving the results

(*New York Times*, February 12, 1995, p. F8). By the mid 1990s, many thought AK Steel was among the lowest cost integrated firms (*New York Times*, December 21, 1994, p. D8).

In 1999, AK Steel and Armco merged. This combination put together the integrated mills at Middletown and Ashland with the specialty shops at Butler and Baltimore and the EF plant in Mansfield. By 2001, AK Steel was one of the few integrated firms that remained solvent.

As of 1989, Inland Steel was the sixth largest steel company in production. In that year, it produced 4,700,000 tons. Historically, Inland Steel had been known as a strong, efficient company (*New York Times*, December 2, 1989, p. D2). While it lost money during the early 1990s recession, it made money in the mid 1990s. In the early 1990s, Inland entered into a joint venture with Nippon Steel, which built two finishing facilities, I/N Tek and I/N Kote, in New Carlisle, Indiana.

In 1997, Inland experienced a stockholder quarrel similar to that of U.S. Steel. Alfred Kingsley, the chief partner of Greenway Partners, LP, proposed that Inland Steel Industries, the parent company of Inland Steel, spin off its steel service center, Ryerson-Tull. Kingsley's arguments were that separating the companies would increase the stockholder's value.

Inland resisted Kingsley's proposal, but it came up with a plan that he might have liked. In 1998, the parent company, Inland Steel Industries, sold the steel-producing division to Ispat, an English-Dutch company. This action left the parent only with Ryerson-Tull, the steel service center company. Ispat was a large international steel company with plants in Europe and Asia; it was owned by the Indian tycoon, Lakshmi Mittal. Like the U.S. Steel purchase of VSZ, this acquisition was indicative of the internationalization of the American steel industry.

The smaller integrated firms

As of 1989, nine other firms operated integrated mills. These firms produced roughly 20,000,000 tons of steel. It is difficult to determine the exact amount they made because some firms operated both BOF and EFs, but this figure gives one a rough idea of what the smaller integrated firms produced. By 2000, eight smaller integrated firms remained. Two, Lone Star and Sharon Steel, had dropped out of the market, and there was one additional firm, Republic Technological Industries, LLC, which had been spun off by U.S. Steel.

Of these nine firms working in 1989, four had been spun off earlier by larger companies. The steel plant at Geneva, Utah had been abandoned by U.S. Steel; Gulf States Steel and WCI Steel had been sold by LTV as a result of antitrust and bankruptcy proceedings; Weirton Steel had been sold to its employees by National Steel. The other independents were Acme Steel, Lone Star, Sharon Steel, Wheeling-Pittsburgh, and Rouge Steel. The latter firm had been sold off by the Ford Motor Company.

These firms experienced quite similar problems. Due to competition from the larger firms, EFs, and imports, they had to keep costs quite low. This led them to install more efficient technology.

Often, even these measures did not prevent the firms from running into financial difficulties. They had to sell steel at a price high enough to not only cover production cost, but also cover interest payments on the modernization loans. This led to the Wheeling-Pittsburgh, Rouge Steel, and Weirton Steel bankruptcies in 2002.

The lack of scale economies and the competition from the EF and imports made the survival of these firms problematic. The experience of Geneva Steel illustrates the problem. A group of Utah businessmen bought the equipment of this firm from U.S. Steel. Early on, as an independent firm, the plant was able to take advantage of its western location to sell plate on the Pacific Coast. In the late 1990s, however, the minimill firms, Nucor and Oregon Steel Mills, built new low-cost plate plants, which cut into Geneva's sales. This led to its bankruptcy in 2002.

Consequently, the smaller integrated firms had a difficult time in the 1990s leading some to drop out.

EF firms: Nucor

While technologically the EF companies, whether old firms like Lukens and Lone Star or minimills firms like Roanoke and Georgetown, were very similar, their focuses were often quite different.

One firm, Nucor, worked on such a different strategy in the 1990s that its story needs to be told separately. Historically, the company had been a pioneer in minimill technology. It got into the business in the 1960s in order to supply the steel requirements of one of the company products, joists.

The company found that it could compete effectively in products such as rebar, angles, and other simple construction items. Building its own plants and instituting its own managerial system, Nucor expanded into other parts of the country from its original location in North Carolina, building steel minimills in Nebraska, Texas, and Utah.

Essentially, it set up a chain of minimills with conventional products to fill geographical niches. In the late 1980s, Nucor went in another direction, finding new steel products for the EF. First, they entered a joint venture with Yamato Steel of Japan to make large structural beams in Blythesville, Arkansas. The future president of Nucor, John D. Correnti, headed this effort.

Second, Nucor built a plant at Crawfordsville, Indiana to make sheets. This was notable for two reasons. First, sheets were about the last product that the minimill companies had not entered. Second, Nucor used a new technology, a thin slab caster from the German firm, SMS Schloemann-Siemag A.G. Rolling a thinner slab, this machine allowed sheets to be made at a much lower capital cost than the conventional process.

After some initial difficulties, this plant succeeded in making sheets that were competitive, in most uses, with the integrated firms. The manager of the Crawfordsville plant was Keith E. Busse, who went on to found another minimill company, Steel Dynamics. Even before the success of Crawfordsville was clear, Nucor started to build another sheet plant at Hickman, Arkansas. This plant was also successful.

As of 2001, Nucor had built another sheet plant in South Carolina, and it was contemplating a sheet mill in the Pacific Northwest. Carrying the product pioneering approach further, Nucor entered the plate market with a plant in Hertford County, North Carolina.

Nucor did not always succeed in its innovative endeavors. Fearing that it might be squeezed by rising scrap prices, Nucor entered into a joint venture with a Brazilian firm to make iron carbide in Trinidad. Due to technical problems and falling scrap prices, this venture was abandoned in 1999.

Even with this one misstep, much has been made of Nucor's success, and most analysts give too much credit to the minimill technology and not enough to the peculiar nature of the firm. Nucor's strength was not just that it was a minimill. Rather, Nucor derived its success from the special abilities of managers and workers. Outstanding among the managers were Ken Iverson, Keith Busse, John D. Correnti, and the finance expert, Samuel Siegel (Preston, 1992). Being non-union, the company treated its workers almost as management, paying them on an incentive basis. While the EF minimill was one way to succeed in steel, it did not necessarily guarantee success.

EF firms: the others

Much of the glow associated with EF firms, and especially minimills, arose from the story of Nucor. Unfortunately, many others did not do as well. While some firms succeeded, others ran into the problems.

To see the situation of the EF firms, one must understand the numerous types of firms in this class. First, some of these companies, such as Lukens and Lone Star, had originally been fully integrated firms. Second, some firms were companies primarily interested in other products that went into steel making to get sources of supply. Among them were Worthington and Timken. Other firms were joint ventures between companies that were diversifying out of their particular geographic and product niches. Among them were Trico, a sheet maker which was a joint venture between LTV, British Steel, and the Japanese Sumitomo Steel and Gallatin Steel, a sheet firm which was a joint venture between the Canadian firms, C-Steel and Defosco. There were also multiplant firms such as Nucor, itself, North Star, and Florida Steel, later renamed Ameristeel.

The very number of minimill firms contributed to their first major problem by making the market competitive. This was especially true for items such as rebar, rods, wire, and rails. In addition, imports were always the available in these products. Therefore, even minimill companies often had difficulties making a profit.

The second problem faced by the minimills was the uncertainty associated with the price of scrap, the major material input for these companies. Table 10.2 shows the behavior of scrap prices between 1987 and 2001. While prices dropped in the early 1990s, they rose until 1996 and remained high through 1998. This led to a great fear that the EF firms would be squeezed between the competitive product pricing and the rising scrap costs (Standard & Poor's, May 23, 1996, p. S22). The drop in scrap prices in the late 1990s lessened this problem (Standard & Poor's,

January 17, 2002, p. 10). By 2001, scrap prices did not present a major problem to the EF firms, but the competition threatened their health. As with the integrated firms, there were a number of bankruptcies: among them Trico, Laclade Steel, and Birmingham Steel.

Imports

The last source of competition in the 1990s was imports. While imports from the traditional sources, Japan and Europe, leveled off, other countries such as Taiwan, Brazil, Russia, and the Ukraine started selling steel in the United States. These foreigners were often subsidized by their governments, and they very likely dumped product into the United States.

Especially vulnerable to these incursions were the smaller integrated firms and minimills who made the simpler products such as plate, rod, wire and rebar. In the late 1990s, a recession in the South Asian economies enhanced imports into this country. This situation led all types of steel firms, not just the old integrated ones, to demand some form of government protection from imports.

Summary

Even though steel production and demand was stable, this period was not a comfortable one for the steel firms, and toward the end of it, many went into bankruptcy. Among these firms were not only the traditional integrated companies such as Bethlehem, LTV, and Geneva Steel, but also minimills such as Trico and Birmingham Steel.

Substitutes

Steel basically held its own in the 1990s against substitute materials. To see what happened, we reexamine four sectors where there was a potential for significant substitution: automobiles, construction, containers, and appliances. Then, we analyze the market for steel's chief substitute, aluminum.

In the automotive sector, the trend against steel that had occurred in the 1970s and 1980s attenuated. Table 10.5 shows the average amounts of steel, iron, aluminum, and plastics in an American automobile for 1977, 1990 and 2001. While the

Table 10.5 The amounts (by pounds) of steel, iron, aluminum, and plastics in the average American automobile, 1977, 1990, and 2001

Year	1977	1990	2001
Steel	2,202	1,564	1,781
Iron	540	398	345
Aluminum	97	158	257
Plastics	168	222	253

Sources: Standard & Poor's, July 4, 2002, p. 13 and Hogan, 1994, p. 127.

amounts of steel and iron dropped, the amounts of aluminum and plastics increased. In the 1990s, however, steel started to increase its weight, and the increase in plastics subsided. Helping steel was the trend toward the large sports utility vehicles (SUV).

Furthering this increase was a concerted effort by the steel industry to develop products that could be used by the auto industry. Hogan (1994, p. 125) stated: "An attempt on the part of the steel industry to reduce car weight has extended to the complete design of the automobile, rather than just reducing the weight of individual parts. This is known as an holistic approach."

Last, the limitations of the major substitutes for steel may have stopped its decline in automotive use. Plastics were often cheaper, lighter, and resistant to corrosion, but it was difficult to attach plastic pieces to the other components of the car and it was hard to shape plastic pieces into some forms (Cyert and Fruehan, 1996, p. 47). Aluminum had many advantages, but the major limit on aluminum was availability. In 2000, the American auto industry used 16,063,000 tons of steel, but world aluminum production was only 24,464,000 tons. It is doubtful whether the aluminum industry could or would divert very much metal from its other uses to autos in the near future.

Historically, the major substitute for steel in construction was concrete. By the 1980s, steel and concrete reached an impasse whereby each was taking about one half of the market (Hogan, 1994, p. 130). High lumber prices and the lack of quality in wood posed an opportunity for steel in home construction. Steel was substituted for many lumber uses.

In containers, steel, having lost almost all of the canned beverage market, seemed to hold its own in other uses until 1998. In recent years, more and more canned foods and fruit juices have been put in plastic containers.

In appliances, plastics took the place of steel in the liners for refrigerators and washing machines, but new enameled steels had made the metal more popular for the outsides of the machines. Consequently, "Some switch back to steel has already occurred" (Cyert and Fruehan, 1996, p. 48). Thus, in the 1990s, steel held its own in the major uses except for containers.

An analysis of steel substitutes in the 1990s would not be complete without a look at the structure and behavior of the aluminum industry. The industry became highly concentrated in the 1990s. In 1997, there were only seven firms selling or making aluminum in the United States. The major ones were Alcan (a Canadian firm), Alcoa (the largest), Kaiser Aluminum, and Reynolds Metals. In 2000, Alcoa had bought Reynolds Metals. This move gave it over half of the American market.

Accentuating the effect of the highly concentrated nature of this industry was its ability to use governments to decrease competition. In 1992, the fall of the Soviet Union led to a major redeployment of the Russian and the Commonwealth Independent States (CIS) aluminum industry. Since the Russian military no longer used large amounts of aluminum, the bulk of the CIS aluminum (around 3,000,000 tons) was exported mainly to Europe.

The American, Canadian, and European aluminum companies were able to prevail upon their governments and the European Union to get Russia and the other

CIS countries to sign a Memorandum of Understanding (MOU). Under this agreement, the CIS countries cut their exports by about 25 percent (Standard & Poor's, July 4, 2002, pp. 10–11). This action led to higher aluminum prices and higher profits. It is likely that the industry's ability to engage in such activity lowered its incentive to find new markets and to cut into steel. This possibility calls for further research.

Steel's success in staving off other substitutes can be mainly attributed to its ability to meet customers' wants and, perhaps, also to the lack of incentive of its major competitor, aluminum.

Input supplies

In this period, steel used five major inputs, coal, iron ore, scrap steel, electricity, and labor. Because it involved quite unique issues, labor is treated in a separate subsection, but first, we discuss the issues involving the other four inputs.

Iron ore, coal, scrap steel, and electricity

Iron ore, coal, and scrap steel were the major material inputs into steel, and electricity was the major other nonhuman input. While both coal and iron ore were natural resources with finite total supplies, supplies of these resources seemed adequate to cover the foreseeable future. This was also true of the other two inputs, scrap and electricity, but the price and sales condition of these inputs presented difficulties for some steel makers. Since iron ore presented no special problems, we focus on the problems with coal, scrap, and electricity.

As stated above, there was not any difficulty in obtaining coal *per se*. The United States had enough metallurgical coal to last for centuries. Rather, the difficulty was in obtaining coke for BFs. The pollution caused by the coke process often exceeded the standards allowed by environmental regulations. Regulations limiting these emissions made the profitable operation of coke ovens problematical.

In the 1980s, the United States became an importer of coke. In 1995, the U.S. imported 3,450,000 tons, which was 13 percent of the total consumption of 26,080,000 tons. Historically, American steel firms had produced their own coke, usually at the steel plants, but now this process was often outsourced. Table 10.6 lists the American coke makers and their production capacity as of 1996. Ten of these firms were merchant producers selling their coke to other firms, and nine were steel producers. Of these, some firms made more coke than they used and therefore sold the excess, and some bought coke from others to cover their needs, while one, Gulf States, was self-sufficient (*New Steel*, December 1996, p. 50).

To deal with this lack of coke, the companies used three approaches. The first was to increase coke capacity. The major problem with this course was the very high capital expense of coke plants that could meet environmental standards. It was usually so high that the plant was not profitable.

In 2000, however, two plants of a new type were built at Indiana Harbor, Indiana by the Indianapolis Coke Company and the Indiana Harbor Coke Company. Unlike

Table 10.6 Total capacity of the major American coke producers, 1996

Company	Type of producer[a]	Capacity (in tons per year)	Market share (in capacity)
U.S. Steel	Steel Company[b]	6,440,000	28.3
Bethlehem	Steel Company[b]	3,520,000	15.5
LTV	Steel Company	2,560,000	11.3
National	Steel Company	1,440,000	6.3
AK Steel	Steel Company	1,290,000	5.7
Wheeling-Pittsburgh	Steel Company[b]	1,280,000	5.6
Koppers	Merchant Producer	940,000	4.1
Geneva	Steel Company	700,000	3.1
Jewell	Merchant Producer	650,000	2.9
Citizens	Merchant Producer	640,000	2.8
ABC	Merchant Producer	610,000	2.7
Gulf States	Steel Company[b]	520,000	2.3
Acme	Steel Company[b]	480,000	2.1
New Boston	Merchant Producer	370,000	1.6
Sloss	Merchant Producer	370,000	1.6
Shenango	Merchant Producer	350,000	1.5
Tonawanda	Merchant Producer	230,000	1.0
Erie	Merchant Producer	200,000	0.9
Empire	Merchant Producer	130,000	0.6
Total		22,720,000	100.0

Source: *New Steel*, December 1996, pp. 52–53.

Notes

a A "Steel Company" is a firm that makes steel and uses some or all of its coke in production. A merchant producer makes no steel, but sells its coke to other firms.

b These firms were either self-sufficient in coke or sold surplus on the market.

the traditional by-product coke ovens of the twentieth century, these plants produced nothing but coke. Hence, they were called nonrecovery plants. A similar nonrecovery plant was built at Vansant, Virginia.

The second approach was to substitute other inputs for coke. It was found that injecting coal dust and natural gas could lower the amounts of coke needed to produce pig iron. Additionally, using different mixes of iron feedstock, among them iron ore pellets, sinters, scrap, and direct reduction iron, and iron carbide dust also lowered the coke requirement. The result of such substitution was a 28 percent reduction in the amount of coke needed for a ton of pig iron. One authority stated: "The quantity of coke required to smelt one ton of iron fell during this period [1975 to 1995] from 1,222 pounds (0.611)to 874 pounds (0.437)" (*New Steel*, November 1996, p. 64).

The third way to deal with the lack of coke was to move away from the BF altogether. As described above, over time a larger and larger proportion of the steel in the United States was being made in scrap-fed EFs.

The concern about coke helped foment interest in the direct reduction iron (DRI) and iron carbide processes. Thus, DRI and iron carbide have been used, not only to feed the EF and BOF, but also on occasion to supplement iron ore in the BF.

Motivating most of the industry was also a fear of high scrap prices. They did fluctuate a great deal in the 1990s. As shown in Table 10.2, the price of No. 1 heavy melt scrap rose to a height of $141.98 per ton in 1995. By 2001, however, it had dropped to $76.18 in 2001. In the late 1990s, the interest in DRI and iron carbide attenuated due to the falling scrap prices. Thus, scrap steel remained the dominant iron input into the EF and continued to account for about one-third of the metallic input into the BOF Furnace.

The growth of the EF in the 1990s had led to concern about the availability of scrap. In fact, some experts felt that this would limit the growth of this process (Standard & Poor's, July 24, 1997, pp. 8–9). The continued growth of minimills and other EFs confounded these predictions, and the drop in scrap prices lowered this interest and led to the abandonment of some projects.

The extent of the input problems, lack of coke, and fluctuating scrap prices, did much to determine the nature of the steel industry in 2001. The coke problem was never really solved, and consequently, the integrated firms had limits on their growth. Not only were no new integrated mills built, but also some of the older ones were abandoned. Thus, while the coke problem, the major barrier to the growth of integrated mills, remained unsolved, the major impediment to minimill growth, high scrap prices, had at least been attenuated.

The fourth major nonhuman input into steel, electricity, was more important to the EF sector than to the integrated plants, but its supply could be problematic for all the mills. The major difficulty was the uncertainty as to the price and availability of electric power. The regulatory structure of the electric industry was under going continuous change. On average, this would have led to greater flexibility in pricing and delivery contracts. The major thrust of the reforms could work to the advantage of large users like steel companies. They were now able to choose electrical suppliers through the wheeling of power from more distant utilities through the local company. This gave the steel firms more bargaining power.

The advantages from the resulting price breaks often had a cost in that the supplier had the right to interrupt the service (*New Steel*, January 1996, pp. 22–9). Consequently, while steel companies would benefit from the regulatory reforms, firms often faced price and supply uncertainty. In 1998, Steel Dynamics called for an investigation of electricity pricing in Indiana (*New Steel*, August 1998, p. 8). Some firms found that if they got a profitable electricity rate, the service could be interrupted, but the higher non-interruptible rate might not be profitable. Charter Steel (of Wisconsin) executive Louis Allegra stated: "If we pay the higher rates, our operating costs go up, and our customers will not accept a price increase, . . . If we cut production, we have less to sell. Either way, it affects the bottom line" (*New Steel*, August 1998, p. 9).

Labor

Two issues were important in the steel labor market in the 1990s; the first is the loss in employment, and the second is the role of the United Steelworkers. The trends in employment in the 1970s and 1980s continued in the 1990s. Table 10.7 shows that

Table 10.7 Average number of employees of SIC 3312, blast furnaces and steel mills for the years 1990–2001

Year	All employees	Total production	Production per employee
1990	276,000	98,906,000	358
1991	261,000	87,896,000	337
1992	254,000	92,949,000	366
1993	238,000	97,877,000	411
1994	234,000	100,579,000	430
1995	242,000	104,930,000	434
1996	238,000	105,309,000	442
1997	235,000	108,561,000	462
1998	233,000	108,752,000	467
1999	222,000	107,395,000	484
2000	225,000	112,242,000	499
2001	210,000	99,321,000	473

Source: U.S. Bureau of the Census, 1960–2005.

steel industry employment decreased from 276,000 in 1990 to 210,000 in 2001. Some blamed the loss on imports, and some ascribed it to increased productivity.

One aspect of the situation differed from the past: there was no trend in total steel production. It went from 98,906,000 tons in 1990 to 99,321,000 tons in 2001, fluctuating from a low in 1991 of 87,896,000 tons to a high of 112,242,000 tons in 2000. Thus, the employment loss cannot be attributed to falling production.

It is impossible to make an accurate estimate of how much of the employment loss could be attributed to each of the other two variables. Without imports it is not clear that the American steel industry could provide for all the steel consumption of the United States. The *Wall Street Journal* (March 27, 1998, p. A1) asserted:

> At the same time, the U.S. economy has grown faster than domestic steelmakers' ability to supply the American market. U.S. demand for steel is running about 124 million tons a year, but U.S. producers only ship 100 millions tons to American customers . . .

Given this caveat on production limits, three counterfactuals suggest themselves. One estimates employment assuming that there were no imports whatsoever; the second assumes that imports stayed at their 1990 levels, and the third assumes that labor productivity stayed at its 1990 level.

The first counterfactual gauging the impact of imports on steel industry employment assumes that there were no imports whatsoever. Furthermore, it assumes that labor productivity would grow at its actual rate. If there had been no imports whatsoever, the production level in 2001 would have been 129,401,000 tons instead of 99,321,000 tons. Given the labor productivity of 473 tons per employee, the no-imports simulation indicates that there would have been 63,575 additional steel workers. This all assumes that the industry would have had the capability of producing the additional steel that was imported.

A second simulation of imports assumes that imports remained at the 1990 level and productivity rose at the actual rate. The simulation indicates that the employment loss due to increased imports from 1990 was 26,974 for 2001 at the end of the period, compared with an actual employment loss of 66,000.

To see the change in employment due to increasing productivity, a third simulation assumes that steel productivity stayed at the 1990 level. By this assumption, the influence of productivity change can be isolated. To produce the 2001 production level with the 1990 productivity would take 277,432 workers. This counterfactual, then, implies that productivity gains alone were responsible for a loss of 67,432 jobs. Thus, while it is difficult to separate out the effects of imports and productivity, the simulations imply that productivity change accounted for most of the employment loss in the steel industry in the 1990s.

In the 1990s, the United Steelmakers (USW) continued to control most of the production workers in the steel industry. In the light of the above-described loss in employment, the union faced a difficult task in protecting its workers. Even with these difficulties, it is not clear that the union followed the best policy.

As in the earlier period, the USW workers were concentrated in the integrated mills. Only two major integrated mills were non-USW: the Middletown plant of AK Steel and Weirton Steel's one plant in Weirton, West Virginia. The members of Independent Steelworkers Union (ISU), the Weirton Steel union, were among the owners of the plant. Armco Employees Independent Federation was the union at the Middletown plant.

In the early 1990s, there was a spirit of cooperation between the union, and both the union integrated and EF companies. Beginning with the 1980s, the union negotiated unilaterally with each company. Early in our period, the union negotiated two sets of contracts, one in 1989 and one in 1993. The former were usually for four years, while the latter were set up for six years, but they had options for either party reopening provisions of the contracts. The USW allowed the companies to change the work rules in exchange for somewhat higher total compensation. For most of these contracts, the companies agreed to keep the defined benefit pension plans.

While the negotiations went well in the early 1990s, the cooperative atmosphere was ended by three issues: the desire by the USW to keep all plants of a given company in the union, the incentive pay structure, and pensions. Still, the union and U.S. Steel, LTV, Bethlehem, National Steel, and Inland Steel were able to reach mutually acceptable agreements. With one exception, these firms seemed to work out their relations with the USW in a quiet if not amiable manner.

The exception was LTV, and the USW reacted as it had to the former's investment in the minimill, Trico. As described above, LTV entered a joint venture with British Steel and Sumitomo to build an EF mill called Trico. The LTV union members expressed resentment at the company's investing in Trico instead of putting capital into its older union mills (*New Steel*, July 1995, p. 10 and *Wall Street Journal*, April 2, 1996, p. A4). The major result of the controversy was the insertion of a "neutrality" clause in the contracts with the major integrated companies in 1999 (See *New Steel*, September 1999, p. 10). These provisions stipulated that the companies would not interfere in the election at plants on whether to unionize or not.

The smaller steel companies faced a number of strikes on the issues of pensions and incentive pay. Among them were WCI Steel, Wheeling-Pittsburgh, and the minimill firm, Bayou Steel. Examining the circumstances of these strikes gives one an idea of the state of labor relations in the 1990s. WCI Steel was struck by the USW in 1995 for two months; the issues were mainly wages and work rules. After the strike, the new WCI Steel president made efforts to enlist the workers in the company's goal of increasing productivity (*New Steel*, April 1999, p. 47). A strike at Wheeling-Pittsburgh Steel lasted ten months from October 1995 to August 1996, the main issue being pensions. The union demanded that the company re-institute its pre-bankruptcy defined benefit plan. The strike ended when the company agreed to set up a defined benefit plan that they claimed had the same cost as the plan they originally proposed (*New Steel*, September 1997, p. 8).

In many ways the most contentious strike was that at the minimill Bayou Steel which lasted from March 1993 to September 1996. It was the longest strike in USW history. The major issue was the company incentive plan. As originally proposed, the workers would take a cut in base pay in order to divert funds to an incentive system which would encourage greater productivity. The final result of the strike was a six-year contract that provided the following: no wage increase, an incentive plan, a cost-of-living provision, an accommodation on contracting out of particular jobs, and new health care and pension plans (*New Steel*, November 1996, p. 8).

Aside from its direct negotiations with the companies, the USW pushed its agenda on other fronts. In 1993, George Becker succeeded Lynn Williams as president of the United Steelworkers. He continued the policies of Williams which emphasized political activity in support of contract negotiations with the companies.

Becker began a campaign of mergers. The first attempt, however, was unsuccessful. The USW tried to merge with the independent union at AK Steel's Middletown, Ohio plant. The AK members turned the plan down.

One USW foray outside of the steel industry was successful, but the other failed. In May 1995, the USW merged with the United Rubber Workers. This merger added 94,000 members to the 565,000 members of the USW. In return, the USW helped the financially strapped Rubber Workers who had had to pay for a long strike with Bridgestone/Firestone Inc. The USW planned to merge with two other very large unions, the United Automobile Workers (UAW) and the International Association of Machinists and Aerospace Workers (IAM), but this merger fell through (*New York Times*, July 28, 1995, p. A1 and *Automotive News*, August 26, 2002, pp. 1 and 2).

Political activities supplemented the collective bargaining. Generally, the union took three routes. First, it attempted to obtain legislation strengthening the bargaining position of the unions through changing National Labor Relations Board rules. Second, the union attempted to undermine companies against which it was striking by encouraging customers to switch and dissuading stockholders and bankers from providing capital. For instance, it attempted to get Bayou stockholders to withdraw support from management. Furthermore, the union tried to get the governments, either federal or state, to scrutinize the company environment and safety practices.

Third, the union petitioned for tariff relief from foreign competition cooperating with the companies in a number of antidumping cases.

These activities indicate that the focus of the union activity had moved away from direct confrontation with the steel companies to developing a political environment conducive to greater union control. Given that individual companies were often so strapped for cash that there was little latitude in negotiations, the union believed that changing the entire political-social environment would give it more ability to help its workers.

This raises one question. While undermining a company with its customers or capital suppliers can get more favorable strike settlements, what does it do to the firm in the long run?

There may be political activity where the union could help the companies and maybe the country. For instance, environmental restrictions have forced the United States to import coke, even though it is well-endowed with coal. The fact that much of this coke was imported from Japan and Canada, countries with environmental standard as high as the United States, indicates that there must be something inefficient about the American rules. In cases like these, the union may have been able to help the companies, and perhaps the nation as a whole. To further assess the effect of these problems, we now examine the interconnections between the steel industry and the government.

The influence of government

During the 1990s, four issues dominated the relationship between the American government and the U.S. steel industry: trade policy, the federal private pension insurance, environmental laws, and safety regulation. In this section, we examine these issues, starting with trade policy.

While little changed in the international steel trade, this period saw a major change in the way steel imports were regulated by the government. In July 1989, President George H. Bush agreed to continue this import quota system for another 2.5 years until March 1992, increasing the quotas for some countries. Bush promised to negotiate multilateral agreements with other nations to limit the dumping and subsidization of foreign steel.

In March 1992, the Bush administration decided against renewing the quota, but it had not been able to negotiate any agreement with other steel-producing nations (Moore, 1996, *Iron Age*, October 1991, p. 32, *New York Times*, April 1, 1992, p. D6). Many scholars took this action as a sign that the steel industry had lost its political influence, but subsequent events undermined this conclusion (Moore, 1996).

At this point the nature of the trade regulation changed. In June 1992, several large steel companies brought trade suits against dumping and subsidization by foreign countries. Under the American trade laws, it was illegal for offshore firms to export products to the United States at prices under their average cost and/or the price in their domestic market. Furthermore, it was illegal for a foreign firm to sell at a low price in the American market if it was receiving a subsidy from its government. Proving these charges was often quite difficult, and it took a great deal of time and resources to adjudicate these cases. Instead of working out quotas and price minimums for foreign imports, the Bush administration merely allowed the cases to proceed.

In June 1992, several large steel companies brought trade suits against dumping and subsidization by foreign countries. In November of that year, the Commerce Department in response to the above cases put duties running from 0.64 percent to 90.09 percent on a number of steel products (*New York Times*, December 1, 1992, p. D1 and *Iron Age*, January 1992, p. 8). In January 1993, the new president, William J. Clinton, confirmed the Department of Commerce's decision and imposed still more tariffs on steel products (*New York Times*, January 28, 1993, p. A1).

The Clinton administration also attempted to revive the multilateral discussions with other countries on the problem of dumping and subsidization (*Iron Age*, April 1993, p. 8), but the trade cases proceeded. In June 1993, the Department of Commerce put tariffs on imported rolled steel (*New York Times*, June 23, 1993, p. D1). On July 27, 1993, however, the International Trade Commission ruled that about half of the tariffs imposed by the Department of Commerce were unjustified, and consequently, the duties were taken off (*New York Times*, July 28, 1993, p. D1, *Wall Street Journal*, July 28, 1993, p. A3, and *Iron Age*, September 1993, p. 10). Essentially, the ITC found that dumped and subsidized imports of some cold rolled products had materially hurt the American industry, but none of the hot rolled imports had damaged the industry (*Iron Age*, September 1993, p. 10). This decision was a disappointment to the American companies (Moore, 1996).

While the domestic industry did not get all that it wanted from the decision, tariffs were still continued on half of the products. Thus, it was not a total defeat for the industry. The cases often had an indirect effect. Even the unsuccessful trade suits could lead to lower U.S. exports. The cases tended to be long and drawn out; the 1992 complaint took over a year to adjudicate. Furthermore, there was a likelihood of further appeals. Consequently, foreign firms were reluctant to enter the U.S. market because they did not know what tariffs or fines they might face. This possibility alone might have made even an unsuccessful trade case profitable for the domestic firm. Thus, even though they were "disappointed," the American companies may have succeeded in keeping some foreign steel out, even when the ITC ruled against them (*Wall Street Journal*, March 27, 1998, p. A1).

In the three years after the ITC decision, there was not much activity on trade cases. The steel industry boomed, and many thought that the industry was facing capacity constraints (*Wall Street Journal*, April 11, 1995, p. A21). In 1995, a huge rise in world demand for steel actually led to a fall in U.S. imports because steel was going elsewhere.

These and two other events led some to believe that the steel industry was not so concerned with imports. First, the rod producers, mainly minimills like Georgetown and North Star, withdrew a dumping complaint against the Canadians in 1994 (*New Steel*, June 1994, p. 9). Second, the American steel industry greeted the institution of the North American Free Trade Agreement (NAFTA) with enthusiasm. They thought that the abolition of duties between Canada, the United States, and Mexico would increase their sales (*New Steel*, January 1994, p. 8). From this attitude, some might have inferred a new view of trade.

Events in 1997 and 1998 refuted this inference. In February 1997, talks on steel trade broke down (*New Steel*, February 1997, p. 8). Second, in 1996, Geneva Steel and Gulf States Steel brought antidumping suits against China, Russia, South Africa, and the Ukraine on steel plate. In December 1996, the ITC determined that injury had occurred and set about calculating the commensurate tariffs (*New Steel*, April 1994, p. 124). Not satisfied with the relief from that suit, Geneva Steel brought a so-called private dumping suit against firms from those countries. Under a 1916 Act, private suits allowed for easier standards of import damage. The problem with plate was not only foreign competition, but also increased penetration of the market by the minimills such as Nucor and Oregon Steel. Thus, even in the boom times, not all firms were inactive in the area of trade litigation.

In 1998, imports increased to a record 41,520,000 tons, apparently as a result of the depression in East Asia. This triggered a flood of trade cases. On September 30, 1998, twelve steel companies and two labor unions brought an antidumping complaint on hot rolled sheets (*New York Times*, October 1, 1998, p. C4 and *New Steel*, November 1998, p. 8). The complainants included not only traditional integrated companies such as Bethlehem and Weirton, but also minimills such as Gallatin and Steel Dynamics. Interestingly, five of the companies were at least partially owned by foreigners, California Steel Industries (formerly Kaiser Steel), Gallatin Steel, Ipsco, Ispat-Inland, and National Steel.

In February 1999, the Department of Commerce ruled that this case had merit (*New York Times*, February 13, 1999, p. C1 and *Wall Street Journal*, February 16, 1999, p. 1). The ITC agreed to investigate the impact of the imports in this case and approved punitive tariffs for the hot rolled sheets (*New York Times*, April 3, 1999, p. C3 and June 12, 1999, p. C3). As a result of this case, the Clinton administration made agreements with Russia and Brazil, limiting the imports of hot rolled sheets (*New Steel*, August 1999, p. 8).

This case was not the end of the steel industry trade actions. In April 1999, three minimills brought a trade case on structural beams. Notably among them was Nucor-Yamato. First, in the past, the Nucor parent had been a vocal opponent of trade cases, and second, among the foreign companies affected by the case was Yamato Steel, the other parent of Nucor-Yamato. Thus, most minimills were now amenable to trade cases, and American companies were not averse to bringing action even against their foreign parents (*New Steel*, May 1999, p. 8). Additionally, Wheeling-Pittsburgh, following the lead of Geneva Steel, went forward with a private dumping case against several steel traders and foreign manufacturers (*New Steel*, May 1999, p. 9).

In 1999, a number of dumping cases were brought. The large steel companies brought a case on dumping cold-rolled sheets (*Wall Street Journal*, June 3, 1999 p. 1, *New Steel*, August 1999, p. 9, *Wall Street Journal*, March 6, 2000, p. 1 and *New York Times*, March 4, 2000, p. C1). In October 1999, Weirton Steel initiated a case on tin-plate steel (*New Steel*, December 1999, p. 10). In August 2000, Ameristeel,

Nucor, and several other minimill firms brought a trade case on rebar (*New Steel*, August 2000, p. 6).

In February 2000, the Clinton administration responded to the petitions of the wire and rod makers by bringing what was known as a Section 201 case. With this type of case, if the administration sees that the domestic industry is threatened with substantial harm, it can impose protective tariffs even though the ITC and the Department of Commerce had not made determinations. Essentially, Clinton imposed a 10 percent duty on wire rod and a 19 percent tax on line pipe (*New York Times*, February 12, 2000, p. C2).

In January 2001, George W. Bush became president, and he soon followed Clinton's lead by bringing a Section 201 case, only Bush's case covered a much wider set of products. In effect, Bush set up a quota system for various steel products, imposing substantial duties on imports above those quotas. Those duties ran from 8 to 30 percent (Cooney, 2003, pp. 23–43). The system was supposed to last three years, from 2002 to 2005.

These executive actions were not being brought in a political vacuum. In Congress, there were a number of relief bills for the steel industry (*New Steel*, March 1999, p. 6). In 1999, the House of Representatives had voted to put quotas on the import of steel, but under pressure from both Republican and Democratic party leaderships, the Senate rejected the bill (*New York Times*, March 18, 1999, p. A1 and March 19, 1999, p. C3, March 24, 1999, p. C6 and June 23, 1999, p. A1).

Ironically, there had been a reversal of the policies favored by the executive branch of government from the previous twenty years. In the 1970s and 1980s, the Johnson, Nixon, Carter, and Reagan administrations set up quota systems in order to prevent the companies from going through trade cases that would lead to tariffs. In 1999, 2000, and 2001, the Clinton and Bush administrations decided to rely on the trade cases to prevent Congress from imposing other restrictions.

The second major problem faced by the government and the steel firms in the 1990s was the funding for defined benefit pension funds. In 1983, the federal government set up the Pension Benefit Guaranty Corporation (PBGC) to insure that pensioners receive a pension no matter what the fortunes of the company for which they worked. The companies paid a premium for this insurance, but early on, the extent of the PBGC protection was not clear. In the steel industry, most of these funds were negotiated between the integrated firms and the USW. Many firms had to call on the PBGC to meet their pension obligations. Five of the ten largest claimants were integrated steel firms, Bethlehem Steel, National Steel, Wheeling-Pittsburgh Steel, Sharon Steel, and LTV. While only one of these claims was made in the 1990s, the possibility of defaults affected the operations of the steel industry.

Pensions were instrumental in some of the major strikes. The Wheeling-Pittsburgh and Oregon Steel Mills strikes turned on the union desire to reinstate defined benefit plans that the companies opposed. Pensions were also issues at the WCI Steel and Bayou Steel strikes.

There was litigation between the PBGC and certain steel companies, the major one being LTV Steel. LTV went bankrupt in 1986, and the PBGC took over its pension payments. When the firm emerged from bankruptcy, the PBGC wanted

LTV to resume the payments on its pension plans. LTV resisted, but a 1991 Supreme Court ruling forced LTV to resume paying these pensions. While the decision hurt LTV, many experts felt that the decision made the PBGC funding system more secure.

The long-term funding problems with these pensions did not come to the fore in the 1990s as they did in the subsequent six years. Rather, the major concern in the 1990s was the difference in liabilities between the firms who had defined benefit plans and the ones who had defined contribution pension plans. (With the latter plans, the benefits depend on the amount contributed and the financial management of the funds.) Many felt that the old integrated firms were operating at a disadvantage because they had to cover the defined benefit plans (*Iron Age*, April 1993, p. 7 and *New Steel*, May 1995, p. 30). The costs of these pensions, along with the medical benefits for retired workers, were called legacy costs. *New Steel* (May 1995, p. 30) stated: "These legacy costs, primarily for pensions and retirees' health-care benefits, significantly hinder the competitiveness of the integrated producers. Unlike outdated equipment or poor labor management relations, legacy costs cannot be managed or invested away."

Just how large the disadvantage was can be seen in the very number of the pensioners. In 1995, both U.S. Steel and Bethlehem had considerably more retirees than they did employees, and they were not alone (*New Steel*, May 1995, p. 30).

The minimills usually had defined contribution plans which imposed a much smaller burden on the companies. Being relatively new, most of these companies also had much younger work forces. Thus, even those with defined benefit plans had smaller legacy costs.

The USWA was keenly aware of the legacy cost problem, and it attempted to alleviate it. First, in the strikes at Wheeling-Pittsburgh and Oregon Steel, it attempted to impose defined benefit plans that the managements did not want. At Wheeling-Pittsburgh, the union succeeded in getting such a plan. At the Pueblo, Colorado plant of Oregon Steel Mills, the union wanted a restoration of the defined benefit plan that had existed when the plant was CF&I. The union did not get its fund.

The union tried to persuade the federal government to impose an excise tax on all steel firms to cover the legacy costs (*Iron Age*, April 1993, p. 7). Understandably, minimills opposed this measure. Since most companies operated in the black, little was done about the situation. A solution to the problem was left to later times.

The third regulatory problem for the steel industry in the 1990s was environmental protection. While the steel industry had done much to clean up its effusions into the water supply and atmosphere, there were still difficulties in complying with some environmental laws. Consequently, more resources had to be devoted to solving these problems. Two trends led to increased scrutiny of the industry. First, the public was becoming less tolerant of pollution, and second, medical studies demonstrated stronger links between pollutants and health (*New York Times*, January 21, 1997, p. A10).

There were several federal statutes regulating pollution in the steel industry. The industry emitted a large number of other substances that the EPA considered harmful (U.S. Environmental Protection Agency, 1995, pp. 32–43). While there were ways to minimize the effects of these materials and sometimes they could even be eliminated, it was not clear that the necessary procedures were always carried out.

In the 1990s, the EPA identified two parts of the steel process as areas where emissions could be lowered significantly, coke ovens and the EFs. The coke ovens emitted benzene, sulfur tar sludges, and dirty water. Several ways have been suggested for alleviating these problems. First, the emission of the current types of ovens could be lowered. Second, the coke battery, a new type of oven that emits less pollution, was being researched and introduced in certain mills. While this technology eliminated some valuable by-products, it greatly lessened the emissions into the air and water storage. Third, in contrast to the nonrecovery process, some authorities suggested using more of these materials, thereby eliminating the need to dispose of the harmful waste material. A fourth method of lowering coke oven emissions was to use other material, such as pulverized coal or tar sludge, in the BFs (U.S. Environmental Protection Agency, 1995, pp. 47–9).

For the EPA, the second major problem of the time was the impact of the EF. The major pollutant from EFs was a dust that consisted partly of iron, zinc, lead, and cadmium. The EPA asserted that most of these materials could be recycled (U.S. Environmental Protection Agency, 1995, pp. 349–50 and *New Steel*, December 1997, p. 8). With the spread of minimills and the increase in furnace sizes, the agency needed to ascertain the exact environmental impact of these plants. Unlike the coke ovens, however, the environmental difficulties did not seem to impede the growth of EF technology.

The EPA used both an enforcement and a cooperative approach to getting the companies to lower emissions. It brought many suits against the steel companies. Additionally, in many situations, the companies cooperated with the agency to comply with the regulations (*New York Times*, June 21, 1989, p. B5, *New York Times*, May 16, 1991, p. D3, and *New Steel*, July 1997, p. 64). Nevertheless, there were often unique obstacles to compliance. First, the economy often made for very low profits, which constrained the resources that could be devoted to environmental matters. Second, sometimes new technology made compliance difficult because of the uncertainty of the resulting emissions (*New Steel*, December 1999 p. 27).

Overall, the major difficulty for the steel companies was the coke requirements. Until the introduction of the battery, it seemed that coke production was being eliminated from this country.

The fourth regulatory problem faced by the steel industry was worker safety. While some evidence indicated that the steel industry was much safer in the 1990s than in past decades, there was still a feeling that the danger level may have stopped falling (*New Steel*, October 1995, p. 50).

Fatality data lent some credence to the unease about safety in steel. Table 10.8 shows the incidence of fatal injuries in the steel industry for selected years in the last decade of the twentieth century. By 1990, both the number of fatalities and the number per 100,000 workers had dropped far below what they had been previously, even in the 1980s. Part of the drop could be attributed to lower activity.

Nevertheless, both the gross number and the intensity rose in the middle 1990s until in 1996, the fatalities per 100,000 were very close to what they were in 1950: 21.9 as opposed to 22.7.

Table 10.8 Fatal occupational injuries in the steel industry, selected statistics, 1950–2001

Years	Number of OSHA inspections	Fatal occupational injuries	Fatal injury per 100,000 SIC 3312 employees
1950		126	22.7
1950s Average		103	*
1960s Average		72	*
1970s Average		62	*
1980s Average		25	*
1990	280	12	7.3
1991	290		
1992	253	18	12.9
1993	242	24	18.9
1994	219	26	20.7
1995	218	17	13.9
1996	243	26	21.9
1997	233	17	15.2
1998	186	16	14.6
1999	224	14	13.6
2000	269	12	12.1
2001	188	10	11.4
Average 1992–2001	228	18	*

Sources: U.S. Department of Labor, Bureau of Labor Statistics, Census of Fatal Occupational Injuries All Worker Profile, 1992–2002 and *Iron Age*, December 1992, p. 17.

* Calculating averages for a decade can be misleading in that both fatality and employment figures fluctuate widely from year to year.

Whatever the source of the unease, it led to more safety analysis. Mike Wright, director of health, safety, and environment for the USW, attributed the perceived increased risk in the steel mills to four factors (*New Steel*, October 1994, p. 19 and *New Steel*, July 1999, p. 26). The first was the high capacity utilization rate that occurred in the relatively prosperous years of the mid 1990s: "What you have happening, we believe, is a bottleneck of people taking extraordinary, and sometimes unsafe, steps to maintain that capacity" (*New Steel*, October 1994, p. 19).

Second, a greater amount of overtime work in this period could have led to greater carelessness due to fatigue. Third, the proportion of people doing new jobs increased. Wright's fourth factor was the "influx of new technology." The new technology led to different ways of doing things, and it took time for workers to adjust to the new conditions.

While these arguments have some plausibility, there was little statistical evidence for or against them. While the USW claimed that union shops were safer places to work, again there was little evidence for or against the hypotheses.

The perception of greater danger for steel workers was supported by a series of major accidents in the 1990s. On January 20, 1994, one person died of exposure to carbon monoxide at the Inland Steel plant in East Chicago, Indiana and three others suffered overexposure to the gas (*New Steel*, October 1994 p. 20). On December 5, 1995, a series of explosions in the AK Steel's plant at Middletown, Ohio injured fourteen workers (*New Steel*, January 1996 p. 8).

One of the most publicized incidents occurred at Nucor's Crawfordsville, Indiana plant on January 24, 1990. A ladle full of molten steel dropped onto the plant floor where the hot steel combined with ground moisture causing an explosion. One person died of horrible burns. As a result of this accident, Nucor was cited for several OSHA violations, and the company added a large number of safety features to the plant (Preston, 1992, pp. 250–66).

Toward the end of the 1990s, the fatality rate indicated that safety efforts may have paid off. The rate, after reaching a peak in 1996, started to drop. Both the total number of fatalities and the rate per 100,000 dropped off each year between 1996 and 2001. While employment fell in those years, production actually rose until 2000.

In all four areas, trade policy, pension insurance, the environment, and safety, there were still unsettled issues in 2001, and developments in later years would create more problems for the companies and government.

Conclusion

While the steel industry did not undergo major structural changes, the bankruptcies and chaos that followed in the subsequent five years were at least partially caused by conditions during this period. Having examined the major events of the 1990s, this chapter now draws some preliminary conclusions on the demise of so many companies in the early twenty-first century. Six things are worth examining: imports, changing technology, environmental regulations, unions, the pension system, and management mistakes.

Many analysts see imports as the major problem of the industry. This chapter has shown that only a portion of the employment loss can be attributed to imports, but the weak financial position of some companies could very well have resulted from foreign competition. The steel companies and the unions had two major complaints about foreign steel companies, dumping and subsidization. There may be some justice in these complaints. Nevertheless, the benefits of having some firms still solvent has to be balanced against the costs of higher steel prices and the problems that autarchic trade restrictions would create for international relations.

Some have attributed the problems of the steel industry to its inability to adopt new technology. This charge does not seem to hold for the 1990s. Essentially, the BOF integrated technology lost share to the scrap-based EF. Some have argued that the integrated company management did not respond optimally to the competition of the minimills. This premise has two problems; first, many minimills did not do particularly well in the early twenty-first century, and second two large firms, U.S. Steel and AK Steel, have remained solvent and at times prospered.

This leads us to the problem of environmental regulation. For the most part, environmental regulation did not hurt the industry that much. For one thing, most of the American industry's major competitors, such as Canada, Japan, and the European Union (EU), were faced with similar regulations. One area, however, deserves some attention, the coke ovens. There is evidence that the regulation of these ovens was overly stringent in the United States. Even though the United States was the largest producer of metallurgical coal in the world, steel companies often had to import coke. If Canada and Japan developed regulations allowing coke to be made, why could not the United States?

Many assert that unions, by keeping wages too high and work rules inflexible, caused the downfall of at least some companies. The problem with this hypothesis is that some unionized companies such as U.S. Steel and AK Steel survived, and some non-union firms such as Trico and Birmingham went bankrupt. Thus, the unions in themselves could not have been the cause of the trouble.

The defined benefit pension plans may have been responsible for some bankruptcies. None of the steel company pension plans were funded. Essentially, when companies agreed to set up these plans, they almost never made specific provisions to fund them in the future. Encouraging this behavior was the insurance provided by the Pension Benefit Guaranty Corporation (PBGC). The PBGC, however, did not guarantee the total planned level of these pensions. Consequently, the commitments implied by these pension plans were often beyond the capability of the companies, and at least partially contributed to their bankruptcy. Nevertheless, not all bankrupt companies had guaranteed benefit plans, and some firms with such plans survived.

Consequently, other factors may have contributed to firm insolvency. Actions by managements certainly at least helped some firms to lose out. Hurting some firms were mergers that either just did not work out or diverted resources away from meeting other obligations. Examples were Bethlehem's merger with Lukens Steel and LTV's purchase of Copperweld.

Again this hypothesis is not conclusive, U.S. Steel bought VSZ and survived. Yet the mergers undertaken by those other companies took resources away from other more urgent uses. The very differential in success between companies such as U.S. Steel, AK Steel, and Nucor and the bankrupt firms, both integrated and minimill, suggest that there were differences in management quality.

Thus, four of these factors, imports, coke oven regulations, defined benefit pension plans, and managerial error, could very well have contributed to the bankruptcies of so many steel companies in the last six years. Ascertaining the exact cause of these troubles should be the subject for future research.

11 Conclusion

Introduction

In this chapter, we draw some conclusions about the American steel industry in the 141 years between 1860 and 2001. Before making these conclusions, we first describe the major events in the industry since 2001 in order to add context.

Events in the early twenty-first century

Since 2001, notable events have occurred in four areas: product demand, government policies, labor relations, and industry structure. The last change was by far the most striking. To put it in perspective, we first examine the other changes.

From the depressed conditions of 2000 and 2001, the steel industry experienced a rapid turnaround. Worldwide steel demand rose 37 percent in the first part of the twenty-first century. World production rose from 904 million tons in 2002 to 1.239 billion tons in 2006. The enormous economic growth in first China and then India led to an increase in the world steel demand. Even though China increased its production to 418 million tons, this growth strained the capacity of the world steel industry. This has meant prosperity for the surviving American companies.

This boom and pressure from American customers led President George Bush to end the 2002 Section 201 tariffs that had been imposed at the end of 2003 (*New York Times*, December 5, 2003, p. A1 and *Wall Street Journal*, December 5, 2003, p. A3). This was the major change in government policy.

The third event was the United Steelworkers' (USW) acceptance of lower retirement and medical benefits. In mergers and negotiated contracts, the union agreed to lower benefits from the companies (*Wall Street Journal*, July 10, 2002, p. A2, December 24, 2002, p. A2, May 20, 2003, p. A6, June 27, 2003, p. A9, and February 26, 2004, p. A2). This pliability led to the organization of firms that could survive in the new environment.

The fourth event was the consolidation in the steel industry in the last five years. First, the stronger companies acquired weaker and often bankrupt firms. Second, two outside entrepreneurs moved into the industry. The strong acquiring companies included both minimill and integrated firms. Among the former was Ameristeel. It bought up a number of rival minimill firms, including the Brazilian company, Gerdau. The company, then, changed its name to Gerdau Ameristeel. Ameristeel had also acquired a 50 percent interest in the Kentucky sheet minimill, Gallatin Steel. In 2004, Gerdau Ameristeel bought the North Star Steel Company. In 2006, the relatively new minimill firm, Steel Dynamics, bought Roanoke Steel and its subsidiary, the Steel Company of West Virginia.

Still, the minimill company that epitomized the policy of the strong buying up the weak was Nucor, which historically had depended on internal expansion. From 2001 to present, however, under Chief Executive Officer Dan DiMicco, Nucor engaged in a very active merger policy. Nucor acquired a number of competitors, Trico, Auburn Steel, Birmingham Steel, Corus Tuscaloosa, Marion Steel, and Connecticut Steel.

Among the integrated firms, the strong also bought the weak. In May 2003, U.S. Steel bought National Steel. Even though it survived the 1990s intact, National Steel went into bankruptcy in March 2003 (Standard & Poor's, January 2, 2004, p. 9). Prior to the merger agreement, U.S. Steel persuaded the USW to allow it to set up a defined contribution retirement plan for the former employees of National Steel. Additionally, U.S. Steel got the Pension Benefit Guaranty Corporation to assume the payments of the acquired company's retirees.

Foreign companies also acquired American steel firms. In 2003, the Russian firm, Severstal, purchased the former Ford Motor steel plant, Rouge Steel (*Wall Street Journal*, December 23, 2003, p. A2 and December 29, 2003, p. A2). In August 2008, Severstal also bought Wheeling-Pittsburgh Steel Corporation.

The second force consolidating the steel industry was outside entrepreneurship. Originally, the most important was Wilbur L. Ross, an investment banker who bought up the assets of the bankrupt LTV Steel. He negotiated an agreement with the USW that tied medical and pension benefits to company performance (*Wall Street Journal*, December 24, 2002, p. A2). His new firm, called the International Steel Group (ISG), then prospered with the boom in steel demand.

In 2003, Ross merged ISG with Bethlehem Steel by buying the Bethlehem assets and making a similar deal with the USW on benefits. In the subsequent year, 2004, ISG bought Weirton Steel. ISG then bought Acme Steel and Georgetown Steel.

In April 2005, Ross sold ISG to Mittal Steel, the English-Dutch steel firm owned by the Indian tycoon, Lakshmi Mittal. Mittal had consolidated a number of steel mills in Indonesia, Trinidad, the Netherlands, and Kazakhstan into a huge firm. In the United States, Mittal already owned Ispat-Inland. With this combination of Inland and ISG, Mittal became the largest steel firm in the United States. In 2006, Mittal merged with Arcelor, the largest steel firm in Europe. This gave Mittal a total steel-making capacity of over 100 million tons worldwide, with about 24 million in the United States.

Thus, an Indian entrepreneur now controls the largest steel firm in the United States. With the partial Japanese ownership of AK Steel and the U.S. Steel mills in Slovakia, the American steel industry has become internationalized. The steel company ownership structure has come to resemble other American industries. It is similar to oil, where Exxon-Mobil competes against Royal Dutch Shell, and autos where General Motors competes with Toyota.

This description has brought events up to date as of December 2006. We can now draw some conclusions.

Conclusions

To conclude, we look at some themes that have recurred in the history of the steel industry. They were technological change, insecurity leading to consolidation, international competition, and the interconnections between different events. Before the advent of steel, technological change was a dominant characteristic of the American iron industry in the early nineteenth century. Subsequently, the advent of the Bessemer and open hearth processes played a major role in the industry.

Process innovation and new products continued to be important. In the first three decades of the twentieth century, the rolling mills were electrified, Henry Grey introduced a new type of construction beam, and John B. Tytus developed the wide steel sheet. In the late twentieth century, the basic oxygen process, the electric furnace, and the continuous caster revolutionized the market.

Throughout the history of the American steel industry, from the iron sector of the early 1800s to the steel market in the twenty-first century, financial insecurity due to fluctuating demand and changing technology plagued the industry. This led to three major periods of consolidation. The first was in the 1890s; it resulted in the founding of U.S. Steel. In the second period, between 1910 and 1930, the second-tier companies emerged. This group included Bethlehem, Republic, and National Steel. In the 1970s and 1980s, a third consolidation period resulted in the founding of LTV Steel and the enlargement of National Steel and Armco. Finally, in the last five years, Mittal obtained control of a number of formerly independent companies, and other firms bought up small competitors.

While these consolidations might alleviate the problem of firm insecurity, they could have led to above-competitive pricing. Therefore, the antitrust authorities have often stopped mergers that furthered the consolidation trend.

The third theme in this history is international competition. In the early nine-teenth century, the British iron industry exported much product to the United States. The American industry expended much effort, persuading the government to erect tariff barriers. The American dominance in the late nineteenth and early twentieth centuries put trade issues into the background until the 1960s. The recent growth and innovations in Japan and other countries resulted in imports into the United States and clamors for protection from the American companies.

While the internationalization of the steel industry led to a more competitive environment, the struggle for market share between domestic and foreign competi-tors often created layoffs. Accentuating the problem was the changing technology that could quickly turn prosperous firms into money-losers. Overall, increasing productivity and efficiency decreased employment. Thus, while prices often dropped and product quality improved, the position of both the company and the employee became very insecure.

It was this insecurity that led to the federal government protection measures such as tariffs and quotas. Unfortunately, these initiatives did not stop the drop in steel employment. While the industry as a whole has become very good at adopting new technology and responding to customers, steel firms' employees and stockholders have not necessarily done that well. Often, jobs were lost, and stock values went to zero.

This problem points to the interconnection between different events. Trying to bring economic security by protecting or "rationalizing" an industry usually does not work. Perhaps, a general system of economic income insurance can be developed that could still leave an incentive for individuals to produce. Nobel Prize economist, Michael Spence, says,

> . . . it is better to protect people and incomes rather than jobs and firms. The latter approach impedes the competitive responses of firms in the private sector and, in the context of the global economy, becomes very expensive.
>
> (Wall Street Journal, January 23, 2007, p. A19)

Still, from the history of the steel industry, some interesting insights can be educed. Often actions in response to one set of problems create other problems. For instance, Elbert Gary's emphasis on placating the government may have prevented U.S. Steel from keeping up with the latest technology. The urgent build-up of capacity during World War II provided the industry with so much capacity that it may have had little immediate incentive to build efficient greenfield BOF plants. The emphasis of the American integrated firms on old technology may have prevented them from exploiting the electric furnace.

These examples indicate that often it is impossible to see the long-run effect of particular actions. This makes it very difficult to make overall plans for these sectors – whether from private groups like the Morgan and Gary managements or from government regimes like the Clinton and Bush administrations. This suggests that a reasonably competitive market system may be the best way to organize the production, even with the insecurity resulting from technological change.

This does not preclude the government from correcting externalities such as environmental protection, and it does not mean that government actions cannot sometimes increase competition. Still history suggests that trying to direct the exact course of the steel market may be beyond the capability of any central authority – be it government or private.

Bibliography

Adams, W. (1950) *The Structure of American Industry: Some Case Studies*, New York: Macmillan.

Adams, W. and J. Dirlam (1964) "Steel Imports and Vertical Oligopoly Power," *American Economic Review*, LIV(5): 626–655.

Adams, W. and J. Dirlam (1966) "Big Steel, Inventions, and Innovation," *Quarterly Journal of Economics*, LXX(2): 167–189.

Adams, W. and J. Dirlam (1966) "Steel Imports and Vertical Oligopoly Power: Reply," *American Economic Review*, LVI(1/2): 160–168.

American Iron and Steel Institute (1910–1975) *Annual Statistical Report*, Washington D.C.: American Iron and Steel Institute.

American Metal Market (1974) *Metal Statistics 1974*. New York: American Metals Market Fairchild Publications, Inc.

Anderson, N. (1990) *North American Coke Today: Red Hot Coke for Red Hot Iron*, privately published.

Ankney, T. L. (1993) *The Pendulum of Control: The Evolution of the Weirton Steel Company, 1909–1951*, Ann Arbor, MI: University Microfilms.

Ashton, T. S. (1968) *Iron and Steel in the Industrial Revolution*, New York: A. M. Kelley.

Atack, J. and P. Passell (1994) *A New Economic View of America: History from Colonial Times to 1940*, New York: W. W. Norton.

Automobile Manufacturers Association (1950) *Freedom's Arsenal: The Story of the Automotive Council for War Production*, Detroit, MI: Automobile Manufacturers Association.

Back, B. D. and Ray, E. J. (1973) "Tariff and Comparative Advantage in the Iron and Steel Industry: 1870–1929," *Explorations in Economic History*, 2(1): 1–23.

Backman, J. (1970) *The Economics of the Chemical Industry*, Washington D.C.: Manufacturing Chemists Association.

Barnett, D. F. and R. Crandall (1986) *Up From the Ashes: The Rise of the Steel Minimill in the U.S.*, Washington D.C.: Brookings Institute.

Barnett, D. F. and L. Schorsch (1983) *Steel: Upheaval in a Basic Industry*, Cambridge, MA: Ballinger.

Bell, T. (1976) *Out of this Furnace*, Pittsburgh, PA: University of Pittsburgh Press.

Bendix, R. and F. W. Howton (1963) "Social Mobility and the American Business Elite" in Lipset, S. M. and R. Bendix, *Social Mobility in Industrial Society*, Berkeley: University of California Press, pp. 114–143.

Bennett, J. P. (1966) "Cyclical Determinants of Capital Expenditures: A Regression Study of the United States Steel Industry," *Southern Economic Journal*, 32(3): 330–340.

Bernstein, I. (1971) *The Turbulent Years: A History of the American Worker, 1933–1941*, Boston: Houghton Mifflin.

Berry, J. P. (1974) *Ships of the Great Lakes, 300 Years of Navigation*, Berkeley, CA: Howell-North Books.

Blonigen, B. A. and W. W. Wilson (2005) "Foreign Subsidization and the Excess Capacity Hypothesis," Cambridge, National Bureau of Economic Research, Working Paper 11798.

Bodnar, J. (1977) *Immigration and Industrialization: Ethnicity in an American Mill Town, 1870–1940*, Pittsburgh, PA: University of Pittsburgh Press.

Bodnar, J. (1980) "Immigration, Kinship, and the Rise of Working-Class Realism in Industrial America," *Journal of Social History*, 14 (Fall): 45–65.

Bolling, R. W. and J. Bowles (1982) *America's Competitive Edge: How to Get Our Country Moving Again*, New York: McGraw-Hill.

Borth, C. (1941) *True Steel: The Story of George Verity and his Associates*, Dayton, OH: Otterbein.

Brandes, S. D. (1976) *American Welfare Capitalism, 1880–1940*, Chicago, IL: University of Chicago Press.

Bridge, J. H. (1972 [1903]) *The Inside History of the Carnegie Steel Company: A Romance of Millions*, New York: Arno Press.

Bridges, H. (1952) *Iron Millionaire: Life of Charlemagne Tower*, Philadelphia: University of Pennsylvania Press.

Brody, D. (1960) *Steelworkers in America: The Nonunion Era*, Cambridge, MA: Harvard University.

Brooks, R. R. (1968, c.1968) As Steel Goes, . . .; Unionism in a Basic Industry, New Haven, CT: Yale University Press.

Broude, H. W. (1963) *Steel Decisions and the National Economy*, New Haven, CT: Yale University Press.

Buire, J. A. (1975) "Barrels to Barrows, Buckets to Belts: 120 Years of Iron Ore Handling on the Great Lakes," *Inland Seas*, 31: 266–277.

Campbell, C. D. (1971) *Wage-Price Controls in World War II, United States and Germany*, Washington D.C.: American Enterprise Institute.

Campbell, R. F. (1948) *The History of Basic Metals: Price Controls in World War II*, New York: AMS Press.

Carlton, D. W. (1983) "A Reexamination of Delivered Pricing Systems," *Journal of Law & Economics*, 24: 51–70.

Catton, B. (1948) *The Warlords of Washington*, New York: Greenwood Press.

Chandler, A. D. (1962) Strategy and Structure: *Chapters in the History of the Industrial Enterprise*, Cambridge, MA: MIT Press.

Chandler, A. D. (1990) *Scale and Scope: The Dynamics of Industrial Capitalism*, Cambridge, MA: Belknap Press.

Cheape, C. (1996) "Tradition, Innovation, and Expertise: Writing the Steel Code for the National Recovery Administration," *Business and Economic History*, 25(2): 69–87.

Clark, G. L. (1988) "Corporate Restructuring in the Steel Industry: Adjustment Strategies and Local Labor Relations," in Sternlieb, G. and J. W. Hughes, *America's New Market Geography: Nation, Region, and Metropolis*, New Brunswick, NJ: Rutgers, The State University of New Jersey, Center for Urban Policy Research.

Clark, P. F., P. Gottlieb, and D. Kennedy (1987) *Forging a Union of Steel: Philip Murray, SWOC, and the United Steelworkers*, Ithaca, NY: Cornell University Press.

Colander, D. C. (2006) *Economics*, Sixth Edition, Boston, MA: Irwin McGraw-Hill.

Colvin, W. H. (1950) Crucible Steel of America: 50 Years of Specialty Steelmaking in U.S.A., New York: Newcomen Society of America.

Comanor, W. S. and F. M. Scherer (1995) "Rewriting History: The Early Sherman Act Monopolization Cases," *International Journal of the Economics of Business*, 2(2): 263–289.

Cooney, S. (2003) *Current Issues in the Steel Industry*, New York: Novinka Books.

Crandall, R. (1981) *The U.S. Steel Industry in Recurrent Crisis*, Washington D.C.: Brookings Institution.

Cummings, S. (1988) *Business Elites and Urban Development: Case Studies and Critical Perspectives*, Albany: State University of New York Press.

Cyert, R. M. and R. J. Fruehan (1996) *Meeting the Challenge: U.S. Industry Faces the 21st Century: The Basic Steel Industry*, Washington D.C.: Office of Technology Policy.

Davenport, M. (1943) *The Valley of Decision*, New York: Charles Scribner's Sons.

Davis, A. E. (1988) "Politics of Prosperity: The Kennedy Presidency and Economic Policy," Ph.D. Dissertation, Columbia University, New York.

Deily, M. E. (1991) "Exit Strategies and Plant-Closing Decisions: The Case of Steel," *RAND Journal of Economics*, 22(2): 250–263.

Deily, M. E. and W. B. Gray (1991) "Enforcement of Pollution Regulations in a Declining Industry," *Journal of Environmental Economics and Management*, 2: 260–274.

Dew, Charles B. (1966) *Ironmaker to the Confederacy: Joseph R. Anderson and the Tredegar Iron Works*, New Haven, CT: Yale University Press.

Dickerson, D. C. (1986) *Out of the Crucible: Black Steelworkers in Western Pennsylvania, 1875–1980*, Albany, NY: State University of New York Press.

Dilley, D. R. and D. L. McBride (1967) "Oxygen Steelmaking – Fact Vs. Folklore," *Iron and Steel Engineer*, 44 (October): 131–152.

Domhoff, W. (1987) "The Wagner Act and Theories of the State: A New Analysis Based on Class-Segment Theory," *Political Power and Social Theory*, 6: 159–185.

Duke, R., R. Johnson, H. Mueller, P. Qualls, C. Roush, and D. Tarr (1977) *The United States Steel Industry and its International Rivals: Trends and Factors Determining International Competitiveness: Staff Report*, Washington D.C.: Federal Trade Commission, Bureau of Economics, U.S. Government Printing Office.

Edsforth, R. (2000) *The New Deal: America's Response to the Great Depression*, Malden, MA: Blackwell Publishers, Inc.

Eggert, G. G. (1981) *Steelmasters and Labor Reform, 1886–1923*, Pittsburgh, PA: University of Pittsburgh Press.

Enke, S. (1942) "Price Controls and Rationing," *American Economic Review*: 842–843.

Evans, P. (1982) "The Effects of General Price Controls in the United States during World War II," *Journal of Political Economy*, 90(5): 944–966.

Fisher, D. A. (1946) *Steel in the War*, New York: United States Steel Corporation.

Fisher, D. A. (1963) *The Epic of Steel*, New York: Harper & Row.

Fitch, J. A. (1969) *The Steel Workers*, New York: Arno.

Fogel, R. W. and S. L. Engerman (1969) "A Model for the Explanation of Industrial Expansion during the Nineteenth Century: With an Application to the American Iron Industry," *Journal of Political Economy*, 2: 306–328.

Folsom, B. W. (1987) *Entrepreneurs vs. The State*, Reston, VA: Young America's Foundation.

Friedman, M. and A. J. Schwartz (1963) *A Monetary History of the United States, 1867–1960*, Princeton, NJ: Princeton University Press.

Galbraith, J. K. (1946) "Reflections on Price Control," *Quarterly Journal of Economics*, 60(4): 475–489.

Galenson, W. (1960) *The CIO Challenge to the AFL: A History of the American Labor Movement, 1935–1941*, Cambridge, MA: Harvard University Press.

Gandre, D. A. (1971) "Recent Changes in the Flow Pattern of Iron Ore on the Great Lakes," *Inland Seas*, 22: 246–259.

Garraty, J. A. (1960) *Right-Hand Man: The Life of George W. Perkins*, New York: Harpers.

Gaskins, D. (1971) "Dynamic Limit Pricing: Optimal Pricing Under the Threat of Entry," *Journal of Economic Theory*: 306–322.

Giarratani, F. and D. B. Houston (1989) "Structural Change and Economic Policy in a Declining Metropolitan Region: Implications of the Pittsburgh Experience," *Urban Studies*, 26: 549–558.

Girdler, T. M. and B. Sparkes (1943) *Boot Straps: The Autobiography of Tom M. Girdler*, New York: Charles Scribner's Sons.

Gold, B., W. S. Pierce, G. Rosegger, and M. Perlman (1984) *Technological Progress and Industrial Leadership: The Growth of the U.S. Steel Industry, 1900–1970*, Lexington, MA: Lexington Books.

Gold, B., G. Rosegger, and M. G. Boylan (1980) *Evaluating Technological Innovation*, Lexington, MA: Lexington Books.

Gold, B., G. Rosegger, and M. Perlman (1984) *Technological Progress and Industrial Leadership: The Growth of the U.S. Steel Industry, 1900–1970*, Lexington, MA: Lexington Books.

Goldberg, W. (1986) *Ailing Steel: The Transoceanic Quarrel*, New York: St. Martin's Press.

Gordon, C. (1994) *New Deals: Business, Labor, and Politics in America, 1920–1935*, Cambridge: Cambridge University Press.

Gordon, R. B. (1996) *American Iron, 1607–1900*, Baltimore, MD: Johns Hopkins University Press.

Gregory, F. and Neu, I. D. (1952) "The American Industrial Elite in the 1870's: Their Social Origins," in Miller, W., *Men in Business: Essays in the History of Entrepreneurship*, Cambridge, MA: Harvard University Press, pp. 193–211.

Gulick, C. A. and H. R. Seager (1972 [c.1929]) *Trust and Corporation Problems*, New York: Arno Press.

Gutman, H. G. (1969) " The Reality of the Rags-to-Riches 'Myth': The Case of the Paterson, New Jersey, Locomotive, Iron, and Machinery Manufacturers, 1830–1880," in Stephan Thernstrom, S. and R. Sennett, *Nineteenth-Century Cities: Essays in the New Urban History*, New Haven, CT: Yale University Press, pp. 98–124.

Hacker, L. M. (1978) *The World of Andrew Carnegie: 1865–1901*, Philadelphia, PA: Lippincott.

Hacker, L. M. and H. S. Zahler (1952) *The United States in the 20th Century*: New York: Appleton-Century-Croft.

Haddock, D. D. (1982) "Basing-Point Pricing: Competitive vs. Collusive Theories," *American Economic Review*, 72: 289–306.

Hale, R. D. (1970) "An Economist's Analysis of a Vertical Acquisition: The Inland–Ryerson Merger," *Indiana Law Journal*, 45(2): 180–194.

Hall, C. G. L. (1997) *Steel Phoenix: The Fall and Rise of the U.S. Steel Industry*, New York: St. Martin's Press.

Hawley, E. W. (1966) *The New Deal and the Problem of Monopoly*, Princeton, NJ: Princeton University Press.

Herling, J. (1972) *Right to Challenge: People and Power in the Steel Workers' Union*, New York: Harper and Row.

Hessen, R. (1975) *Steel Titan: The Life of Charles M. Schwab*, New York: Oxford University Press.

Hexner, E. (1941) "American Participation in the International Steel Cartel," *Southern Economic Journal*, 8: 54–79.

Higgs, R. (1987) *Crisis and Leviathan: Critical Episodes in the Growth of American Government*, New York: Oxford University Press.

Hoerr, J. P. (1988) *And the Wolf Finally Came: The Decline of the American Steel Industry*, Pittsburgh, PA: University of Pittsburgh Press.

Hogan, W. T. (1950) *Productivity in the Blast-Furnace and Open-Hearth Segments of the Steel Industry: 1920–1946*, New York: Fordham University Press.

Hogan, W. T. (1971) *Economic History of the Iron and Steel Industry in the United States*, Lexington, MA: D. C. Heath.

Hogan, W. T. (1972) *The 1970s: Critical Years for Steel*, Lexington, MA: Lexington Books.

Hogan, W. T. (1983) *World Steel in the 1980s: A Case of Survival*, Lexington, MA: Lexington Books.

Hogan, W. T. (1984) *Steel in the United States: Restructuring to Compete*, Lexington, MA: Lexington Books.

Hogan, W. T. (1986) *Steel Industry Future*, Duluth, MN: D. N. Skillings.

Hogan, W. T. (1987) *Minimills and Integrated Mills: A Comparison of Steelmaking in the United States*, Lexington, MA: Lexington Books.

Hogan, W. T. (1991) *Global Steel in the 1990s: Growth or Decline*, Lexington, MA: Lexington Books.

Hogan, W. T. (1994) *Steel in the 21st Century*, New York: Lexington Books.

Hogan, W. T. (2001) *The POSCO Strategy*, New York: Lexington Books.

Hone, G. A. and S. Schoenbrod (1966) "Steel Imports and Vertical Oligopoly Power: Comment," *American Economic Review*, LVI(1/2): 156–160.

Hoopes, R. (1963) *The Steel Crisis*, New York: Day.

Howell, T. R., W. A. Noellert, J. G. Kreier, and A. W. Wolff (1988) *Steel and the State: Government Intervention and Steel's Structural Crisis*, Boulder, CO: Westview Press.

Hughes, J. and L. P. Cain (2003) *American Economic History*, Sixth Edition, Boston, MA: Addison Wesley.

Ingham, J. N. (1976) "Rags to Riches Revisited: The Effect of City Size and Related Factors on the Recruitment of Business Leaders," *Journal of American History*, 63(3): 615–637.

Ingham, J. N. (1978) *The Iron Barons: A Social Analysis of an American Urban Elite, 1874–1965*, Westport, CT: Greenwood Press.

Ingham, J. N. (1991) *Making Iron and Steel: Independent Mills in Pittsburgh, 1820–1920*, Columbus: Ohio State University Press.

Iron Age (1922) "Tracing the History of Pittsburgh Basing," *Iron Age*, 110 (November 16): 1287–1289.

Iron Age (1947) "Oxygen Firm Outlines its Research Program for Steelmaking Applications," *Iron Age* (June 12): 109–110.

Iverson, K. (1998) *Plain Talk: Lessons from a Business Maverick*, New York: Wiley.

Jones, K. A. (1986) *Politics vs Economics in World Steel Trade*, London: Allen & Unwin.

Kaelble, H. (1980) "Long Term Changes in the Recruitment of the Business Elite: Germany Compared to the U.S., Great Britain, and France since the Industrial Revolution," *Journal of Social History*, 13(3): 404–423.

Kahn, A. E. (1950) " The Chemical Industry," in W. Adams, *The Structure of American Industry: Some Case Studies*, New York: The Macmillan Company, pp. 197–230.

Kahn, A. E. (1961) " The Chemical Industry," in W. Adams, *The Structure of American Industry: Some Case Studies*, Third Edition, New York: The Macmillan Company, pp. 197–230.

Kanawaty, G. D. (1963) "Concentration of the Steel Industry," Ph.D. Dissertation, University of Illinois, Urbana.

Katzman, M. T. (1988) "From Horse Carts to Minimills," *Public Interest*, 92: 121–135.

Kennedy, D. M. (1999) *Freedom from Fear: The American People in Depression and War, 1929–1945*, New York: Oxford University Press.

Koistinen, P. A. C. (2004) *Arsenal of World War II: The Political Economy of American Warfare, 1940–1945*, Lawrence, KS: University Press of Kansas.

Lages, J. D. (1967) "The CIO-SWOC Attempt to Organize the Steel Industry, 1936–1942: A Restatement and Economic Analysis," Ph.D. Dissertation, Iowa State University.

Lamoreaux, N. R. (1985) *The Great Merger Movement in American Business*, Cambridge: Cambridge University Press.

Lauderbaugh, R., A. (1976) "Business, Labor, and Foreign Policy: U.S. Steel, the International Steel Cartel, and Recognition of the Steel Workers Organizing Committee," *Politics & Society*, 6(4): 433–436.

Lauderbaugh, R. A. (1980) *American Steel Makers and the Coming of the Second World War*, Ann Arbor, MI: UMI Research Press.

Leary, T. E. and E. C. Sholes (1987) *From Fire to Rust: Business, Technology and Work at the Lackawanna Steel Plant, 1899–1983*, Buffalo, NY: Buffalo and Erie County Historical Society.

Lerner, R., A. K. Nagai, and S. Rothman (1996) *American Elites*, New Haven, CT: Yale University Press.

Lester, G. E. (1883) *Life and Character of Peter Cooper*, New York: John B. Alden.

Livesay, H. C. (1975) *Andrew Carnegie and the Rise of Big Business*, Boston, MA: Little, Brown.

Longenecker, C. (1936) "Corrigan, McKinney Steel Company," *Blast Furnace and Steel Plant*, 24 (January): 75–81.

Longenecker, C. (1940) "Weirton Steel Company," *Blast Furnace and Steel Plant*, 28 (August): 773–777.

Lynn, L. H. (1982) *How Japan Innovates: A Comparison with the U.S. in the Case of Oxygen Steelmaking*, Boulder, CO: Westview Press.

Maeva, M. (1977) *Truman and the Steel Seizure Case*, New York: Columbia University Press.

Mancke, R. (1968) "New Determinants of Steel Price in the U.S., 1947–65," *Journal of Industrial Economics*, 16(2): 147–160.

Mangum, G. L. (1961) "Interaction of Contract Administration and Contract Negotiation in the Basic Steel Industry," *Labor Law Journal*, 12 (September): 846–860.

Mansfield, E. (1963) "Size of Firm, Market Structure, and Innovation," *Journal of Political Economy*, 71(6): 556–576.

McAdams, A. K. (1967) "Big Steel, Inventions, and Innovation, Reconsidered," *Quarterly Journal of Economics*, LXXXI(3): 457–474.

McConnell, G. (1963) *Steel and the Presidency, 1962*, New York: Norton.

McCraw, T. K. and F. Reinhardt (1989) "Losing to Win: U.S. Steel's Pricing, Investment Decisions, and Market Share, 1901–1938," *Journal of Economic History*, 49(3): 593–619.

McDonald, D. (1969) *Union Man*, New York: Dutton.

McHugh, J. (1980) *Alexander Holley and the Makers of Steel*, Baltimore, MD: Johns Hopkins University Press.

McManus, G. (1967) *The Inside Story of Steel Wages and Prices, 1959–1967*, Philadelphia, PA: Chilton.

Meyer, P. B. "Episodes of Collective Invention," BLS Working Paper No. 368, Office of Productivity and Technology, U.S. Department of Labor Statistics.

Misa, T. J. (1995) *A Nation of Steel: The Making of Modern America, 1865–1925*, Baltimore, MD: Johns Hopkins University Press.

Moore, M. O. (1996) "The Rise and Fall of Big Steel's Influence on U.S. Trade Policy," in Krueger, A. O., *The Political Economy of Trade Protection*, Chicago, IL: University of Chicago Press, 1996.

Mueller, H. (1984) *Protection and Competition in the U.S. Steel Market: A Study of Managerial Decision Making in Transition*, Murfreesboro, TN: Business and Economics Research Center, Middle Tennessee State University.

Nation (1975) "An Insurgent's View," *Nation*, 221 (September 6): 173–175.

Orr, J. A. (1973) "The Rise and Fall of Steel's Human Relations Committee," *Labor History*, 14 (Winter): 69–82.

Parsons, D. O., and E. J. Ray (1975) "The United States Consolidation: The Creation of Market Control," *Journal of Law and Economics*, 18(1): 181–219.

Paskoff, P. F. (c.1983) *Industrial Evolution: Organization, Structure, and Growth of the Pennsylvania Iron Industry, 1750–1860*, Baltimore, MD: Johns Hopkins University Press.

Paskoff, P. F. (1989) *Encyclopedia of American Business History and Biography: Iron and Steel in the Nineteenth Century*, New York: Facts on File.

Pension Benefit Guaranty Corporation (1996–2003) *Annual Reports, 1996–2003*.

Pension Benefit Guaranty Corporation (2002) *Pension Insurance Data Book 2002*.

Peterson, R. H. (c.1991) *The Bonanza Kings: The Social Origins and Business Behavior of Western Mining Entrepreneurs, 1870–1900*, Norman: University of Oklahoma Press.

Piore, M. J. (1984) *The Second Industrial Divide: Possibilities for Prosperity*, New York: Basic Books.

Polanyi, K. (1957) *The Great Transformation*, Boston, MA: Beacon Press.

Porter, M. E. (1980) *Competitive Strategy: Techniques for Analyzing Industries and Competitors*, New York: Free Press.

Porter, M. E. (1998) *On Competition*, Boston, MA: Harvard Business School Publishing.

Preston, R. (1992) *American Steel*, New York: Avon Books.

Rees, J. (2004) *Managing the Mills: Labor Policy in the American Steel Industry During the Nonunion Era*, Dallas, TX: University Press of America.

Reutter, M. (1988 and 2004) *Sparrows Point: Making Steel: The Rise and Ruin of American Industrial Might*, New York: Summit.

Rippe, R. D. (1970) "Wages Prices and Imports in the American Steel Industry," *Review of Economics and Statistics*, 52: 34–46.

Rockoff, H. (1981a) "The Response of the Giant Corporations to Wage and Price Controls in World War II," *Journal of Economic History*, 41(1): 123–128.

Rockoff, H. (1981b) "Price and Wage Controls in Four Wartime Periods," *Journal of Economic History*, 41(2): 381–401.

Rodengen, J. L. (1997) *The Legend of Nucor Corporation*, Ft. Lauderdale, FL: Write Stuff Enterprises.

Rogers, R. P. (1983) "The Behavior of Firms in an Oligopoly Industry: A Study of Conjectural Variations," Ph.D. Dissertation, The George Washington University, Washington D.C.

Rogers, R. P. (1987) "Unobservable Transactions Price and the Measurement of a Supply and Demand Model of the American Steel Industry," *Journal of Business & Economic Statistics*, 5(3) (July): 407–415.

Rogers, R. P. (2001) "The Effect of Plant Configuration on the Integrated Steel Mill Sector in the United States," in Zhongliang Shi and Jiajun Wu, *China's Industrial Development and Enterprise Reform*, Beijing: Economic Management Publishing House, pp. 287 306.

Rostow, W. W. (1971) *Politics and the Stages of Growth*, Cambridge: Cambridge University Press.

Rowley, C. K. (1971) *Steel and Public Policy*, London: McGraw-Hill.

Sanger, M. F. S. (1998) *Henry Clay Frick: An Intimate Portrait*, New York: Abbeville Press Publishers.

Santos, M. (1978) "Laboring on the Periphery: Managers and Workers and the A.M. Byers Company, 1900–1956," *Business History Review*, 52 (Spring): 113–133.

Saville, J. P. (1976) *Iron and Steel*, Hove, UK: Priory Press.

Scheuerman, W. (1986) *The Steel Crisis: The Economics and Politics of a Declining Industry*, New York: Praeger.

Schroeder, G. G. (1953) *The Growth of Major Steel Companies, 1900–1950*, Baltimore, MD: Johns Hopkins Press.

Seely, B. E. (1994) *Iron and Steel in the Twentieth Century*, New York: Facts on File.

Serjeantson, R., R. Cordero, H. Cooke, S. Sexton, and S. Jordain (1988 and 1974) *Iron and Steel Works of the World*, Surrey, UK: Metal Bulletin Books.

Serrin, W. (1992) *Homestead: The Glory and Tragedy of an American Steel Town*, New York: Vantage Books.

Slesinger, R. E. (1966) "Steel Imports and Vertical Oligopoly Power: Comment," *American Economic Review*, LVI(1/2): 152–155.

Smith, G. D. (1988) *From Monopoly to Competition: The Transformation of Alcoa, 1888–1986*, New York: Cambridge University Press.

Smith, J. R. (1922) *The Story of Iron and Steel*, New York: D. Appleton.

Sobel, R. (1972) *The Age of Giant Corporations: A Microeconomic History of American Business, 1914–1970*, Westport, CT: Greenwood Press.

Standard & Poor's (1993–1996) *Standard & Poor's Industry Surveys: Metals Industrial*, New York: Standard & Poor's.

Standard & Poor's (1997–2003) *Standard & Poor's Industry Surveys: Steel and Heavy Machinery*, New York: Standard & Poor's.

Sternlieb, G. and J. W. Hughes, *America's New Market Geography: Nation, Region, and Metropolis*, New Brunswick, NJ: Rutgers, The State University of New Jersey, Center for Urban Policy Research.

Stevenson, A. (1952) "Philip Murray: The Nature of Leadership," *New Republic*, 127 (December 15): 10–12.

Stigler, G. J. (1951) "The Division of Labor is Limited by the Extent of the Market," *Journal of Political Economy*, 59(3): 185–193.

Stigler, G. J. (1965) "The Dominant Firm and the Inverted Umbrella," *Journal of Law and Economics*, 8: 167–172.

Stocking, G. (1954) *Basing Point Pricing and Regional Development: A Case Study of the Iron and Steel Industry*, Chapel Hill, NC: University of North Carolina Press.

Stoddard, D. J. (1906) *Prominent Men: Scranton and Vicinity, Wilkes-Barre and Vicinity,*

Pittston, Carbondale, Montrose and Vicinity, Pennsylvania, Scranton, PA, privately published.

Stone, K. (1974) "The Origin of Job Structures in the Steel Industry," *Review of Radical Political Economics*, 6: 61–97.

Strohmeyer, J. (1986) *Crisis in Bethlehem: Big Steel's Battle to Survive*, Bethesda, MD: Adler & Adler.

Sumrall, J. B. (1982) "Diffusion of the Basic Oxygen Furnace in the U.S. Steel Industry," *Journal of Industrial Economics*, XXX(4): 421–437.

Sweeney, V. (1956) *The United Steelworkers of America: Twenty Years Later, 1936–1956*, Pittsburgh, PA: United Steelworkers of America.

Szekely, J. (ed.) (1973) *The Steel Industry and the Environment*, New York: Marcel Dekker.

Tarbell, I. M. (1933) *The Life of Elbert H. Gary: A Story of Steel*, New York: D. Appleton-Century.

Tarr, D. (1977) "The Minimum Optimal Scale Steel Plant in the Mid–1970s," FTC Working Papers, 3 (March).

Tarr, D. (1984) "The Minimum Optimal Scale Steel Plant," *Atlantic Economic Journal*, 12(2): 122.

Tebbel, J. (1963) *The Human Touch in Business: The Story of Charles R. Hook*, Dayton, OH: Otterbein.

Temin, P. (1964) *Iron and Steel in Nineteenth-Century America: An Economic Inquiry*, Cambridge, MA: MIT Press.

Tiffany, P. A. (1984) "The Roots of Decline: Business–Government Relations in the American Steel Industry," *Journal of Economic History*, 44(2): 407–419.

Tiffany, P. A. (1988) *The Decline of American Steel: How Management, Labor, and Government Went Wrong*, New York: Oxford University Press.

Tornell, A. (1997) "Rational Atrophy: The U.S. Steel Industry," Cambridge, National Bureau of Economic Research, Working Paper 6084.

Ulman, L. (1962) *The Government of the Steel Workers' Union*, New York: Wiley.

United States v. *United States Steel Corporation et al.*, 223 Fed. 35 (1915).

United States v. *United States Steel Corporation et al.*, 251 U.S. 417 (1920).

United States Federal Trade Commission v. *Cement Institute et al.* (1948) 333 U.S. 683, 712–721.

United States Steel Corporation (1940) *T.N.E.C. Papers: Comprising the Pamphlets and Charts Submitted by United States Steel Corporation to the Temporary National Committee*, Vol. I, New York: United States Steel Corporation.

Urofsky, M. I. (1969) *Big Steel and the Wilson Administration: A Study in Business–Government Relations*, Columbus: Ohio State University Press.

U.S. Bureau of the Census (1960–2005) *Statistical Abstract of the United States*, Washington D.C.: Government Printing Office.

U.S. Bureau of the Census (1961) *Historical Statistics of the United States, Colonial Times to 1957*, Washington D.C.: U.S. Government Printing Office.

U.S. Department of Labor, Bureau of Labor Statistics, Census of Fatal Occupational Injuries, All Worker Profile, 1992–2002, found at www.OSHA.gov.

U.S. Environmental Protection Agency (1995) *EPA Office of Compliance Sector Notebook Project. Profile of the Iron and Steel Industry*, Washington D.C.: U.S. Government Printing Office.

Vukmir, R. B. (1999) *The Mill*, New York: University Press of America.

Wall, J. F. (1970) *Andrew Carnegie*, New York: Oxford University Press.

Wannski, J (1978) *The Way the World Works*, New York: Touchstone.

Webb, W. P. (1959) *The Great Plains*, Boston: Ginn.

Weiss, L. W. (1971) *Case Studies in American Industry*, Second Edition, New York: Wiley.

Wendt, L. and H. Kogan (1981 [c.1948]) *Bet a Million!: The Story of John W. Gates*, New York: Arno Press.

Wickham, S. and C. D. C. Rogers (1970) *Manufacturing Policy in the Steel Industry*, Homewood, IL: Richard D. Irwin.

Wollman, D. H. and D. R. Inman (1999) *Portraits in Steel: An Illustrated History of Jones & Laughlin Steel Corporation*, Kent, OH: Kent State University Press.

Yamawaki, H. (1985)"Dominant Firm Pricing and Fringe Expansion: The Case of the U.S. Iron and Steel Industry, 1907–1930," *Review of Economics and Statistics*, 68(1): 429–437.

Yetter, J. B. (1974) *Steelton Pennsylvania*, Harrisburg, PA: Triangle Press.

Zimring, C. A. (2005) *Cash for Your Trash: Scrap Recycling in America*, New Brunswick, NJ: Rutgers University Press.

Index

Printed in the United States
by Baker & Taylor Publisher Services